Marjorie N. Boyer 2215

20-

W9-CKM-682

RESEARCH IS A PASSION WITH ME:

THE AUTOBIOGRAPHY OF MARGARET MORSE NICE

Original Drawings by the Author selected
from her Published Works

Edited by Doris Huestis Speirs

Foreword by Konrad Lorenz

RESEARCH IS A PASSION WITH ME
see page 41

MARGARET MORSE NICE

RESEARCH IS A PASSION WITH ME

FOREWORD BY
KONRAD LORENZ

© Copyright:　The Margaret Nice Ornithological Club
and
Consolidated Amethyst Communications Inc. 1979

ISBN 0-920474-16-0
ISBN 0-920474-15-2

No portion of this book, with the exception of brief
extracts for the purpose of literary review, may be
reproduced in any form without the permission of
the publisher.

*Drawings appearing in this autobiography from the
book "Development of Behavior in Precocial Birds"
(1962) by Mrs. Nice, are printed by special
permission of The Linnaean Society of New York.*

Published by
Consolidated Amethyst Communications Inc.
12 Crescent Town Road, Unit 310
Toronto, Ontario M4C 5L3

Printed and Bound in Canada
by
Haynes Printing Co. (Cobourg) Ltd.
880 Division Street, Cobourg, Ontario

Contents

Foreword

Margaret Morse Nice was a naturalist in the truest sense of the word. She combined a poet's appreciation of nature's beauty with a scientist's analytical mind. Her simple and artless description of natural things often achieved an effect reminiscent of Thoreau's writing. Her greatest gift was an infinite joy in observation for its own sake which, unbiased and free from any hypotheses or prejudice, is the very best basis for the understanding of animal behaviour.

Another outstanding trait of her character was her engaging simplicity stemming from true pureness of heart, a property which is rarely found in combination with an intelligence such as hers. Her attitude towards nature remained — up to her high old age — that of a child's wide-eyed wonder, combined with a childlike curiosity which is exactly what a scientist's attitude ought to be, but so very seldom is.

When I first met Margaret Morse Nice in 1934 at the International Ornithological Congress held in Oxford, I was at once impressed by her deep understanding of ethology, its methods and its approach. Her particular gifts and her attitudes towards nature predestined her to be an ethologist. We happened to sit side by side in a charabanc driving the members of the Congress from Oxford to Tenby in Pembrokeshire; we fell to talking and we have been close friends ever since.

*At that time, she had already begun her field-studies on the song sparrow **Melospiza melodia**, which occupied her for many years and which turned out to be a major break-through in the methods of studying animal behaviour. Her paper on the song sparrow was, to the best of my knowledge, the first long-term field investigation of the individual life of any free-living wild animal. She has been followed by many students of animal behaviour since* *and all these "longitudinal" studies of wild animals have proved extremely fruitful.*

Although most of her own papers are concerned with the "plain tale" of unbiased observation, written much in the same, story-telling style as her charming and instructive autobiography, Margaret Morse Nice was fully conversant with the subtlest and the most difficult problems of modern ethology. Between the lines of her writing one can always read her deep understanding of these problems. Actually, every detail reported by her is relevant to important questions, nor does she ever leave out of her account anything relevant. (See Appendix # 1.)

Margaret Morse Nice was a very wonderful person indeed, and her sterling qualities become, I think, clearly apparent in this book. In her self-effacing simplicity she tries to put her personality in the background and to centre the reader's interest on that which she has to tell. Nonetheless, anyone discerning enough to read between the lines will appreciate the unique properties united in her; a scientist's seeking for truth, a poet's appreciation of nature's beauty, a sage's humility and a pure heart whose love encompasses everything that is alive.

Altenberg, Austria
February 26, 1975

Konrad Lorenz

Introduction

The Margaret Nice Ornithological Club, for women only, honouring Margaret Morse Nice, was founded in Toronto, Canada, in January, 1952 (see Appendix #2).

In accepting an Honorary Membership Mrs. Nice wrote (in part): " ... the study of nature is a limitless field, the most fascinating pursuit in the world ...

"We must *see clearly, record fully and accurately*, and *try to understand*.

"Emerson wrote: 'I am impressed with the fact that the greatest thing a human soul ever does in this world is to see something and tell what it saw in a plain way. Hundreds of people can talk for one who can think, but thousands can think for one who can see. To see clearly is poetry, philosophy and religion in one.'"

Louise de Kiriline Lawrence was among the few we invited to become corresponding members. In accepting she wrote (in part): from Pimisi Bay, Rutherglen, Ontario:

" ... The founding of the Nice Club ... will be an inspiration to all of us, who will have a part in its work and achievements, and, indirectly, it is to be hoped, for those who are on the outside ...

"The name that has been chosen represents a particular incentive to worthy achievement. The name Margaret Nice is synonymous for inspired thinking, for a meticulous and unremitting search for facts, for unrelenting analysis of conjectures and reasoning, interpretations and evidence and a rigid acceptance of nothing but the truth. She has given us an example, most particularly in her study of the Song Sparrow, of the benefit of making individual study comparative to that of others, the only way, she says, of making true progress. She has shown us that not a single observation, however trivial, is without significance, when repeated often enough. She has pointed to the importance of evidence in every shape and form, not only with which to support the statements and allegations of the researcher, but upon the strength of which *only* to accept the statements of anyone else. Lastly, and always, she affirms the matchless satisfaction and joy of research and creation . . . "

Last winter, as president of the Margaret Nice Ornithological Club, I received a letter from Mr. Edward S. Morse asking if our club would consider sponsoring the publication of his sister's autobiography. This exciting but challenging suggestion was duly weighed and discussed with the club members. The next day, an inner green light having appeared, I was able to long-distance to Mr. Morse the one word: YES.

In the summer of 1964, on our way home from Hawaii with a grand-daughter, we had spent a day with the Nices in Chicago. It was then I saw the first chapters of the autobiography, being requested to read to the family Chapter I. How delighted we were with it! From time to time, then, I would ask how it was progressing. In 1968 a letter arrived saying that it was almost completed. Its author passed on in June, 1974, ninety years old. Little did I dream that day in Chicago that her club would be involved in its publication, but I have a feeling that she would have been very pleased.

Now, concerning the names of the birds in the text, Dr. Margaret Nice frequently used the Third Edition of the A.O.U. Check-list of 1910. For the names of North American birds the editor has accepted as her authority the Fifth Edition of the A.O.U. Check-list of 1957, and the Thirty-second and Thirty-third supplements. For birds outside of North America she used the nomenclature of Edwards (1974) and, in some instances, of Delacour (1974).

Doris Huestis Speirs
Cobble Hill, 1815 Altona Road
Pickering, Ontario L1V 1M6
Canada. April 14, 1979 . . .

A Child of Nature

It was a most curious apple tree at the edge of our Grandfather Ely's young forest, for its trunk, instead of standing up straight like all proper trees, lay upon the ground. It was wonderfully easy for small children to climb and the year that it held a Robin's[1] nest we visited it often. As the fledgelings grew we wondered how, after they had left the nest, we would be able to distinguish these very special birds from all the other young Robins. At length we hit upon the scheme of painting the little birds' backs with bright colours; so armed with paintbox, brushes, and a cup of water, my little brother, Harold, and I sallied forth. When we reached the tree, our subjects had flown! So ended my first attempt at marking birds.

Our family alternated — boy, girl, boy, girl — till there were seven of us. I was the middle child, born December 6, 1883. I like to think that the same year saw the birth of the American Ornithologists' Union, although it was a long time before I, in my ignorance, became aware of the existence of that august body.

We were an enterprising lot of youngsters in the large house set in the two-acre orchard and garden at 28 Northampton Road in the village of Amherst, Massachusetts. My father, Anson Daniel Morse, professor of history at Amherst College, had a deep love for the wilderness, yet at the same time was a devoted gardener, delighting in fine flowers and choice fruits. We learned of nature at first hand, planting and weeding in our own small gardens, perpetually fighting in the family garden against weeds and the hateful

[1]American Robin, *Turdus migratorius*

rose bugs; climbing trees and taking care of old Beauty and learning to ride her.

Amherst lies in a broad valley; to the east are the Pelham Hills, to the north wild Mount Toby and rugged Mount Sugarloaf, to the west the Connecticut River, and to the south the Holyoke Range lying like a couchant dragon. It is fascinating country, with its woods and meadows, its clear streams and friendly mountains. Many were the family trips into the countryside, occasionally behind Beauty, but usually afoot.

My mother, inspired by her course in botany at Mount Holyoke Seminary, taught us the names of the wild flowers. Happy memories come to me of Sunday afternoon walks in the woods with the whole family, and of late April trips for flowers for our May baskets to Mill Valley — the only place in the neighbourhood where we knew that spring beauty grew. One spring, two ladies conducted Saturday morning walks for children. On one never-to-be-forgotten May morning I had helped my brothers escort our cow, Daisy, to her pasture in Daisy's Woods, a mile to the west of our home. On this radiant day of buttercups and daisies, bluets and dandelions, we started a Song Sparrow[1] from her eggs; and when we reached home the flaming flowers of Japanese quince were glorified by another flame — the first Ruby-throated Hummingbird[2] of the season.

The first bird book that came into my life was *Jenny and the Birds* by Mrs. Lucy Guernsey, published in 1860 by the American Sunday School Union, Philadelphia. Mother read it aloud to us as we struggled with the family mending pile and, as far as I can remember, it consisted largely of conversations between Jenny the wren and Jenny the proper little girl. The chief item I recall is that the winter home of the House Wren[3] was a well-kept secret. The moralizings of the two Jennys repelled us children.

The first real bird book with which I became acquainted was John B. Grant's *Our Common Birds and How to Know Them*, published in 1891 by Scribner's. In it, the males of ninety species are described, with sixty-four of them illustrated by photographs of stuffed specimens. Mr. Grant's aim was simplification. "Do not attempt," he writes, "to identify any bird which presents puzzling characteristics or, rather, any which does *not* present some striking mark either of song or plumage." Unfortunately, birds with puzzling characteristics insisted on calling attention to themselves instead of always skulking in the bushes. With no hint as to the

---

[1]*Melospiza melodia.* [2] *Archilochus colubris.* [3] *Troglodytes aedon.*

plumages of females and young, and with no emphasis on the locality covered — the New York City region, some one hundred and fifty miles southwest of Amherst — one small girl was badly led astray.

Our cherry trees were full of birds whose colouring best matched the description of Yellow-breated Chats[1]. I thought it strange that they did not seem the least bit shy and I looked in vain for clownish actions; nevertheless, I can remember that as "Y.b. Chats" they were listed in my earliest records and it was some time before I discovered that they were really female and immature Baltimore Orioles[2]. One notable summer an Indigo Bunting[3] sang persistently in our great blackberry patch, but we could locate no mate, looking as we did for another blue bird. We believed him to be a bachelor until we happened upon the nest and thus discovered his plain brown wife.

One June day, by the little alder-bordered brook in the tangle we called Song Sparrow Jungle, I stumbled upon a tiny yellow bird with a black mask across his face. He was quite unbelievable; it was almost as if I had found a fairy! I remembered the name "Hooded Warbler[4]" from our book. Neither it nor the Maryland Yellowthroat[5] (nor the chat, by the way) was illustrated. I jumped to the conclusion that here was a pair of Hooded Warblers and how proud I was of my discovery! But search as I would, I never could find the nest of the indignant pair, which long afterwards I found had been *Yellowthroats.* Thirty years were to pass before I at last beheld a Hooded Warbler.

Although *Our Common Birds* misled me in some respects, in others it should have served as a trustworthy starting point. Looking at it now, it is gratifying to find under the Northern Shrike[6] a good statement of the modern view of the role of predators; namely, that by removing the old and sickly, they actually *benefit* the prey species. As to my "Yellow-breasted Chats" and "Hooded Warblers," they were indeed strangers to the township of Amherst.

I used to say that I kept my first notes on birds when I was eight, but no records have survived earlier than the spring of 1893, when I was nine years of age. In this first of my extant diaries, the Song Sparrow, prophetically enough, is the first bird mentioned. Robins and hummingbirds also appear, as well as spring flowers;

---

[1]*Icteria virens.* [2]Northern Oriole, *Icterus galbula.* [3]*Passerina cyanea.* [4]*Wilsonia citrina.* [5]Common Yellowthroat, *Geothlypis trichas.* [6]*Lanius excubitor.*

but most items tell of Harold's and my expeditions to get inhabitants for our dishpan aquariums.

Each spring the drowsy trill of the American toad called us and armed with pails and strainers and home-made nets, off we started to the nearby railroad cut. Here we found treasures: strings of toad eggs, pollywogs big and little, sedate newts (which we believed were lizards), back-swimmers and alluring whirligig beetles, drab dragonfly larvae, and most tempting of all, caddis fly larvae in their fantastic houses. Caddis flies had fascinated me ever since I had read about them in Charles Kingsley's *Water Babies* (1863), and it was wonderful to find that these almost mythical creatures of English brooks were our neighbours here in our own waters. (In running water we later met them ensconced in tubes of sand granules, or perhaps in half cases plastered to a rock with a tiny net close by for catching prey brought down by the stream.) But these in the stagnant pools made their houses out of bits of leaves, with perchance a fragment of sawdust. Each case was different from every other one. They were irresistible to us and it was hard not to collect just one more absurd example, although we knew only too well their voracious appetites for our precious water plants.

Our summers were largely spent at my Grandfather Ely's country home in Lyme, Connecticut. Here we children, with cousins and our aunts' dogs, Hugo and Napesy, roamed the fields and pastures, sometimes with pails for blackberries, but usually just for fun. We walked on the precariously balanced stone walls and pulled them down when the dogs had brought a woodchuck to bay; we tramped the cedar-and-bayberry-covered hills; we explored Turtle and Roaring Brooks and we swam in the Connecticut River. Each lichen-covered rock had its individuality for us, from Giant Rock with its crown of polypody ferns to the stones we built with under Maple Home. There were long, slow drives in surrey and buckboard behind Dick and Piper and Dinah to Roger's Lake, where a pair of Ospreys[1] nested, and to the beach at Blackhall on Long Island Sound, where more Ospreys nested and where we gathered sea shells on swimming expeditions.

The wide spaces, uninhabited by man, and our own freedom to explore, made of Lyme a magic place. All our expeditions were on foot or with horses. Thus we gained an intimacy with our surroundings that is impossible nowadays with our incredibly speeded-up transportation that reduces one's impressions to a blur. Ruskin truly said: "There was always more in the world than men

[1]*Pandion haliaetus.*

could see, walked they ever so slowly; they will see it no better for going fast."

Our maternal grandfather, Zebulon Stiles Ely, was a great-great-great grandson of Richard Ely, who came from England in 1660 and settled in Lyme; he and his descendants were for the most part farmers. But in my grandfather's generation a sister had gone with her husband as a missionary to India, while a brother had become a brilliant linguist and scholar, a graduate of Yale University and of Princeton Theological Seminary; he was licensed to preach but, sadly enough, died before going to the mission field. Z. Stiles Ely had been a sugar and coffee merchant, but had retired from business at the age of fifty-four. His winter home was New York City and on our visits to him there we enjoyed the sights of the great city: the horse cars, the hansom cabs, the museums, the zoo in Central Park, and Barnum and Bailey's spectacular circus. His summers were spent on his estate, Lord's Hill, in Lyme, not far from the Ely homestead. He was a genial gentleman, both generous and frugal, a lover of the out-of-doors. His greatest interest lay in missionary enterprises.

My grandmother, Sarah Duncan Ely, a sweet and pious lady, had died of tuberculosis when my eldest brother was a baby. She had Scotch-Irish and French blood; her father, James Duncan, had been a mate on a sailing vessel with ports of call in Europe and China. In 1815 he went west and founded a town in eastern Ohio which his wife, Eliza Tillinghast Villette, named after the distinguished French bishop, Massillon. My grandfather's second wife, Mary Post, had been a friend of the family; we children called her Aunty Stiles.

The most cherished Christmas present of my life came in 1895 — Mabel Osgood Wright's *Bird-Craft* (1895). For the first time, I had coloured bird pictures. Many of these were adapted from Audubon's *Birds of America* (1827); single birds, or occasionally a pair, sometimes in surprising attitudes, were depicted. In later years, when looking at the reproductions of Audubon's original plates, every now and then a picture has given me a little tug at the heart, recalling my childhood years of eager search. The simple descriptions, the charming discussions, the enthusiastic introductory chapters of *Bird-Craft* — all these I pored over and all but learned by heart.

Sometimes an author captures the imagination and so stirs anticipation over a particular species that when the bird is finally met there is a glow of satisfaction, a realization that here is a very special character. Thanks to *Bird-Craft*, those were stirring events,

SARAH DUNCAN
(Margaret's maternal grandmother)
From an oil painting

when I met my first Magnolia[1] and Blackburnian Warblers[2] and, many years later in Oklahoma, the Yellow-breasted Chat and White-eyed Vireo[3]. That these two loud-voiced species had been absent from our haunts in Lyme may well have been due to the close pasturing of the hillsides by the cattle and Angora goats of our neighbour, Kansas Nebraska Bill; in 1931 these croppers were gone, shrubs had flourished, and both of these beguiling species were at home on the Ely acres.

---

[1]*Dendroica magnolia.* [2]*Dendroica fusca.* [3]*Vireo griseus.*

Bird-Craft had been the first great step in my ornithological education; some months afterwards came the second. Playing in our attic on a rainy afternoon, I chanced upon a ragged, coverless, undated, and apparently anonymous pamphlet whose first page announced "An Artificial Key to the Birds of Amherst." Beyond this, I found to my wonderment and delight an annotated list of our local birds, and a notation as to whether each was beneficial or injurious. Part I treated "Birds of Regular and Certain Appearance in Amherst at the Proper Seasons," and this I studied with loving care. Part II, "Birds of Irregular and Uncertain Appearance in Amherst," and Part III, "Birds Extremely Rare or Accidental in the Country," I consulted only occasionally. My parents told me that the author was Hubert L. Clark, son of Colonel William S. Clark, a former president of the Massachusetts Agricultural College, which was situated a mile to the north of our home. Later I discovered that *Birds of Amherst and Vicinity* had been published by J. E. Williams in 1887, when the author was only seventeen.

Bird-Craft gave me descriptions and habits and pictures; *Birds of Amherst* told me what to expect and when. I took my precious copy apart, interleaved it for my own observations, fixed up a cover, and fastened it all together again. Following the dictates of *Bird-Craft*, I corrected Hubert Clark's ideas on economic status of various species. I also recorded notes on nests I had found. My chief interest, however, was in outdoing the book in the matter of dates of earliest arrivals; it was always with a glow of pride when I beat *Birds of Amherst.* This local list, although based on inadequate work, was of the greatest value to me in narrowing my field by showing me what species to expect, and in stimulating me to add my mite to the knowledge of our local birds.

As I faithfully studied this guide, I wondered where the fabulous Adams Pond, haunt of waterfowl, could have been, and I was disappointed to read of the former abundance of hawks, Mourning Doves[1], Barn Swallows[2], and Vesper Sparrows[3]. In later years, Dr. Clark and I became friends, and in response to my persuasions, he wrote an account of how he came to publish this bulletin while still in high school. "How I Became an Ornithologist and How I Fell from Grace" appeared in the *Bulletin of the Massachusetts Audubon Society* in January 1947.

Under the guidance and encouragement of W. A. Stearns, professor of zoology in the M.A.C., Hubert Clark (1883) had published in our weekly newspaper, the *Amherst Record,* a list of the

[1]*Zenaidura macroura.* [2]*Hirundo rustica.* [3]*Pooecetes gramineus.*

"Butterflies of Amherst," when only thirteen years of age! He became an observer of bird migration for the Biological Survey in Washington when fifteen, and the next year received a rifle with which he roamed the fields at daylight every day but Sunday. His ambition was to verify and amplify a list of Amherst birds published by Professor Stearns in 1883, and to prepare an annotated list to be brought out as a pamphlet by the *Amherst Record*. In this effort he was assisted by a sportsman, a taxidermist, and by Professor C. A. Fernald of the "Aggie," who "suggested the form for the artificial keys."

Adams Pond had been situated between our home and the Aggie; it had been formed by the damming of one of our favourite streams — Clam River to us, Tim's River to Hubert Clark, Mill River on the map. The pond had been drained before our explorations began some ten years later, and all we knew in its place were pastures, thickets, and the creek. Dr. Clark kept up his interest in ornithology, particularly in pterylography (the study of the distribution of the feather tracts over the bird's body), but for his life work he turned to starfish and sea urchins, and in this pursuit travelled to the far corners of the earth.

In August, 1896 our family received a cruel blow in the death of my best-beloved brother, Harold; of all of us children it fell heaviest on me. When we drove to Woldwood to choose a plot in the woods, my instant thought on seeing some migrating warblers was, "I must tell Harold." And then I remembered I never again could tell him anything.

This bereavement threw me on my own resources, and I turned to birds with a passion that was not to be matched for many years.

My second surviving diary (from October 25 to December 6, 1896) is full of notes on fall migrants, on nests, the weather, and on my pair of canaries. By this time, I had a good acquaintance with the local birds. I wrote:

Oct. 29 Juncos[1] abundant. Kinglets have come. Warblers have passed.

Nov. 7 Driving up to Wildwood I counted 54 nests in the trees we passed. Coming home, 21 Oriole nests, all built so we could not get them; 29 other nests, including Chippies[2], Robins', Cedar Birds[3] and 1 Vireo's nest.

Nov. 8 Going to church found 5 Vireos' nests and 1 Yellow Warbler's nest. (These must have been all Red-eyed Vireo[4] nests.)

Nov. 9 This is the time to find nests. Saw 47 of them from school to home. Climbed up a maple and got a Vireo's nest.

---

[1]Dark-eyed Junco, *Junco hyemalis.* [2]Chipping Sparrow, *Spizella passerina.*
[3]Cedar Waxwing, *Bombycilla cedrorum.* [4]*Vireo olivaceus.*

My "personally taken" collection of nests was augmented by a windfall. My mother had taken me to call upon two elderly ladies who had a number of nests; upon seeing my admiration, they then and there presented them to me. I arranged all my best nests on a shelf above my bed — the greatest prizes being a bunch of glued twigs of a Chimney Swift[1] and a few straws laid by a Mourning Dove on top of an old Robin's nest. I gloated over my treasures, and every evening, for fear I might forget their identity, I recited their names.

For this Christmas I had written on my list of wanted gifts, "Any book of Olive Thorne Miller's." What was my despair to find my mother had inadvertently bought *Four-handed Folk* (1896)! Life had betrayed this bird-hungry child with a book on *monkeys*! Sarah suggested a trade with Katharine, who had received Mrs. Wright's *Tommy-Anne and the Three Hearts* (1896). Katharine did not mind, and Christmas for me was once more Christmas. This book was fascinating to us, representing as it did a nature-loving girl who had been given "magic spectacles" that enabled her to talk with the wild creatures. Unlike *Jenny and the Birds,* the animals talked in character, we loved it and longed for magic spectacles for ourselves.

Nevertheless, one of Mrs. Miller's books of essays on birds would have been better for me. *Tommy-Anne* led me away from my small start toward serious bird study, as shown in my notes to *Birds of Amherst* and in my tiny booklet on the *Fates and Fortunes of Fruit-Acre Birds,* 1896. In this I recorded the outcome of the twelve nests of robins, Chipping Sparrows, and Least Flycatchers[2] on our grounds in April and May; six of them succeeded in fledging twenty young out of forty-five eggs laid.

Interestingly enough, the percentage of success — 44.4 — corresponds well with that reported by me sixty-one years later; twenty-nine studies by twenty-three people of open nests of altricial birds (those whose young are helpless at hatching) in the North Temperate Zone averaged a fledging success of 46 percent for 21,951 eggs.

---

[1] *Chaetura pelagica.*   [2] *Empidonax minimus.*

II

Our Cherished Hens

Two years of kindergarten followed by five years of elementary instruction were passed by all of us in a little red schoolhouse, the private institution of imposing Miss Perkins and gentle, gray-haired Miss Hills. We then entered the seventh grade of the public school and after three years were ready for high school. The ninth grade proved to be largely a review of what we had studied before.

Time, in this grade, hung heavy on my hands, and I amused myself with starting a newspaper and writing a book — both supposed to be composed by birds. The book is on "Bird Families;" its author, "Hermit Peckwood," a conceited Hairy Woodpecker[1]. There are nine families: "Climbers, Fruit Lovers, Seed Eaters, Fly-catchers, Ground Builders, Pensile Nests, Tinys, Larges, Cannibals." In this last class Cowbirds[2], Shrikes, Blue Jays[3], Crows[4], Hawks, Owls, and Eagles are eloquently castigated for their misdomeanours. The violent prejudice against predators was largely a reflection from *Bird-Craft* and *Tommy-Anne*. These whimsical enterprises of mine "Fruit-Acre News" and "Bird Families" were composed mainly for my own entertainment.

Both grammar and high school were in a large, old building next to a ravine with a little brown brook and a great scarlet oak. This ravine was a favourite place for me during recess. The school building itself was of ornithological interest, for in its attic there was a colony of pigeons; the sound of their cooing mingled with our

---

[1] *Picoides villosus.* [2] Brown-headed Cowbird, *Molothrus ater.* [3] *Cyanocitta cristata.* [4] Common Crow, *Corvus brachyrhynchos.*

Greek and Latin recitations. Occasionally, when the janitor had left the ladder in place, we climbed to the attic and gathered a few squabs which we established in the barn at home. The half-mile walk to and from school at times was richly rewarding. Two days stand out in my memory: one first of May made glad by the return of Rose-breasted Grosbeaks[1] and Baltimore Orioles; a never-to-be-forgotten winter morning when a flock of Pine Grosbeaks[2] perched in the shrubbery, the bright red of the males brilliant against the snow.

In the ninth grade each of us had to write a Thanksgiving story; mine concerned two chickadees[3], their plight when the trees were all covered by a glare of ice, their rejoicing when the ice melted. My pleasant teacher, Miss Abbott, was impressed. She asked me to write a paper for the class on "Winter Birds." This I did and proudly read it. All I remember about it was the glee with which some of the boys fastened upon "Yellow-bellied Sapsucker[4]." "Have you seen a Yellow-bellied Sapsucker lately?" they would inquire, and I would gravely answer "Yes" or "No."

At the time of starting Latin I had been reading Charles Dickens's *Child's History of England* (1853-54) and I reported my impressions in a letter to my father:

"The character that I most admire is King Alfred the Great. He was courageous and persevering, whom misfortunes could not subdue, whom fortune could not spoil, and whose great love of learning did more to preserve the English language than Dickens can imagine."

The Amherst High School at that time had courses in physics and chemistry, but nothing in biology. Latin and Greek, French and German, mathematics, English and history, were the other subjects I remember as being offered. It was a solid program mostly oriented toward preparation for college. When I graduated I had credits for four years in Latin, three in Greek, and one in French, besides four in mathematics and English, and one in Greek and Roman history.

In February 1897, my father went to California for a few months for his health. My letters to him speak of skunk cabbage and pussy willows, arbutus and hepaticas; of Song Sparrows, a Bald Eagle[5], and a "sad and lonely Robin" that "almost never sings": of Robins nesting for the third year in the same crotch of one of our apple trees; of getting "two pretty nests and six eggs of the English

---

[1] *Pheucticus ludovicianus.* [2] *Pinicola enucleator.*
[3] Black-capped Chickadee. *Parus atricapillus.*
[4] *Sphyrapicus varius.* [5] *Haliaeetus leucocephalus.*

Sparrow[1]" from the arc-light man. Also a pair of bluebirds[2] "fixing things very nicely already to lay the eggs" in a last year's flicker's[3] hole, while "the male flicker drums on the Wards' chimney's tintop, waiting for a mate. I guess he will be very angry at finding the bluebirds established there."

The other chief topic of these letters concerns our hens. In the previous fall Sarah and I had acquired a dozen Brown Leghorns; these were all named, cherished and, due to Sarah's insistence that we give them superlative care and that I keep meticulous records on their laying abilities, they absorbed too much of our time and energy. Sarah was ingenious. She devised a system of one-way entrances to the laying pen, so each day we recorded those biddies waiting to be released into their general quarters. They were pets and objects of study. We told the family about their characters and exploits and announced that we learned much from them about human psychology. This attitude was sternly rebuked by our parents as incompatible with the Christian religion. "Peck order" was an everyday fact to us. Once I started a notebook on the characters of our hens, relating how Rexie bossed Prexie, Prexie bossed Queerie but, amusingly enough, Queerie pecked Rexie. By the time I had jotted down accounts of half a dozen biddies, I suddenly thought: What is the use? I'll remember these things all my life. Alas, I did not remember the details. But that was the end of my recorded observations on heirarchy in Brown Leghorns.

More than thirty years later I read in the *Zeitschrift für Psychologie* the doctoral dissertation of a Norwegian — Thorlief Schjelderup-Ebbe on this very subject — *Beiträge zur Sozialpsychologie des Haushuhns* (1922). It seemed too absurd to be reading ponderous statements in German of what we had known so well in our teens. Schjelderup-Ebbe's work, although of uneven value, inspired others to study dominance relations in hens and other animals. Dr. W. Clyde Allee of the University of Chicago and his students became the foremost investigators of this subject. I once told him of my uncompleted records on this matter. "That would have been a first," said he.

When Sarah was at Lyme, I wrote to her of an exciting happening involving my hens:

I saw Three Feather and Caterpillar looking so queer, so I went to see what was the matter. There I saw a snake; taking a stick I beat him to death. Hens were much alarmed at him. I took him on my stick (he was 3 feet, 2 inches

[1]House Sparrow, *Passer domesticus.* [2]Eastern Bluebird, *Sialia sialia.*
[3]Common Flicker, *Colaptes auratus.*

long), laid him down and scattered grain by him. No hen dared touch the food. But Golden came running from a distance, greatly delighted at the food. She stood right on the snake as she gobbled. Suddenly she discovered what was under her feet. She gave a horrified scream, leaping into the air and rushed away.

I deplore my behaviour in killing that poor snake; it must have been due to my hatred of predators derived from Mrs. Wright's books.

The hens lasted until I graduated from high school. They were a trial to my father in their enthusiasm for his garden. Once he wrote me when I was at Lyme: "I think — indeed I know — that the precious creatures at the barn are thriving. The olders ones have been taking tomato-tonic (at my expense) with surprising results — almost a doubling of the number of eggs." They were a trial to my mother, too, who resented the time we consumed in their company. Yet I benefited from them in many ways: from the practical experience in farm work; from the knowledge gained of bird behaviour; from the training in arithmetic (later useful in research); from the keeping of elaborate accounts and records; and finally from the goodly sums earned and put away in the Savings Bank.

In July I had gone to Lyme with my Aunt Data before any of the others of my family; my over-cautious parents forbade me to go out of the ten-acre park surrounding my grandfather's stone "mansion" without a grownup. To compensate for this irksome restriction my nine-year-old cousin, Dick, and I turned to tree-climbing as our chief sport. I wrote to Sarah: "Data thinks I'm made of iron — scrambling up trees by the hour. My arms are all scratched and scraped from climbing so much."

In answer to a gentle remonstrance from my father, I wrote him:

"If all the books about training daughters don't mention tree-climbing and out-of-doors exercise, I ought to write one myself. I think a girl ought to know how to ride, drive (a horse), climb, swim, row, cook, sew, do general housework, take walks, and have a good many pets. Made to go to bed early and get up early. Perhaps I will think of some more later."

I was eager to read the best books — poetry and other classics. My father often read to us at breakfast inspiring passages from books, such as Wordsworth's "Ode to Duty," (1807) Emerson's "The Days," (1867) and *Marcus Aurelius Antoninus to Himself* (1898). One small volume made a strong impression on me — George W. Palmer's *Self-Cultivation in English* (1897). All of his precepts were helpful: his encouragement to cultivate "accuracy, audacity, and range" in our speech, and especially his advice to "seek every opportunity to write," to treat composition "as an opportunity, a chance, and not as a burden or compulsion." I tried to follow his counsel, and since I must have written over thirty thousand letters in my life, I have not lacked for practice.

Two lectures that I heard made lasting impressions. John Tyler, Professor of Zoology at Amherst College, talked to the High School Girls' Club on "Weeds;" he told us that to call a plant a weed is to give it the greatest of compliments for it has shown itself hardy and successful in the struggle for existence. This was a new viewpoint for me who had been taught to hate weeds as pests; who had pulled them up in the family garden at the stipend of three cents an hour, and under the spur of my Grandfather Ely's detestation of the graceful Queen Anne's lace had uprooted "lace weeds" at the rate of one cent for fifty.

On my fifteenth birthday Dr. G. Stanley Hall, President of Clark University at Worcester, Massachusetts, lectured at Amherst on "Love and Study of Nature." In my diary I find these quotations: "Science, art, literature, religion (except Christianity) originate in love of nature. Nature is the backbone of all education. Love is the great principle of nature and life." Little did I imagine that one day I would study nature at Clark University.

One day, Father told us of a visitor to his class who had asked him a question after his lecture. In answering, Father had added the word Sir, whereupon the stranger drew herself up and announced, "Dr. Mary Walker." This indomitable woman had been nurse and surgeon in the Union forces during the Civil War. She was greatly exercised over the unhygenic clothes that women wore — tight corsets and long, heavy skirts that dragged on the ground. To set a good example, she donned male attire. As this was forbidden by law, she was continually being jailed, but she refused to submit.

Despite our long skirts, it is clear that we girls led active, out-of-doors lives, taking long walks, and riding our bicycles, as well as our intelligent but rather temperamental horse Rex. For this last enterprise we wore divided skirts, as we always rode a man's saddle. At Amherst our chief companion was our next-door neighbour, Malleville Emerson, an ardent horse-lover.

Sixty years ago household help was plentiful and inexpensive, while labour-saving devices were few. We, like most of our friends on the faculty, had two maids, who did all the housework, including the washing and ironing. Our house had two coal furnaces in the cellar, and a coal-burning stove in the kitchen. For lighting we had gas in the halls, kerosene lamps for reading, and candles for going to bed. Automobiles were scarce, and how Rex did prance and plunge when he met one! We did not have a telephone before 1898. Movies, black and white and silent, were just starting, and how silly their plots were! For music at home we had our piano.

My childhood had been a very happy one, with wonderful parents, a flock of congenial brothers and sisters, and the glories of nature at Lyme and Amherst. In my teens, however, I often felt depressed. Our parents were old-fashioned and over-protective; my mother perpetuated the attitudes of her parents, while my father was determined to spare us the struggles of his own childhood. They did not believe that their daughters should prepare themselves for professions. To be a "perfect housekeeper and homemaker" was the ideal held before us and how dreary it did seem (although I never imagined then that in adult life I would have to do much housework myself)! We three girls all wished we had been boys, since boys had far more freedom than girls did to explore the world and to choose exciting careers.

Once my brother Will asked what I would like to do in the future. "I wish I could help Nature, make people love Nature more," I replied, with a vague notion of writing essays like Burroughs or Torrey, although composition had never been my forte at that age. I lacked an earnest purpose for my life.

III

When
Wednesday
Was a Holiday

College was an adventure in friendships, in learning, and in the out-of-doors. When I entered Mount Holyoke College at South Hadley, Massachusetts, in September 1901, I had, for the first time, freedom to arrange my life pretty much as I wanted it, unhampered by parental solicitude. College rules were easy to keep: I was glad to go to bed at ten o'clock, and as for not "walking alone outside the village limits," riding Rex was neither walking nor "alone," in my view.

From the founding of the Seminary, Wednesday had been an all-day holiday, and this proved a boon to me for all-day explorations of the countryside. By the greatest good fortune, I had two like-minded companions for these excursions; Ruth Cutter from Brooklyn, New York, during the first two years and Lucy Day from West Newton, Massachusetts, during the last two. Most of the students, in my opinion, wasted Wednesday in studying. My academic work was strictly confined to the five other weekdays and to the evenings from seven to nine-thirty.

Ruth and I had a new region to get acquainted with, even if it was only ten miles south of Amherst. The gentle south slopes of the Holyoke Range are different from the steep north slopes. Moreover, the Connecticut River was much nearer College than it was to my home in Amherst. The country was wilder, less inhabited here than there, and there were two fine brooks — Stony and Bachelor — to be explored.

We kept no notes on birds or flowers. It was nature in general and the fun of walking in such pleasant country that we loved. With Thoreau, our walking was "itself the enterprise and adventure of the day" (1862). During my sophomore year Ruth sat at the same table in Brigham Hall as Miss Jeanette Marks, professor of English Literature, and a rivalry gradually arose between her and us, for she also was a confirmed walker.

One Wednesday, Ruth and I started east and we walked and walked until we came to the Swift River Valley, and there, half hidden in the mist, like a city in a fairy-tale, lay Enfield. We turned back and stopped at the Belchertown Hotel for an ample country dinner; after a rest in the fields we reached College feeling as vigorous after our twelve-hour, thirty-one-mile walk as when we had started.

We boasted of our walk to Enfield. "Enfield, Connecticut?" No one had ever heard of Enfield, Massachusetts. It was plain we would have to go to this other Enfield, and for good measure we decided to go beyond, even to Hartford — forty miles from South Hadley. On June 3rd we started at four o'clock in the morning, after a snack; we walked cheerily south until we reached Springfield where in a small park at eight o'clock we ate a substantial picnic breakfast. Somehow, after this our enthusiasm waned. We toiled on through lengthy Longmeadow and endless Enfield and on and on. Nowhere could we discover a good eating place where we could revive our strength; we could only nibble our crackers and sweet chocolate. It was dull country in comparison to our other walks, relieved once by a colony of Bank Swallows[1], again by an incredibly blue field of blue-eyed grass, and finally by the welcome discovery of wild strawberries.

We felt like Thoreau and his friend on their tramp to Mount Wachusett, "At length as we plodded along the dusty roads, our thoughts became as dusty as they; all thought indeed stopped, thinking broke down, or proceeded only passively in a sort of rhythmical cadence of the confused material of thought" (1843). My chief emotion became envy of those happy householders we passed who could stay at home. At length and at last at six o'clock we caught the train at Hartford for Holyoke — two "over-walkers" fully convinced with Robert Louis Stevenson that "to walk this unconscionable distance is only to stupify oneself." (1907)

One notable day, in June 1902, at a reception at our home for the Amherst College class back for its tenth reunion, whom should I meet but Hubert Lyman Clark! With beating heart I told him I

[1]*Riparia riparia*

had surpassed some of his records for earliest arrivals of Amherst birds. To my delight he said he would be very happy to have them as he was planning a second edition of *Birds of Amherst*. When, four years later, I received a copy of the revised edition, inscribed, "With the compliments of the author," and stating in the preface, "Additional notes on other species, particularly in reference to spring arrivals, have been very kindly furnished me by Miss Margaret Morse," (1906) all of our family were proud indeed.

My college course was interrupted by almost a year in Europe with Aunty Stiles (my step-grandmother Ely), as well as with a lovely friend of hers, Miss Ella Higgins, and one of Aunty Stiles's nieces, Mabel Coulter. We spent an unhurried winter in Naples and Rome, and spring in the hill towns with visits to all the major and some of the minor places in Italy. We studied in leisurely fashion the Italian language, art, architecture, and history. In summer we visited the Tyrol, Switzerland, Germany, Holland, and England.

The European trip was a happy, rich experience with art, architecture, scenery, alpine flowers, and interesting people, but as far as birds were concerned, my eyes and ears were sealed. The only notes on birds in my diary concern gulls in the harbours, nightingales[1] in the ancient Botanical Garden at Padua and at Lago di Garda, and one White Stork[2] at Strassburg.

In September I returned eagerly to college with an enriched background for study and a new appreciation of my opportunities.

Ruth Cutter had graduated, but by the greatest good luck I found another comrade, Lucy Day, an expert canoeist and enthusiastic horseback rider; she was glad to spend Wednesday exploring the countryside. After all, had not Mary Lyon established Wednesday as Recreation Day.

New possibilities were now open. We explored the woods and mountains — Holyoke, Tom, and Norwottuck — on foot and horseback, too, for one winter I had Rex in South Hadley, and the next winter, Dolly, the mare belonging to our good friend, Malleville Emerson. Lucy hired horses from the livery stable.

One galling prohibition of our youth was that against the girls going walking in the woods and fields without a brother; our suggestion that we protect ourselves with a revolver met with strong disapprobation. During my sophomore year I had written home that I would like to purchase a .22 rifle; my father objected as follows: "(1) it is exceedingly dangerous; (2) it brings upon a young woman who is addicted to it the name of being eccentric."

---

[1] *Erithacus megarhynchos.* [2] *Ciconia ciconia.*

THE MORSE FAMILY
PHOTOGRAPH TAKEN ON STEPS OF MORSE HOUSE AT
28 NORTHAMPTON ROAD, AMHERST, MASS.
ON OCCASION OF THE PARENTS' SILVER WEDDING ANNIVERSARY
SEPTEMBER 3, 1903

Front row (left to right): Anson Ely (aged 24). Sarah Duncan (aged 22). Edward
Stiles (aged 11). Katharine Duncan (aged 15). William Northrop (aged 21).
Margaret (aged 20). Back row: Margaret Duncan Morse (Mother, aged 48).
Anson Daniel Morse (Father, aged 57).

In my junior year I bought the rifle and blithely wrote home of Lucy's and my practice with it; we were re-enacting the current Russo-Japanese War in a ravine to the west of College with paper targets on tree stubs. Mother wrote, "I cannot smile, I fear, on your rifle practice; it seems to me dangerous, and not an appropriate pastime for young women."

I did not tell my parents that I had also bought a revolver. Although I never had any excuse for using it — except in our so-called War — it was a great comfort to me in my solitary explorations of the Holyoke Range on horseback and also on foot with Lucy. And the same was true many years later on my eight-mile bird censuses in Oklahoma.

The purchase of a canoe, however, could not be kept secret. After much persuasion my parents consented, but only if our craft were provided with sponsons — bulky air-chambers — on each side. At my suggestion we christened her Thyone, which I untruthfully told Lucy was an Indian name meaning "Leaf-on-the-water" (*most* inappropriate for the awkward thing). Some years later at the Biological Station at Woods Hole, Massachusetts, Lucy was dumbfounded when starting on the study of the bizarre sea-cucumber to discover the real origin of the name. Thyone was housed on the Upper Lake in a tar-paper shack kindly built for her by the College. On pleasant Wednesdays in spring we had her taken in a farmer's cart to the Connecticut River and thus we explored Stony and Bachelor Brooks from their mouths.

The academic courses that were to be of use to me in ornithological research in later years were those in modern languages — French, German, and Italian — and in the natural sciences — geology, botany, and, particularly, zoology. The courses in geology with my friend Miss Mignon Talbot were interesting, but I regret to say, I forgot much of their content. The botany courses I took were mainly concerned with structure and stirred no answering chord in me. There was, however, a field course dealing with plant associations. It was a pity that I did not select physiographic ecology.

In my five courses in zoology under Miss Louise Wallace, Miss Abby Turner, and Dr. Cornelia Clapp, I received an excellent foundation, both practical and theoretical. For the bird study portion of first-year zoology, I bought Frank M. Chapman's *Handbook of the Birds of North America* (1895), a book which did not arouse my enthusiasm. We all kept lists of spring arrivals on the blackboard; thanks to horseback rides through the country-side, my list headed all the others, until at last Miss Wallace got busy and outdistanced me.

Yet this bird study in class, chiefly identification, failed to awaken my former zeal. I felt I knew it all. I was unaware of any problems remaining to be solved, at any rate, any problems that held an appeal to me. I could see very little connection between the courses in college and the wild things I loved. I benefited from the knowledge acquired of varied forms of life, but the approach seemed to me a dead one. I did not like to cut up animals.

The four years at Mount Holyoke College were very happy for me, with excellent courses under stimulating teachers, the companionship of true friends, and carefree exploration of the lovely country. I was fortunate in making real friendships with two of my teachers – Miss Mary Young of the Romance Language Department and Miss Mignon Talbot, Geologist, who had many congenial outdoor interests. Dr. Clapp was a delightful person, full of fun, overflowing with kindness and high spirits. Our president, Mary Woolley, was a constant inspiration to us in her poise, her graciousness, her vision, and her ideals. The majority of the faculty were noble women, primarily interested in things of the mind, vital, and eager for the betterment of the world.

I believe that I was the only one of my class of 150 who graduated without a definite plan for earning her living, either at once or in the future. I did not want to teach school, nor had I taken the courses necessary for this occupation. I saw no future in laboratory zoology. I was not expert in any foreign language. I was to return to Amherst to be a daughter-at-home as my parents wished.

During a six-weeks' stay at the Biological Station at Woods Hole that summer I was again fortunate in finding a congenial girl friend, Emma Longfellow, Mount Holyoke, 1904. Many were the picnic suppers we took together in country that was then little inhabited. I enjoyed the elementary course at the Marine Biological Laboratory and liked to view the sea creatures in their homes. I went swimming nearly every day. There was one notable early morning trip with a lobster fisherman to a small colony of Least Terns[1] nesting on Woopecket Island.

That fall at home my mother and I attended my father's daily class in American History; I cared for my father's greenhouse; I rode horseback; and I told our old coloured cook, Fanny, what to prepare for our meals. Fanny could neither read nor write, nor did she know her age; she had been born a slave and had reached young womanhood when the Civil War ended. She was always

---

[1] *Sterna albifrons.*

giving us children advice. For instance, to cure a child of stuttering, have him drink from a clam shell for a year; this had worked with her brother. An egg laid on Good Friday will never spoil; she had seen such an egg with its contents all dried up. What one does on New Year's Day foretells what one will do the rest of the year, hence with Fanny in the kitchen no New Year's state dinners. To rid our grounds of the hateful rose chafers, fill a small bottle with them and throw it into the Freshman River at Mill Valley. Strangely enough, we proved to be "hard-headed young uns" and disregarded her well-meant admonitions.

In February 1907 my mother, Sarah, Will, and I travelled on the Sante Fe to California to attend my brother's wedding in San Jose. We came home in May by the way of Mexico. The strangeness of the West was fascinating to me — the amazing wind-eroded rock formations on the way to California, the loveliness of that sparsely populated state with its live oaks, redwoods, and Monterey cypresses, its rich sea life, including the astonishing sea lions, and on the land the abundant, fat ground squirrels. My interest in birds, however, was superficial. Mountain Bluebirds[1] in Arizona, Western Meadowlarks[2] and Mockingbirds[3], Killdeer[4], House Finches[5], Golden-crowned Sparrows[6], Valley Quail[7] and cormorants in California — these are the birds that impressed me most.

I was a little disappointed in the songs of the Mockingbirds and Western Meadowlarks; it became clear to me that association plays a large part in our enjoyment of bird song as well as in our own music. Two lectures by Professor William E. Ritter which I visited in the course in bird study at the University of California at Berkeley gave me my first news of Life Zones proposed by C. Hart Merriam (1894). I purchased Mrs. Irene Wheelock's *Birds of California* (1904), a popular book in which "Keys have been avoided and a simple classification, according to habitat or colour, substituted."

In preparation for the trip to Mexico I had bought a beginner's book in Spanish and a small dictionary. A professor at Mount Holyoke College gave me two tutoring lessons and at Berkeley I visited two classed in the subject. Needless to say, my Spanish was deplorable; nevertheless, it helped us mightily in the unspoiled Mexico of 1907. Mother, Sarah, and I travelled to Cordoba, Oaxaca, Mitla, and Mexico City; we saw strange trees and flowers

---

[1]*Sialia currucoides.* [2]*Sturnella neglecta.* [3]*Mimus polyglottos.* [4]*Charadrius vociferus.* [5]*Carpodacus mexicanus.* [6]*Zonotrichia atricapilla.* [7] California Quail, *Lophortyx californicus.*

and wondrous great fireflies, but the only birds I remember were the superabundant vultures – the *Zopilotis*.

Back home in May to the burning question of escape from the toils of home, I was desperately dissatisfied with the aimless life of a daughter-at-home. I thought I would like to teach nature study somewhere, but there seemed to be no such opportunities. I toyed with the idea of social work, for which my only qualifications were a smattering of languages and a kind heart. And then fate took a hand.

The Massachusetts Agricultural College started a summer school that year and I attended. It was in Amherst, a mile from home, and I rode my bicycle there and back. The various nature and gardening courses that I took made little impression on me, but a visitor who gave two lectures had a profound effect on me and gave direction to my whole life. Dr. Clifton F. Hodge of Clark University, Worcester, Massachusetts, told us about studying *live* animals, with the toad as chief example, how much and what they ate, how they affected man. If I could study such things in a university, life would have a real purpose for me. I talked with Dr. Hodge about this possibility and he was most encouraging. He had a problem all ready for me: he had plenty of farm-raised Bob-whites[1], and I could study their food. This was an exciting possibility to me, but my parents were full of doubts.

At last my brother Ted and I were about to realize one of our great ambitions – a tump-line camping trip. When on August 17 we came downstairs to get ourselves a very early breakfast I found a note from my father: "I am verging to the conclusion that in view of all your talents, proclivities, likings and dislikings and accomplishments, it may be advisable for you to specialize in the field of Biology with the purpose of teaching and writing."

So it was with hopes of high adventure in the future as well as in the present that we started off that morning. The success of this trip was largely due to the hard work, ingenuity, and woodcraft of my 15-year-old brother. Faithfully he had studied techniques and equipment in book after book and countless outing journals. He had sewed food bags on the sewing machine; he had experimented with drying corn and blackberries; he planned, assembled, and rejected until at last all was ready. We were to carry house, blankets, kitchen, wardrobes, and larder on our backs by means of tump-lines – broad leather straps over the forehead, the pack resting on the small of the back. One pack weight 28 pounds, the other

[1]*Colinus virginianus.*

varied between 18 and 25 according to the state of our provisions.

We took the train to Hinsdale, New Hampshire, just across the Massachusetts border, and from there we headed for the primeval forest, which I had once visited on a horseback trip. With our wordly goods on our backs, all we needed for a night's lodging were two trees to support our silk tent, and a source of water nearby. The world was before us; we had cast off the shackles of civilization. To us there was something heroic and elemental in this adventure, something that gave us a belief in ourselves that perhaps we never lost.

Through the wonderful great white pines and hemlocks, 400 years old and over 200 feet tall, through ferns and over mosses, we made our way to lonely, beautiful Kilburn Pond. On a bluff overlooking the water we made camp and slept on springy beds of hemlock. All the next day we trudged through the ancient forest, majestic in rain and mist, up and down ridges and through a long swamp until our packs grew heavy and we feared our necks might snap in two. By Broad Brook, glowing with cardinal flowers, we found a resting place; at night there were many little scurryings past our heads, pillowed on our shoes and canvas leggings.

The next morning we found the road, and very happy we were to have reached it. Soon afterwards, we saw Mount Monadnock rising steeply from the plain, "its sublime gray mass, that antique, brownish-gray Ararat colour," as Thoreau had written 50 years earlier (1906). In leisurely fashion we made our way northeast along dirt roads, untroubled by automobiles, from one quiet little lake to another, through avenues of shimmering paper birches and past woods of pine, oak, and beech.

At New Hancock we descended upon my geology teacher, Miss Talbot, and in her tent and the cottage of her friends, the Westons, we were royally entertained. Lake Nubanusit was a wild and lovely place with its spruce-covered shores and its strange, wild cries of Loons[1].

After a few days of luxury, we started once more, heading southeast for Mount Monadnock. Meeting a bull in the path, we climbed the wall and found great ripe blackberries and then fringed gentians. How often in life a defeat brings rich compensation! The night before we climbed Monadnock itself we were awakened by a series of blood-curdling screams, surely from an angry wildcat insulted at the instrusion of our small tent into his domain. We knew well enough that these creatures are normally

[1]Common Loon, *Gavia immer.*

timid; but we remembered tales of exceptionally fierce individuals. Unaccountably, we had forgotten to take the revolver with us! Armed with safety axe and camp knife, Ted crept to the tent door, but could see no enemy in the moonlight. To allay our excitement we ate our breakfast, cold pancakes saved from supper. In retrospect, I imagine the screecher had been a Great Horned Owl[1]. Ted writes me, however, "I think still, that it was a bobcat."

On Monadnock we established a base camp on the south slope near a spring among yellow birches. Unhampered by our packs we climbed to the summit and saw southern New Hampshire spread out before us. That night it started to rain and it kept right on raining. Even Ted's woodmanship failed to get us a fire out of soaking yellow birch, so our rice stayed in its bag. We had miscalculated on provisions, and all that we had all day was a few crackers and a pittance of brown sugar.

So severe had been the pruning of our luggage that we had no reading matter; with conversation (some of it wistful remarks on the bountiful table at home), and gymnastic exercises in our cramped quarters, the wet, hungry day at length came to an end.

The six miles to the station the next morning were quickly covered; our earthly frames had an unaccustomed lightness. We were glad to reach home. We had been gone two weeks and had walked with our packs some 90 miles.

Although as Thoreau writes we were "weary and travel-worn," it had been "sincere experience" (1892). We had learned a more fundamental sense of values; we had new self respect in knowing we could rough it and meet difficulties without complaint. We had new appreciation of the comforts of civilization; never again, we thought, would we take them for granted. We had been brought near to the primal sources of life. This experience might be thought of as a parable of life; a journey, stripped down to essentials and involving struggle and hardship, to see and to love some of the wonders of the world.

---

[1] *Bubo virginianus.*

IV

I Find
My Goal

It was at Clark University that I found a purpose in life. Dr. Hodge, Dr. Hall, and my fellow students showed me that the world was full of problems crying to be solved; at every turn there was a challenge — nature waiting to be studied and understood. For the first time I comprehended the phrase that had so often puzzled me in my youth — "the search for truth." This was the first great step — the orientation to a world that offered discoveries to the searcher, the ability to penetrate the mask of things, to follow hidden paths and find unsuspected beauty and truth. To see and record the what and the how; to venture hypotheses as to the why. Clark University gave me my first awakening. I had found my goal.

Clark University had been founded in 1887 by a successful business man, Jonas Clark, who commissioned G. Stanley Hall to organize a unique university. Dr. Hall was a psychologist, particularly interested in the subject of child development. He had studied in Europe and lectured at Harvard and Johns Hopkins Universities. He gathered together a faculty for a coeducational university purely for graduate students. This did not suit Mr. Clark who, at his death, left his money to found Clark College. In 1907 the college was a small one for men only; college and university used the same rooms and some of the professors taught in both institutions.

G. Stanley Hall, President, and Professor of Psychology, was an extraordinary man. Six days a week, from eleven to twelve-thirty he lectured, giving six different courses each year. His subjects, among others, included religion, child development, sex, abnormal psychology, and social problems. He was the first psychologist in this country to take cognizance of Freud and Jung. On Monday evenings his Seminar lasted from seven to eleven; his students read reports from their theses and Dr. Hall commented on them with marked erudition. In his autobiography (1923) he wrote: "Man is really just starting on his career as an investigator, so that research is not only the apex of creative evolution and the highest vocation of man, but is the greatest joy that life affords to mortals."

In many respects Dr. Hodge and Dr. Hall resembled each other. Both possessed brilliant, original minds; both lacked patience to verify their intuitions. What was said of the psychologist applied as well to the biologist: "never for a moment did he value science save as it gives meaning and value to human life." Dr. Hodge's interests lay in applied biology. In the introduction to his book — *Nature Study and Life* (1902), he tells us that the study of living things is the "sheet anchor of elementary education"; that his purpose was "to bring nature into relation to child life, rather than to school life, to make it a continuous source of delight, profit, and highest education," for "touch with nature at first hand, original research, if you please, is the very breath of mental life."

Dr. Hodge's personality was dynamic; he was always up and doing, and bitter in his scorn of stuffy and timid people who sat in armchairs and followed the books. His zeal was great to save our native fauna and flora (with a few exceptions) and to exterminate pests — flies, mosquitoes, House Sparrows, and cats. It was these last two and especially the arch-demon cat, that were the greatest obstacles to his hopes of multiplying our native birds and of having every garden a sanctuary where the Bobwhite and other birds would take care of the insect problem.

He was one of the first men to raise Ruffed Grouse[1] in captivity; this he achieved from 1901 to 1907. At the meeting of the American Ornithologists' Union in December 1909*, he persuaded Colonel Anthony R. Kuser, a patron of ornithology who later financed William Beebe's *Monographs on the Pheasants* (1918-22), to withdraw his offer of $100 for a freshly killed specimen of a Passenger Pigeon[2] and to offer instead $300 for an undisturbed nesting. There followed a hectic spring with reports from east, north, and west, but all ended in disappointment, the birds all

---

[1] *Bonasa umbellus.* [2] *Ectopistes migratorius.*

---

*The 27th Stated Meeting of the American Ornithologists' Union, American Museum of Natural History, New York, December 7-9, 1909.

proving to be either Rock Doves[1], Mourning Doves, or Band-tailed Pigeons[2]. At the 1910 meeting of the A.O.U.* Dr. Hodge stated: "It now looks as if the worst fears of American naturalists were about to be confirmed and that we are 'in at the death' of the finest race of pigeons the world has produced."

Clark University was a strange and wonderful place in the fall of 1907: devoted entirely to graduate work, with sixteen men on the faculty and sixty-four students, hampered by few rules and imbued with the most democratic spirit, it was a haven from the hurried, worried materialistic world, a place where truth could be pursued in freedom. It was the friendliest place I ever encountered; from the President to Henry the furnace-man, all were on the same social level. Between the men and women students there existed a companionship very welcome to me as a daughter of a professor in a men's college and a graduate of a women's college.

My chief companion was the only other girl student in the Biology Department — Edith Wallace, Mount Holyoke, 1903. Other warm friends were the O. P. Dellingers, a jolly, carefree couple with two small children. Dr. D. was an instructor in biology in the college; as his Ph.D. thesis he had published an important paper: "Comparative study of cilia as a key to the structure of contractile protoplasm."

My problem — the food of the Bobwhite — was based on studies on this subject by the late Sylvester D. Judd, for which he had examined crops and gizzards of 918 specimens collected in 21 states, and from Canada and Mexico. Dr. Judd had been a brilliant, dedicated worker in the Bureau of Biological Survey. I tried to add as many species as possible of weed seeds and insects to Dr. Judd's lists, and also to find out how many of these tidbits a Bobwhite would eat at a meal or throughout a day.

Hunting weed seeds, catching grasshoppers, and feeding them to appreciative Bobwhites; attending lectures, seminars, and journal club; taking informal courses in bacteriology, neurology, and histology; reading in the splendid library; walking in the country and attending parties with fellow students — all these activities made it a happy year.

Since Dr. Hodge was booked for a lecture tour from late June through July, it was arranged that I should care for the Bobwhites during his absence. I busied myself carrying out feeding tests on

---

[1]*Columba livia.* [2] *Columba fasciata.*

*The 28th Stated Meeting of the American Ornithologists' Union, U.S. National Museum, Washington, D.C. Nov. 14-17, 1910.

adults and chicks. There was one tame hen who cooperated willingly. I would sweep the grass with my nets, extract my booty and weigh it in a small can; I would put a fine wire mesh screen over the lady and her prey inside the large pen in which she and her mate lived. She would gobble up the feast and I would count. Meanwhile, her mate would search about, come upon some tiny creature, puff himself out and call with exaggerated fervor, "See what a wonderful treat I've found!" Immediately, Lady, ignoring the bounty spread before her, would rush up and down against the wire, trying to get to her husband's tidbit. Despite such distractions, this bird made history. One day she ate 700 insects, 300 of which were small grasshoppers; another day 1,350 flies (caught in a fly-trap), and — proudest day of all — 1,532 insects, 1,000 of them tiny grasshoppers.

The best thing I got from these weeks at the Hodge Farm was my pet Bobwhite, Loti. He and a dozen brothers and sisters were hatched under a Cochin Bantam Hen and removed to a brooder from which the little balls of fluff adopted me as their parent-companion, cuddling under my hand and following me closely when let out on the lawn. Some disease swept off almost the entire brood, so at nine days Loti was alone, a devoted and beguiling child. He pattered after me in frantic haste as I swept the grass for insects, and when I lay down on the grass he would cuddle in my hand for a while, but suddenly out he would scramble and make a dash for my face to burrow into my eye or ear, or even, once, when as an experiment I held it open, into my mouth! He usually ended up under my neck, snuggling in my hair. He was a wonderful pet as described in my book *The Watcher at the Nest**. In late July Loti and I went home to Amherst, and Katharine cared for him while Ted and I took our long-hoped-for canoe trip up the Connecticut and Deerfield Rivers.

All the rain of the whole summer seemed to fall in the week of our trip. The first night while we were camped on the little island just above the Sunderland Bridge, the river rose and flooded us out. In the middle of the night we had to move to the only clear spot on higher ground. We had more struggles and more hardships than on the Tumpline Trip; indeed, such difficulties and such back-breaking work that I wondered why we did it in the name of *fun*. I decided one must need an earnest purpose for such a trip.

Due to the previous prolonged drought, the Deerfield River became shallower and shallower, so that most of the time we

*1939. New York, The Macmillan Co.: 1-159. (Reprinted by Dover without change in 1967)

waded, pulling Thyone behind us. There seemed no future in this, so we finally cached her in tall weeds and donned our tumplines and packs. On our first trip, we had so carefully avoided civilization that more than once we had run very low on food. This time we were wiser. Again, we had to spend a rainy day in camp, but with a steak for our stomachs and reading matter for our minds, it was luxury in comparison to our final day on Monadnock.

Our last day on this trip was an heroic adventure. First we had seven miles with the tumplines to the canoe, followed by a rapid dash down the Deerfield River to the Connecticut, only to find it full of logs, so we had to hug the shore in shallow water and paddle manfully for many miles. And then a great storm arose in the south and a fierce wind pushed against us. It was night by the time the rain passed, and then the katydids began their tremendous chorus. As we paddled along in the semi-darkness I had the illusion that the centre of the river was higher than we were and that the logs were bound to crush us. At last we reached the boat house in Hadley and were only too thankful to fall asleep on the bare floor.

In September, Loti and I travelled back to Clark University. With Edith teaching at the University of Maine in Orono, and the Dellingers gone to Indiana, Loti was my chief companion. He and I had the girls' laboratory to ourselves. Across the hall were four men students, while in the laboratory next to mine was Dr. D's successor, Leonard Blaine Nice, a graduate of Ohio University, Athens, Ohio. He was instructor in physiology in the college, as well as a graduate student of Dr. Hodge.

Loti was the pride of the building. When the college classes changed, he would rush out into the hall shouting his loudest. Whenever anyone came into our room he would make a great oration. Some people he always fought, but Blaine's friend from Athens' days, Aldie Matheny, greeted Loti with the Bobwhites' rally call and thus became a prime favourite of my pet.

The first time I remember hearing of the American Ornithologists' Union was in the fall of 1907 when Dr. Hodge invited me to join it as an Associate. This I did and soon began to receive the learned journal *The Auk*. A year later I attended the 26th Stated Meeting in Cambridge, Massachusetts in mid-November*, to my surprise, for I had thought Associates were beneath notice, I received a cardboard disk with 79 on it; this corresponded with my name on a printed list of Members Expected to be Present. It

---

*The 26th Stated Meeting of the American Ornithologists' Union, Cambridge, Massachusetts, November 17-19, 1908.

was an easy method of identifying important and interesting-looking persons.

The A.O.U. was founded on September 26, 1883, in response to a call from J. A. Allen, Elliott Coues, and William Brewster, all members of the Nuttall Ornithological Club of Cambridge. This strictly masculine organization, the oldest Natural History society that still exists in this country, was started in 1873. There were 23 Founders of the A.O.U. These called themselves Active Members; they elected 24 other Active Members and 87 Associates at the first meeting. In 1901 the Union advanced the 50 Actives to Fellows and established an intermediate class of 75 Members, while the great majority of members remained Associates.

A study of this list, checked by the Secretary's report of the meeting in the January, 1909, issue of the *Auk*, shows that 16 Fellows were present, seven of them Founders. I knew a few of these notables by reputation. Being unknown to anyone but Dr. Hodge, who came only for the day on which he talked on "Propagation of Bobwhite," and being too shy to go alone to the reception, I remember talking to only one person, a friendly Boston lady.

The officers of A.O.U. at that time were: President, Edward W. Nelson, later chief of the Bureau of Biological Survey; Secretary, John H. Sage, co-author of *The Birds of Connecticut* (1913); and Treasurer, Jonathan Dwight, Jr., famed authority on plumages and moults of passerines, gulls, and other families of birds.

There was plenty of time for discussion, with only 20 papers in two and a half days. Six of these were concerned with matters of conservation: "Canadian Bird Havens," by Ernest T. Seton; "The Part Played by Birds in the Recent Field Mouse Plague in Nevada," by C. Hart Merriam, Chief of the Bureau of Biological Survey; "Pelican Island in 1908," by Frank M. Chapman; "Gulls and Terns of Massachusetts," by Edward H. Forbush, State Ornithologist of Massachusetts; "Ornithological Miscellany from Audubon Wardens" by Beecher S. Bowdish; and "Triumphs of Bird Protection in Louisiana," by Herbert K. Job, State Ornithologist of Connecticut. The last four papers were illustrated by lantern slides.

In "The Tagging of Wild Birds as a Means of Studying Their Movements," Leon J. Cole of New Haven, Connecticut, recounted the beginnings of bird banding in North America; the following year Dr. Cole became the first President of the American Bird-Banding Association. Thomas S. Roberts, who later published the admirable two-volume set of *Birds of Minnesota* (1932), told of a colony of Yellow-headed Blackbirds[1], all of whose eggs and chicks were destroyed by an unknown predator. Charles W. Townsend, author of *Sand Dunes and Salt Marshes* (1913) spoke on "The Position of Birds' Feet in Flight."

The most exciting event to me of the whole meeting was the showing by Frank Chapman of moving pictures of birds, particularly of the catbird[2]. These were the first such I had ever seen and the first to be exhibited at an A.O.U. meeting. I liked them very much, especially as they seemed so true to life in contrast to the speeded-up commercial movies then in vogue. It was not until three years later that moving pictures were again mentioned in the reports of the meetings, this time shown by Clinton G. Abbott, author of *The Home Life of the Osprey* (1911). It was many years before movies in colour were to be shown at the meetings.

Of the officers and speakers at the 1908 meeting mentioned above, I never met Dr. Nelson, nor Dr. Merriam, but all the others became my friends in later years. I looked with interest at William Brewster of Cambridge, because I knew of his leadership in conservation struggles, and at Dr. A. K. Fisher, author of the notable *Hawks and Owls of the United States in Their Relation to Agriculture,* (1893). The importance of three other men I came to know later - Dr. J. A. Allen, distinguished editor of the *Auk* for 28 years; Henry W. Henshaw, explorer and worker for conservation whose complete set of the *Auk* I was to purchase 12 years later; and, finally, Arthur Cleveland Bent, whose great *Life Histories of North American Birds* were to appear from 1919 to 1968.

William Brewster gave a reception for the gentlemen of the Union at his museum, while the ladies of the Union were invited to the home of Mrs. Charles F. Batchelder, whose husband was the retiring President of the A.O.U. Evidently, the role of the ladies was expected to be largely ornamental.

The name of distinguished naturalist and tireless original student of nesting habits - Althea H. Sherman of National, Iowa, is on the list, but not on the program. She gave papers at the two next A.O.U. meetings: "At the Sign of the Northern Flicker," in New York City, and "Nest Life of the Screech Owl[3]," in Washington, D.C.

"Whenever the truth is injured, defend it," wrote Emerson. I did defend it in the first item in my ornithological bibliography,

---

[1] *Xanthocephalus xanthocephalus.* [2] Gray Catbird, *Dumetella carolinensis.* [3] *Otus asio.*

the only one published by Margaret Morse. Indignation over a misguided lady's attributing the great deeds in weed-seed consumption of our native Tree Sparrow *(Spizella arborea)* to the introduced House Sparrow *(Passer domesticus)* roused me to setting her right in a carefully-worded and well-documented letter to the newspaper, the *Springfield Republican;* this appeared October 22, 1908.

My intention on going to Clark University had been to get an M.A. on "The Food of the Bobwhite." I was so happy there that I decided to use this subject for a Ph.D. thesis; this in spite of strong family opposition, for my parents urged me unceasingly to return and again be a daughter-at-home. In my second year I continued my feeding tests on Loti, and for the early summer of 1909 I had planned to carry out a large series of such tests with baby Bobwhites at the State Hatchery at nearby Sutton. In August there was to be a canoe trip with Ted in "really wild country."

These plans were changed. Instead of raising Bobwhites, I was married; instead of working for a Ph.D., I kept house. Sometimes I rather regretted that I had not gone ahead and obtained this degree, as we stayed in Worcester for two more years until Blaine got his Ph.D. But no one had ever encourged me to study for a doctor's degree; all the propaganda had been against it. My parents were more than happy to have me give up thoughts of a career and take up home-making, and in every way they helped us in this new venture.

After a simple wedding in August at my home in Pelham, Massachusetts, to which Lucy Day, Edith Wallace, the Hodges, and Mathenys all came, Blaine and I travelled to his home on a farm in southeastern Ohio. He was the second son in a family of five boys and four girls. His great-grandfather, Philip Nice, had come from Germany when a child and had served in the War of 1812. His son Philip, married Scotch-Irish Rebecca Meek, and they had 18 children, of whom the 16th, Fred, was Blaine's father. He married Romina Adams of English ancestry and they pioneered on 167 acres in Athens County. The Nices are a hardy strain, proud, hospitable, and "work-brickle."

Blaine's father was an industrious, ambitious farmer and lumberman. His mother was a fine woman, devoted to her family, and especially to her grandchildren, of whom at this time there were six. Their farm was in hilly, picturesque country; it possessed a brook and a 30-acre tract of primeval hardwoods.

Blaine had had an active, hard-working, frugal childhood and youth, with a great deal of practical experience on the farm and in the lumber camp. For some years the family had lived in a log cabin. Here the boys slept in the loft which in summer they shared with a pair of Bewick's Wrens[1], the birds nesting in a great ball of carpet rags. Early each morning the Wrens would discover the boys and indignantly scold them as they slept. When Blaine was 14 the family built a roomy, two-storey house for themselves and surrounded it with shrubs and trees; this was the wonder of the neighbourhood. For many years we were to visit the farm on our journeys between my family home in Massachusetts and our home in Oklahoma.

Blaine had attended, off and on, the ungraded country school, after which he spent a year at the New Marshfield High School, four miles distant from his home. The next year he taught the country school and had among his pupils his four sisters and two of his younger brothers. All the children called him "Blaine." His salary was $180 for the six-month term and now with money in his pockets, he entered the preparatory school of Ohio University at Athens, eight miles from his home. Eager to earn money for a college education, he persuaded the county officials to establish a new rural mail route (which, incidentally, would serve his home); for half a year he carried mail on this route.

Ohio University then was a small, but excellent, institution, founded in 1804. Tuition in Blaine's day cost only $5.00 a term and by waiting on tables he helped pay for his board. He derived pleasure and comradeship from membership in the fraternity of Beta Theta Pi. With the hope of becoming a physician he specialized in zoology and graduated in 1908 with a Bachelor of Philosophy degree. One of his teachers, Frank Copeland, had received his Ph.D. under Dr. Hodge in 1907, and it was through Frank's suggestion that Blaine received his assistantship in physiology at Clark University.

It was fun to keep house in our roomy flat with absurd Loti under foot. But Loti did not appreciate Blaine; indeed, he would greet him with pecks on his feet. Afraid that he might step on the precious bird, Blaine would get out a broom and Loti would hurry to shelter. I attended a weekly cooking class and also learned from Blaine, for he had cooked for his father's lumber camps. My technique of housework, then and afterwards, was based on efficient preparation of good and simple meals, scalding water instead of dish towels, sending out the washing and ironing, and dispatch in

[1] *Thryomanes bewickii.*

the matter of cleaning. Most of my time was free for activities of more lasting value.

My first project was to work up my material on the food of the Bobwhite. Dr. Hodge wrote an introduction to it in which he said my paper "presented the most complete and convincing statement of the food of any bird," and he pointed out the dangers confronting this valuable species, especially from the cat. He sent the paper to the *Auk*. It was returned by the editor, Dr. J. A. Allen, who said it was too long, but might be accepted if abbreviated.

About this time Mr. E. P. Felt, editor of the *Journal of Economic Entomology,* called on Dr. Hodge, saw the paper, and offered to publish it in full. It appeared in June, 1910. Shortly thereafter, Mr. Felt sent Dr. Hodge a letter from Mr. W. L. McAtee, economic entomologist of the Biological Survey, which began: "I must protest against the undue praise given by Dr. Hodge" to the paper. He pointed out the fallacy of drawing conclusions about the food of a wild species by what a captive individual will eat; for instance, anteaters in zoos live upon hard-boiled eggs. Caged birds of a number of species refuse foods freely taken by their wild congeners. He ridiculed the value of discovering that a Bobwhite would eat clothes moths, mosquitoes, and house flies. "Such experiments," he declared, "are even more disappointing when data as to the quantity of food consumed by wild birds is desired. The paper fails as a contribution to knowledge of the economic value of the Bobwhite."

I asked Dr. Hodge what answer he was going to make; he said that he would write of his hope to have the Bobwhite in semi-domestication everywhere so that household pests *could* be eaten by such birds. However, he never got around to writing his reply, and McAtee's condemnation appeared in the next issue of the journal, in solitary grandeur.

I agree with much of McAtee's criticism, but when he wrote that the experiments on the *quantity* of food consumed were "even more disappointing" than those on the objects eaten, he could not have noticed how closely my results tallied with those of Dr. Judd. I must confess that it gave me considerable satisfaction to realize that these strictures were safely buried in a journal read by few bird enthusiasts, while my paper spread its message far and wide through the 300 reprints I had purchased for $8.00. They went to friends, relatives, and to state and government game departments.

"Food of the Bobwhite" made quite a stir. Whenever I read that these birds eat 129 different kinds of weed seeds, and as many as 12,000 to 30,000 seeds in a single day; whenever I saw that a Bobwhite ate 568 mosquitoes at a meal and 5,000 plant lice in a day, I knew that my studies had borne fruit. Dr. Hodge quoted my most spectacular feeding tests in a Nature Study pamphlet on *The Bobwhite* and in an article in the *Nature Study Review* (1910); Edward H. Forbush did likewise in an Audubon Bulletin. *Forest and Stream* ran two articles on the subject; Col. G. O. Shields of New York City quoted liberally from my article in his speeches on conservation and William T. Hornaday gave a page and a half to my findings in his book *Our Vanishing Wild Life* (1913).

Loti's special friend at the University, W. A. Matheny, who became Professor of Botany at Ohio University, lectured far and wide throughout the state on the value of the Bobwhite, illustrating his talks with pictures and tales of Loti. A telling cartoon by Billie Ireland appeared in the *Columbus Dispatch*; it was entitled "Bugs or Birds – *Ohio Can Have Its Choice.*" In a barren landscape a desperate farmer is treed by an army of bugs, one of whom cries, "Come on, boys; the birds are gone." In an inset, however, a covey of Bobwhite is shown in flourishing vegetation with this note: "Mrs. L. B. Nice, of Clark University, after a most careful and complete investigation proved that a 'Bobwhite' hen will eat on an average in one season 75,000 insects, and 5,000,000 weed seeds. Can Ohio afford to open the season on Quail?" Dr. Maheny always believed that Loti and I did much toward putting the Bobwhite on the Songbird List in Ohio in 1912. Despite repeated efforts by the gunners, there it remained for 47 years. In 1959 Quail shooting was again legalized, this time under strict supervision on less than 1 per cent of the state's area.

Even in 1945 I found in a folder for an Illinois bill, aimed at restraining cats, this sentence, "One Quail at a meal (sic) will eat 1,000 grasshoppers and 532 other insects of the most deadly varieties." Little did I realize that I was taking my life in my hands in catching those creatures!

V

The Journey to Oklahoma

After two years in Cambridge, where Blaine had an instructorship in physiology at the Harvard Medical School, it was a pleasant adventure for us in September 1913, to settle in the prairie town of Norman, Oklahoma, where Blaine had been appointed Professor of physiology and pharmacology in the University of Oklahoma. We were enchanted with the new, open country, the clear air, the prairie wild flowers, the Scissor-tailed Flycatchers[1], Mockingbirds and Cardinals[2], with the friendliness of the people, and the mild winter weather. At that time there was no gas in town; the streets were largely unpaved and only two members of the faculty possessed automobiles.

For three years we were most fortunate in the student who lived with us in the roomy rented house we called the Yellow Pumpkin. Gladys Hilsmeyer was a fine and loyal friend. Besides helping with the housework, on Sunday afternoons she stayed with Marjorie and Constance so Blaine and I could explore the country. The favourite goal of these walks was the South Canadian River, three to four miles distant. This usually meandered as a small stream over its immense bed of sand, but on occasion it became a mighty flood. In our big backyard we installed hens, bees, and a garden, while pets from the laboratory came and went — frogs, guinea pigs, and a procession of rabbits.

What about birds in this new region? I had obtained a copy of *Field, Forest and Stream in Oklahoma*, a beautiful and fascinating

[1]*Muscivora forficata.* [2]*Richmondena cardinalis.*

volume by the late Frederick S. Barde (1912) put out by the State Game and Fish Department as its 1912 *Annual Report*. This contained a list of birds recorded from Oklahoma — 244 species and three sub-species. The authority for most of these was Professor George W. Stevens of the Northwestern Normal School at Alva, but the names of 23 that were followed by G.S. had been reported by the Oklahoma Geological Survey. The status of Professor Stevens' birds was briefly noted but seldom with any indication as to where the bird might be expected in this state that extends some 522 miles from the southeastern to northwestern corner. Moreover, some of the statements were clearly erroneous, so the list offered small help in telling us what to look for in central Oklahoma.

One day I met the Professor of Zoology, who gave a course in ornithology at the University. He asked me whether we had seen Scissor-tailed Flycatchers, Bewick's Wrens and Painted Buntings[1]. He warned me against Barde's list. "Pay no attention," said he, "to anything with 'G.S.' after it; some students went out and thought they saw this and that, and *that* is the basis of these records. For instance, they have the *Song Sparrow* listed!"

I accepted this verdict, little dreaming how mistaken our friend was. Instead of opening my eyes and finding Song Sparrows wintering in the thickets from October to April, I felt it was impossible to know what birds were supposed to be here. I gave up trying to find out what to expect and contented myself with enjoying the most conspicuous species. Here Blaine knew more than I, for having grown up in southeastern Ohio, he was very familiar with the ways and songs of Cardinals, Tufted Tits[2], and Carolina Wrens[3].

From early spring we were fascinated with the prairie flowers. Gladys was studying botany in the University, and she told us all their names.

Largely in order to give Constance child companship, I had conducted a little Montessori Nature Study School from January through May in our home and on our grounds. The six small children loved the bunny, the frogs, and great fat toad so much that they fought over them. And how proud they were of their gardens!

In June 1914, I travelled 250 miles northwest to Alva to watch for two weeks a proper Montessori School. The flowers along the railroad right-of-way were glorious in their brilliance and variety. At the Normal School I visited Professor Stevens with samples of

---

[1] *Passerina ciris.* [2] Tufted Titmouse, *Parus bicolor.* [3] *Thryothorus ludovicianus.*

new flowers I had found in the vicinity; all of these he named for me. Strangely enough, I asked him *nothing about birds* here in the headquarters of the Mississippi Kite[1]. We travelled back together on the train to Oklahoma City, and the next day he came to dinner at our house. He showed us, with disapprobation, a pamphlet entitled *The Oklahoma Bird Day Book* in which the *speckled* eggs of the Bobwhite were mentioned. He told us that he was writing a book on the birds of Oklahoma.

The next two years Professor Stevens spent at Harvard University working on a doctoral thesis on the flora of Oklahoma. This lists over 1600 ferns and seed plants, nearly all of which were collected over the state. "It is unfortunate," wrote Drs. Jeffs and Little, "that the entire flora was never published, as it would have done much to encourage further Botanical exploration in the state."

Professor Stevens did not return to Oklahoma, going instead to Central Missouri State Teachers' College at Warrensburg. From there he wrote me on August 5, 1922, that he was strongly emphasizing nature study in the college, saying, "We are trying to interest our teachers in birds as a means of improving civic righteousness in the state." He added: "The seeming impossibility of obtaining the Reed pictures from Doubleday Page and Co., for which I had a contract before the war, gives me, at present, the impression that I may not publish my MS. on Birds of the Western Mississippi Valley!" This impression proved true.

As a former student of Dr. Hall it had been natural that I should make a study of Constance's speech development. Further stimulated by studies of two fathers of their daughters' vocabulary attainment, I wrote a paper on "Development of a Child's Vocabulary in Relation to Environment" (1915), in which I analyzed her vocabularies at 18 months and at three and four years. Dr. Hall accepted it for the *Pedagogical Seminary*, at the same time writing, "It brings a new point of view and a new epoch in this line of work, and I congratulate you on doing such an admirable thing."

This paper did set a fashion in vocabulary studies for a while. It was with it as a thesis that in 1926 I was granted a degree of Master of Arts "as of 1915" from Clark University. Encouraged by Dr. Hall's interest I kept records of my children's mastery of language, and for 13 years averaged a paper a year on speech development of my own and of others' children. These studies involved much reading of German and French, a great deal of arithmetic, and considerable creative thought.

[1] *Ictinia mississippiensis.*

In March 1916 we were called to Grey Rocks by the illness and death of my dear father. He had so greatly loved this wilderness that it was sad he could not have stayed longer with his forests, brooks, and mountains. His was a rare character, compounded of gentleness, courtesy, strength, and a passion for the best that man has achieved. He was a man of the noblest ideals, devoted to his family, his friends, and to the betterment of mankind.

Our three small daughters and I stayed on with my mother and had the happiness of the late winter, the spring, and summer in Pelham.

In 1917 we became more active in our nature interests. In January Blaine and I were inveigled into supporting a bill for a ten-year closed season on Bobwhite; when the hearing was scheduled the sponsor failed to appear, leaving us as the sole advocates of an impossible proposition. We did, however, try to exert an enlightening influence on the legislature, but without success.

In the spring we consulted with Mr. Charles W. Shannon as to forming a Nature Study group for adults. Mr. Shannon was Director of the Oklahoma Geological Survey, and author of a bulletin on *The Trees and Shrubs of Oklahoma* (1913). He called a meeting of people interested in nature and we took a number of Saturday afternoon walks. These were pleasant but interest was not sustained. On May 12 I went to our meeting place and found no one there. So I took a "wonderful walk by myself along Bird Brook. Brown Thrasher's[1] nest, Cardinal's with two of her own eggs and two Cowbird's eggs, *White-crowned Sparrow*[2] (a transient), *Blue Grosbeak*[3] (a new bird for me), Bells' Vireo[4] (?), Carolina Wren; Dove's nest, Red-bellied Woodpecker's[5] nest, box turtle, two lizards." I had begun to suspect the identity of our commonest vireo from a description in Chapman's *Handbook* (1895).

On May 24th I was taken on a "bird-nesting" walk on the campus by a zoology student. She showed me in the osage orange hedges nests of Brown Thrashers, Mockingbirds, Bronzed Grackles[6], Catbird, Mourning Doves, Loggerhead Shrike[7], Red-headed Woodpecker, and in a post the three babies of a Carolina Chickadee[8].

In 1917 we moved from a rented house to a bungalow which we owned. In 1918 we moved next door to another bungalow, slightly larger, with three bedrooms and a sleeping porch. However in the

---

[1] *Toxostoma rufum.* [2] *Zonotrichia leucophrys.* [3] *Guiraca caerulea.* [4] *Vireo bellii.*
[5] *Melanerpes carolinus.* [6] Common Grackle, *Quiscalus quiscula.*
[7] *Lanius ludovicianus.* [8] *Parus carolinensis.*

fall of 1918, with four children aged six months to eight years, in what seemed to be cramped quarters, no one enjoying housework, and much of the time without even a college girl to come in an hour a day to wash the dishes, with no means of transportation but our own legs and the baby carriage, and no free Sunday afternoon for tramps to the river, I was truly frustrated. I resented the implication that my husband and the children had brains, and I had none. He taught; they studied; I did housework.

Even though our meals were simple, the washing and ironing always sent out, and though I averaged an hour a day on research on speech development, my life became so cluttered with mere *things* that my free spirit was smothered. My desires were modest enough, inexpensive enough — an occasional walk to the river.

I decided it would be better to be a bird. Birds are very busy at one period each year caring for babies, but this lasts only a few weeks with many of them, and then their babies are grown and gone. Best of all, they leave their *houses* forever and take to camping for the rest of the year. No wonder they are happy.

On March 10, 1919 I wrote in my notebook:

Research is a passion with me; it drives me; it is my relentless master. Ten days ago I finished and sent off "A Child's Imagination" [1919], and then turned to my mussed-up house and clamoring neglected duties. Many of these odds and ends I have done. Yet now I find myself longing, yea pining, to begin on my paper on Constance and nature.

Relief came through three channels: my finding birds again; Eleanor's growing out of babyhood; and in the spring of 1920 our purchase of an ancient car.

VI

The
Awakening

Until 1919 we had always travelled each summer to Grey Rocks. But that year the railroads markedly increased their fares so, for the first time, we resolved to spend the summer in Oklahoma. This decision proved of signal importance to our family.

A newspaper item that summer was responsible for my becoming an ornithologist. Mourning Doves, protected entirely in the state from 1913 to 1917, for the last two years had not been mentioned in the State game laws, and Federal game laws fixed the start of the open season in Oklahoma on September 1. On a morning in early August the *Daily Oklahoman* reported that Ben Watts, State Game Warden, advocated an open season on doves from August 1 or "even August 15 when all the young doves are off the nest and strong fliers."

I felt that he was wrong on his facts; surely I had read that Mourning Doves nest through August. So that evening we packed our supper into the carriage with the baby and trundled off to the campus. Sure enough we located three doves on nests. A week later we found three more. At once I wrote protesting letters to the Oklahoma City and Norman newspapers entitled, "Doves Must Not be Shot in August." I also told the story to the Oklahoma Game Department and to the United States Biological Survey.

August 20 chanced to be cool, and I escaped by myself to the river along one of our favourite paths with its tangled vines and bushes, its mistletoe-laden elms, its Cardinals, orioles, and gnatcatchers[1], its display of wayside flowers. Many of these flowers were armed with spines — the exquisite great white prickly poppy, the rosin weeds, golden prionopsis, weedy horse nettle, and fierce tread-softly with its coarse spotted leaves. A large hawk flew to shelter in some cottonwoods pursued by six kingbirds[2] and a dashing Scissor-tailed Flycatcher. One of the kingbirds was so excited that he attacked an inoffensive Turkey Vulture[3].

At Low Brook, just east of the river bed, myriads of little moths rose around me, while a great black and white beetle with antennae two inches long buzzed as it flew by. It seemed like fairyland with new flowers at every step. Many of these belonged to the pulse family — partridge pea, wild creeping pea with long narrow pods poking out under the bright pink bonnet of the flower, tick trefoil, pink and yellow bird's foot trefoil. There was a little pink fog fruit and, loveliest of all, a wonderful deep blue gentian, *Estoma Russellianum*, far larger than the fringed gentian of the East, and as stately as a wood lily. And for the last touch of enchantment, the hauntingly sweet refrain of the Field Sparrow[4].

Under the great elms and cottonwoods on the river bank I watched the turbulent Canadian River and dreamed. The glory of nature possessed me. I saw that for many years I had lost my way. I had been led astray on false trails and had been trying to do things contrary to my nature. I resolved to return to my childhood vision of studying nature and trying to protect the wild things of the earth.

I thought of my friends who never take walks in Oklahoma, "for there was nothing to see." I was amazed and grieved at their blindness. I longed to open their eyes to the wonders around them; to persuade people to love and cherish nature. Perhaps I might be a sort of John Burroughs for Oklahoma.

This August walk was a turning point in my life. It was a day of vision and prophecy. But what the future really held in store for me would have seemed to me utterly fantastic.

I now turned seriously to learning the local birds, a somewhat difficult matter since information was scattered and some of it unreliable. I bought Florence Merriam Bailey's *Birds of the Western United States* (1902), and studied it. I asked the Professor of Zoology which meadowlark nested with us. "The Western," he replied. The next spring we found it was the Eastern[5]. "What is

[1]Blue-gray Gnatcatcher, *Polioptila caerulea.* [2]Eastern Kingbird, *Tyrannus tyrannus.* [3]*Cathartes aura.* [4]*Spizella pusilla.* [5]Eastern Meadowlark, *Sturnella magna.*

that little vireo that is so common on the campus?" (His students merely wrote "Vireo" on their nest censuses.) "Red-eye," he hazarded. This I knew to be wrong, and after checking again with Chapman's description, decided definitely it was Bell's.

Our dove investigations were prosecuted vigorously. We searched the campus more thoroughly, the children climbing the trees to report the contents of the nests. In a special notebook I kept records of each nest, noting the kind of tree in which it had been built and the behaviour of the parents, some of which left the nest quietly, while others went through elaborate broken-wing demonstrations. More nests were discovered in August, making a total of 14. Moreover, we found 28 new nests in September, in three of which the young were not fledged until October!

In the meantime a slightly injured juvenile Mourning Dove had been given us. The children called him Flower. He was a pleasant pet and accompanied family expeditions perched on the baby carriage. We adopted another dove just out of the nest. Daisy was a timid creature and showed plentiful lack of sense in persistently begging from Flower, who attacked Daisy's head until it became completely bare.

Once again I gathered weed seeds and carried out feeding tests, weighing the birds night and morning. However, remembering McAtee's criticism with regard to dietary preferences of wild and captive birds, I did not exert myself over-much in collecting seeds; it was simpler to buy canary seed. Observations on the development, behaviour, and feeding tests of Flower and Daisy were presented before the Oklahoma Academy of Science in February 1920, and published in Volume I of the *Proceedings* (1921). Nine years later I reported the results of the feeding tests in a note in the *Auk* (vol. 46:233-234), since my experience did not corroborate assumptions of a bird-bander who had calculated food consumption from night and morning weights of trapped birds.

About half a mile to the west of our home ran the sluggish little stream we called Snail Brook; bordered by large elms and cottonwoods, willows and hackberries, coralberry, poison ivy and grape vines, it offered us a woods in miniature, the best place near town for finding birds. We had always visited it at intervals; now I began to haunt it, slipping away for an hour at a time and studying the birds earnestly. Not only was it a laboratory for learning the birds of the region, but my frequent trips into its solitudes brought much contentment. In mid-December it occurred to me to make a special study of the bird population by means of censuses, when I was able to traverse the whole half mile between West Boyd Street and Lindsay Avenue, whereas shorter visits might add new species to the list.

In my notebook "Snail Brook Descriptions," I wrote:

Dec. 13, '19: The children and I went to Snail Brook, the day being one of marvelous ice effects, every twig weighed down with its casing of glass and the sun sparkling through it all. I took a dozen pictures.

Dec. 19: Today I went birding alone and had much better success than when the small fry were along. Day bright and mild, while a *Song Sparrow* — wonderful sound — sang most of his song! After careful study I discovered that the common, shy, brush-hiding Sparrows were my old friends, the Song Sparrows. They are common along Snail Brook wherever there are piles of brush.

Among the reasons why it took me so long to find Song Sparrows in Oklahoma: the zoology Professor's conviction of their absence; their shyness and comparative silence here in migration and winter quarters, and finally, the fact that their songs might easily be mistaken for those of Bewick's Wrens.

I now felt that Blaine and I knew the winter birds well enough to attempt a Christmas census for *Bird-Lore* (1920) and I was more than eager for the time to arrive. Despite the warning of dreams — that I had to retrace my steps from halfway down Snail Brook, that I could find no room to write in my notebook, and that the only bird I saw was a bedraggled-tail Robin — and despite a gloomy, bleak day with a north wind and the temperature just above freezing, nevertheless, our first Christmas Bird Census was a success. For we saw 33 species and 1120 individuals. Constance and I went south in the morning, finding 25 species and 834 individuals; Blaine went west in the afternoon, recording 21 species and 286 individuals.

The morning trip followed Snail Brook down to the flood plain of the Canadian River; we visited Persimmon Pond, and in the Olivers' woods met a flock of hundreds of redwings, one a partial albino. On the way home along the road in the face of the north wind, we saw one bird — a meadowlark. Blaine's hike to Bird Brook rewarded him with a bewildering array, and he added to our list, Mourning Dove, Cedar Waxwing, Red-shafted Flicker[1], and a Sharp-skinned Hawk[2] that dashed into the midst of a flock of small birds that Blaine was studying.

---

[1]Conspecific with the Yellow-shafted Flicker, *Colaptes auratus:* now Common Flicker. [2]*Accipiter striatus.*

It was hard to wait for spring now that my eyes and ears were opened; now that I was really aware of nature. In my new line-a-day diary nearly every day was crowded with entries. With walks to Snail Brook, Bird Brook, the river, and Bishop Creek east of town, I was filling in my picture of the winter bird life. In contrast to New England, spring came to the plant world long before there was any movement of the birds. By February 12 elms were blooming, and by the 23rd we found chickweed, bluets, spring beauty and anemone in flower. On March 5th there was a light snow, but brave bluets and wild pansies raised their bright heads regardless. By the 8th I had seen no spring birds but Killdeer, Loggerhead Shrikes, and Fox Sparrows[1], and all of these species sometimes wintered.

A week later I had an unforgettable experience.

Mar. 15th, spring is here. Strange frog voices are grunting and wheezing. Robins, Redwings[2], Savannah Sparrows[3], and most wonderful of all — four enchanting Green-winged Teal[4]!!! They flew up from Reed Pool and alighted on Snail Pond; when I followed them there, back they flew to the Pool. This time I returned very slowly and cautiously. While looking at some Song Sparrows I heard a rustling, and there were my birds waddling along the brookside, for all the world like tame ducks! I advanced with great care, and when near the bank, crept on hands and knees. At first I could see only the female lying quietly in the water; on creeping closer I saw the three males with the beautiful green on their cheeks and their bright chestnut faces. It was a wonderfully exciting experience seeing these lovely wild ducks within a few yards. I don't understand how anyone could kill anything so beautiful.

I was so uplifted by this adventure that I wondered how I could bear the glory of the coming of the birds. They came gradually and each one was welcome. Yet the migration in central Oklahoma consists primarily in the return of summer residents and we miss the spectacular waves of warblers that were then such a happy part of spring in the East.

My list of the birds of the region grew steadily, and several mysteries were solved. Lincoln's Sparrow[5] had puzzled me, since the descriptions in the books did not emphasize what seemed to me its most impressive character — the buffy breast; it was a specimen in the University Museum that enabled me to identify it. The wintering and migrating towhees[6] I had assumed to be our old

---

[1] *Passerella iliaca.* [2] Red-winged Blackbird, *Agelaius phoeniceus.*
[3] *Passerculus sandwichensis.* [4] *Anas crecca.* [5] *Melospiza lincolnii.*
[6] Spotted Towhee, conspecific with the Rufous-sided Towhee, *Pipilo erythrophthalmus.*

friends of the East — the Red-eyed; gradually I became perturbed by noting the large amount of white on their backs and I discovered they must be "Arctic Towhees," of all crazy names for a bird that nests in Montana and southern Alberta and winters from Colorado to Texas! On the campus I met one day a pale new sparrow with the squeakiest excuse for a song — my first view of a Clay-coloured Sparrows[1], a migrant in this region.

One day by Bishop Creek I heard the most amazing, incredible shouts and squawks — *yip bob cheer yank bob cheer where yeep bob cheer yeep bob cheer bob bob bob* — at last I had heard a Yellow-breasted Chat! The bright yellow breast and olive-grey back were very different from those young Baltimore Orioles I had called chats in my childhood. And the song — it was too ridiculous to believe. Other chats heard later used different phrases. One near the Canadian River exclaimed *chip chip purp chip pip purp purp purp*, while another shouted *hur hur hur hur hur hur wheepelet ink chee*.

These new experiences called for more knowledge. I asked my friend, Dr. Wallace Craig at the University of Maine, to nominate me as an Associate of the A.O.U.; long before at Edith Wallace's suggestion he had sent me his "Voices of Pigeons Regarded as a Means of Social Control" (1908). Once again the *Auk* came to me, this time to be eagerly studied. We also invested in *Birds of America* (1917) three volumes edited by T. Gilbert Pearson; the chief value of these lay in the coloured plates by Louis Agassiz Fuertes painted for Elon H. Eaton's two-volume *Birds of New York* (1910).

One of my great problems was which *subspecies* of many species should occur in Oklahoma. It was most unfortunate that Chester Reed's *Pocket Guide* (1909), included subspecies, giving me the erroneous impression that they could be identified in the field. How I puzzled over Field and Tree, Lark[2] and Savannah Sparrows, as I tried to decide whether or not they belonged to the western forms, said to be paler or slightly paler than the eastern forms. As to Mockingbirds, Blue Grosbeaks, Downy[3] and Hairy Woodpeckers, I felt woefully ignorant because I was not sure whether I should dub them Eastern or Western, Northern or Southern.

At that time *Bird-Lore* had an Advisory Council, and listed the ornithologist for each state to whom the beginner might appeal for assistance. Accordingly, I wrote to Dr. A. K. Fisher in Washington

---

[1] *Spizella pallida.*   [2] *Chondestes grammacus.*   [3] *Picoides pubescens.*

asking him which form of 11 species occurred in central Oklahoma. At length a reply came from one of his colleagues, Dr. Harry C. Oberholser of the United States Biological Survey, to whom Dr. Fisher had given my letter. Immediately I responded with questions on seven more species, and after some months received a categorical reply. In the meantime I had become a collaborator of the Biological Survey, keeping migration records for them and taking a nesting census of Snail Brook.

Life was full of happiness for all of our family. Bluebirds had adopted our box as soon as we had put it ip. Bewick's Wrens were nesting in the children's play house — a former chicken house. Four pairs of Purple Martins[1] had settled in the new house Blaine had put up for them. As for Flower and Daisy, they both proved to be males, so as soon as we could get bands from the Biological Survey we released them, and that was the last we ever heard of them. Meanwhile the children and I were busy with our study of Mourning Doves nesting on the campus; here maps of the campus, given us by the University were a help in keeping the multitudes of nests distinct from one another in my records.

At length I had found my vocation, and life held endless opportunities of discovery. What had converted me? The high railroad fares that kept us in Oklahoma that summer, Ben Watts' iniquitous demand to shoot doves in August, and that memorable walk when the beauty of nature engulfed me — all these had played a part.

The dove problem had presented a challenge: did these birds nest in August? We found they nested well into October. So we hastened to the defense of truth and the helpless birds. It is curious how all the pleasant, positive stimuli had proved unavailing, and that it was finally the determination to refute error and save the young doves from a lingering death that aroused me to action. Perhaps it was that no *problem* in regard to wild birds had ever really been posed to me until then. The keen interest in the doves awakened me to interest in all the birds, and the impact of my lone walk to the river gave me the determination to fight to preserve some wildness on the earth.

---

[1]*Progne subis.*

VII

'Summer Birds of Oklahoma'

In April 1920 our next door neighbour wished to build himself a garage; he proposed to construct a double one with such help as Blaine could provide in his spare time. A garage calls for an occupant, and promptly we had a Dodge, an open touring car, second hand to be sure, but said to be in the pink of condition. That very day we made an expedition, and I received my first lesson in driving. Prophetically enough, we had a flat tire.

The car was a boon to us, accustomed as we were to travelling on foot with the two youngest in the baby carriage or wagon. Two-year-old Eleanor could hardly be extracted at the end of a trip, for she would hurry to the far end of the seat and bury her face in the upholstery. Our range of operations was much increased, for we could now explore the countryside to the east with its black jack oaks, and also to the south farther than we had ever walked. Our greatest adventure was finding a Barred Owl's[1] nest with two eggs along Rock Creek east of Norman. Constance shinnied up a pole next the tree and reported on the contents. At our last visit she let down the two owlets by means of ropes so that the rest of us could admire and photograph them before she returned them to their home.

Our longest trip that spring was 60 miles northwest to Kingfisher to visit two families of Blaine's relatives; here we were delighted with absurd Burrowing Owls[2], handsome Western Kingbirds[3] and abundant Grasshopper Sparrows[4] and Dickcissels[5]. As these last

[1]*Strix varia.* [2]*Athene cunicularia.* [3]*Tyrannus verticalis.* [4]*Ammodramus savannarum.* [5]*Spiza americana.*

birds tirelessly chanted their unmusical *jig-jig jig-jig-jig* from barbed wire fences or telephone wires, Constance suggested we play a new kind of roadside euchre by counting them on a five-mile stretch. We found six to eight Dickcissels per mile. Constance's ambitions grew; she proposed that we count *all* the birds as we chugged and bumped along at less than 20 miles an hour. So our roadside census started — a technique that in those days of slow cars, unpaved roads, and blessedly "unimproved" roadsides, provided information on the commoner, more conspicuous birds in each region in Oklahoma which we later visited.

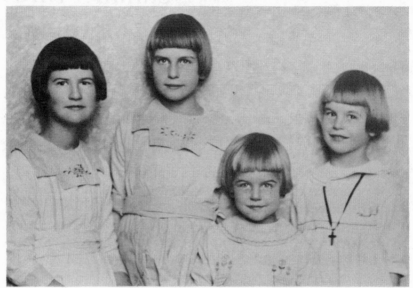

Constance, Marjorie, Eleanor and Barbara

Now that we had a car our thoughts turned to camping. One day Blaine came home saying that Mr. Charles W. Shannon wished he could find someone to work on the birds of the state. This sounded like an exciting prospect, and we went to talk to Mr. Shannon. He told us that the original name of his bureau had been the Department of Geological and Natural History, and that two bird projects had already been sponsored: one in 1901-02, the other from 1913-14. He would be glad to lend us camping equipment, help us with advice, and pay our expenses. So here was an opportunity for a camping trip with a serious and important goal.

Mr. Shannon gave us the reports on the earlier projects.

The first consisted of an unannotated list by Dr. A. H. Van Vleet (at this time head of the Botany Department at the University) of

178 species collected by C. D. Bunker. Many of these were taken on a trip by these two men to the south-western corner of the state in the summer of 1901. Dr. Van Vleet's notes, and 92 of the mounted birds, were destroyed by fire in January 1903. The other specimens were extant, and to my amazement I discovered that the "(G.S.)" notes in Barde's list were based, not on sight records of untrustworthy students, but on these specimens! (Several of these had been misidentified, as we later found out by sending them to Washington; for instance, a "Traill's Flycatcher"[1] turned out to be an Acadian Flycatcher[2], a "Baird's Sparrow"[3] a Western Savannah.) Mr. Bunker, a "collector in Zoology," later went to the Natural History Museum of the University of Kansas; in 1929 he sent me some information on his experiences in Oklahoma. Alexander Wetmore of the Smithsonian Institution in Washington wrote me in 1924 that Mr. Bunker "had in mind a catalog of the birds of the state but was anticipated by Van Vleet's skeleton list."

The other source of information that Mr. Shannon gave us was a copy of Edward D. Crabb's manuscript on the birds of Oklahoma. Under the sponsorship of the Geological Survey he had collected 369 specimens from October 15, 1913 to December 5, 1914, in central, eastern, and southwestern Oklahoma. A beginning had been made on an elaborate report consisting of detailed descriptions of plumages and long quotations from the U.S. Biological Survey on the food of each species. There was very little on the range or status or habits of the birds in the state. We did learn, however, of the many species of warblers nesting in eastern Oklahoma. The money had given out, and the work stopped. The collection was stored in a temporary structure in which a grade school was housed; one of the pupils, averse to education, set fire to the building, and one fourth of the specimens and all the notebooks, including the keys to the place and date of capture, were reported to have been destroyed.

We now had two incomplete lists (Barde's and Van Vleet's) of the birds of Oklahoma and two partial collections of specimens in the University Museum. What seemed to be most needed was information on what birds occurred where in this far-flung state with its astonishing diversity of physiography, rainfall, and flora. Mr. Shannon suggested we go southwest to the Wichita Mountains, then to the Arbuckle Mountains in the south-central Oklahoma, then to the Kiamitia Mountains in the southeast, and finally to the

[1]Willow Flycatcher, *Empidonax trailii*. [2]*Empidonax virescens*. [3]*Ammodramus bairdii*.

northeastern corner of the state. Since considerable collecting had already been done, and since we much preferred live birds to dead ones, we planned to depend as much as possible upon our eyes and ears rather than on the shotgun lent us by Mr. Shannon.

Our books were Mrs. Bailey's *Birds of the Western United States*, Frank Chapman's *Color Key to North American Birds* (1903), and my old Reed's *Guides*, purchased when the colours of the plates were still unworn. Mr. Shannon lent us a heavy, awkward tent that had to be put up with poles. He also lent us cots and cooking utensils, besides a supply of elegant notebooks. We purchased the rest of our outfit at army stores, prepared blanket sleeping bags, put bars on one side of the car to provide storage place in lieu of a car trunk, non-existent in those days, and made countless other preparations. We had planned to leave the two- and four-year-olds with our good neighbour, Mrs. Hedley, who watched the flock and *mended* for them when we went out in the evening, but at the last minute she was called to Texas to care for sick relatives. So we decided on a trial trip to the Wichitas; if the children throve, we would start out again on the rest of our itinerary.

And then began our perfect week in the Wichita National Forest. We were welcomed by our friend Frank Rush, Chief Forester, who showed us the colony of Barn Swallow under the bridge by Head-quarters and a Bewick's nest in a cow's skull. He also promised to supply us with milk. We set up camp on Elm Island and went to sleep under the stars.

The Wichita Mountains rise abruptly 700 to 900 feet above the plateau; they are jumbles of grey granite boulders with scattered black jack and post oaks and red cedars pushing through the rocks. Scarlet gilia lighted the scanty woods, while the close-cropped cattle range was clothed with showy gaillardia and several kinds of coreopsis. On the rocks by the roadside lay brilliant lizards — little blue-sided swifts and gorgeous "mountain boomers" (collared lizards) with yellow heads and brilliant green-blue bodies and tails.

It was a new world to all of us — the strangeness and wildness of the mountains and plains with the flowers, beasts, and birds. We, too, were part of it, living in it and seeking to understand it. We had a burning zeal to learn all we could, especially of the birds, and to share our knowledge with others. At last I was camping again and this time with an earnest purpose.

So earnest, indeed, that at the last cry of the Chuck-will's-widow[1] just before dawn we pulled on our shoes and canvas

---

[1]*Caprimulgus carolinensis.*

leggings (worn as protection from rattlesnakes) and started out to seek birds. Two hours later we would return to camp and the children, and cook bacon and eggs for all of us. Blaine was chief fire-maker and cook, the children were the wood-gatherers and dishwashers. They liked to scrub the tin plates with sand in the creek, for as seven-year-old Marjorie explained, "The fish are just delighted with our crumbs," Four-year-old Barbara decided she wanted "to camp always," even in winter. "Why don't we move here?" she asked. "Move really?" We swam in Cache Creek while Eleanor watched with astonishment and amusement. Blaine and I rode on Mr. Rush's buffalo horses in the tall blue stem of the pasture to visit the bison herd; we clambered up Elk Mountain, Bat Cave Mountain, and Little Baldy, and we met two rattlesnakes. My army breeches were my pride; I was amazed to find with what agility I could leap from rock to rock. By this time women in America were beginning to don male attire for outdoor activities.

The most abundant bird, both in the woods and on the prairie, was the Lark Sparrow. Woodpeckers were uncommon, but Great Crested Flycatchers[1], Tufted Titmice, Carolina Chickadees, and bluebirds were all abundant; apparently they found favourable nesting sites in the knot holes of oaks. Each morning there was a chorus of Wood Pewees[2] uttering their beautiful twilight songs. This species was on the western edge of its range; we found none here on later visits — in 1923, 1926, 1929, 1937 and 1955.

As we explored the boulders at the foot of the mountains we soon discovered our first Rock Wrens[3], absurd little things with their harsh, graty vocalizations, so appropriate to their environment. But what was this large, olive-grey, sparrow-like bird with its chestnut crown and black line down its throat? "This ought to be a Rock Sparrow," said I. Lo and behold, according to Mrs. Bailey's *Handbook*, Rock Sparrow it was! We had never before even heard of the existence of such a bird. We were very proud to think we had discovered a new bird for the Oklahoma list. Later, however, I found the Wichita Mountains included in the breeding range in the 1910 A.O.U. *Check-List of North American Birds*; Vernon Bailey had taken one on Elk Mountain in 1906. Interestingly enough, Bunker in 1901 and Crabb in 1914 had both collected specimens in the Wichitas; these lay, unidentified, in the University Museum. (In the 1957 A.O.U. *Check-List* this fine bird has lost its distinctive name; it is listed with seven other subspecies under the Rufous-crowned Sparrow, *Aimophila ruficeps*.)

---

[1]*Myiarchus crinitus.* [2]Eastern Wood Pewee, *Contopus virens.* [3]*Salpinctes obsoletus.*

We came home to a different bird world — to a morning chorus of Robins, Brown Thrashers, Catbirds, Mockingbirds, Orchard Orioles[1], and Cardinals. When we started out again I felt pity for everyone who could not go camping to study the birds of Oklahoma. And then I remembered that, strange as it might seem, hardly anyone in Norman but ourselves would *want* to do it.

Sixty miles south of Norman lie the ancient, deeply eroded Arbuckle Mountains. Here matchless streams dashed over water-carved travertine rocks where every nook and cranny were filled with ferns. Stately sycamores stood along the streams while in the water grew parrot-feather and watercress, and where rapids flowed over step-like rocks, myriads of caddis fly larvae wove their tiny nets.

Situated 100 miles east of the Wichitas, less elevated and less arid, these more genial conditions were reflected in the bird life. We had found no warblers in the Wichitas; here there were four species. Rock Sparrows frequented the stony tops of the eroded "mountains," but the country was not rugged enough for Rock Wrens. A new bird for us was the engaging little Black-capped Vireo[2]. We came upon a nest three feet up in a redbud; in it were three new infants and a partly hatched egg. The parents protested my presence, but the father came to the nest and gently billed his babies.

From our camp at Price's Falls one day we trundled across the high pastures where the strata are all on end as regular as furrows in a plowed field. Turner's Falls on Honey Creek was a noble sight.

A wood rat adopted our car as its den; each morning when we opened the hood there it sat looking at us with its bright eyes, surrounded by the stuff it had brought in during the night — scraps of wood and string, acorns, and even some of my hairpins. One evening a Chuck-will's-widow started singing outside the tent. Eleanor, who had been prancing about while the rest of us were trying to get to sleep, was arrested; she leaned forward on the cot, intently peering into the dark, and exclaimed again and again in her sweet little voice, "Birdie hay tuck-will-widdie!"

Leaving our enchanting Arbuckles, for a day and a half we ploughed through a sandy road that wound through woods and after 100 miles discovered we had left the West and arrived in the South. Log cabins and plank shanties, razor-backed hogs and other stock running loose, Martin houses by every dwelling, horseback riding the chief means of travel, no provisions in the country stores but salt pork and cornmeal, and splendid oaks girdled for

[1]*Icterus spurius.* [2] *Vireo atricapilla.*

the sake of corn and cotton — these were the outstanding features of civilisation in these woods and mountains.

With all the dead trees it was a land of Woodpeckers — Red-headed[1], Red-bellied, Hairy, Downy, and the astonishing great Pileated[2], called "Woodchucks" by the natives. In one swampy valley, from bushes draped with trumpet creepers, we heard an amazing *twich-u-wail-chit* and I knew that here at last was my White-eyed Vireo, a bird I had longed to meet since, as a child, I had read about him in Mrs. Wright's *Bird-Craft*.

In Pushmataha County, 17 miles north of Antlers, we set up our tent in a wild and beautiful spot beneath the great yellow pines. Milk and water we obtained from a friendly family at a nearby cabin; they told us that we wouldn't be troubled by "varmints," although "timber wolves" (perhaps red wolves *Canis niger*) had carried off half their hogs. Their little boy of two was fat and cheerful and ate all day long. "But he's poor to what he was; in the winter his little old cheeks hung down like a little old hog's." The family said that the Choctaw Indians living thereabouts did not suffer from malaria and rheumatism and all the other diseases that afflicted the white folk. The grandfather told us that in some ways stock have more sense than folks; he said he always talked to his horses when he rode and the horse understood everything he said. "Why, it takes a year for a man to learn the Choctaw language, but it only takes a horse six weeks!"

Birds were everywhere in the primeval forests of pine and oaks, hickories, winged elms and sweet gums. Old friends — Wood Pewees, Blue-gray Gnatcatchers. Red-eyed Vireos, Summer Tanagers[3], and Carolina Wrens. And new friends, too: Chipping Sparrows, familiar door-yard birds in Massachusetts, and migrants in Norman, were here nesting in the deep woods. Warblers were a wonder and a delight — no less than nine species! Two exciting finds were birds of the southeastern pine forests here at the western limit of their range; several Red-cockaded Woodpeckers[4] and a single Brown-headed Nuthatch[5] — the first record for Oklahoma! Day and night there was song — the beauty of the Wood Thrush[6] , the earnestness of the Indigo Bunting, the absurdity of the White-eyed Vireo, the lullaby of the *Chuck will's widow*, and finally the deafening din of katydids in the dark.

Camping fare was varied by an occasional squirrel, a snapping turtle, and bullfrog legs, and once the children dug us a mess of

---

[1]*Melanerpes erythrocephalus.* [2] *Dryocopus pileatus.*

[3]*Piranga rubra.* [4] *Picoides borealis.* [5] *Sitta pusilla.* [6]*Hylocichla mustelina.*

mussels. The car was not thriving on pioneer life and Blaine exclaimed in disgust. "As soon as we get home I'm going to sell it." Barbara piped up, "Oh, I hope that won't be till we're grown up!"

This hope was not to be fulfilled. We drove up and over Winding Stair Mountain quite to the detriment of our poor dear. Our perfect weather came to an end. The rains poured down and the roads became quagmires, and driving a protracted agony. When two of us caught cold, we gave up our plans for northeastern Oklahoma and turned home.

What were the results of our great expedition? A few specimens, unskilfully prepared by myself, much information as to distribution of Oklahoma birds, and a number of discoveries of new summer birds. Besides this, we had really lived during those weeks; we had been a part of the life of the Wichitas, the Arbuckles, the Kiamitias; we had had adventures, we had gained knowledge and a deep love for this wild, strange country.

After we had recuperated a little from this fantastic trip, I went to consult with Mr. Shannon. Our plan had been to write a report on the birds we had found, comparing them with those in our home county and correlating distribution with geography, altitude, latitude, longitude, rainfall, and vegetation. I was dumbfounded to have Mr. Shannon cheerily talk of our writing a bulletin on *The Birds of Oklahoma*. I protested that we knew hardly anything of the birds of the state. He reassured me by telling of his proposed auto trip through northwestern Oklahoma and the Panhandle on which he would keep notes on the birds encountered. At length we agreed on a preliminary report on *Summer Birds* of the state, designed to arouse interest in bird study and protection. He urged us to prepare it at once for publication that fall.

This was a staggering proposition and we looked for all the help we could find. We wrote to the Biological Survey in Washington, and they most kindly sent us addresses of their cooperators in the state as well as copies of nest censuses taken in 1916 in several localities. We prepared a four-page questionnaire on the status of some 50 species; this we sent to members of the Biological Section of the Oklahoma Academy of Science and to anyone else we suspected of having an interest in birds.

Very little utilizable information came from most of the questionnaires. Three men, however, all strangers to us, were earnest bird students and responded with heart-warming generosity.

Theordore R. Beard studied birds in the Sapulpa region during his last two years in High School; he sent us a list of the birds of

Creek County for 1919-20 that was very good for a boy with no guidance but that of a few books. Sadly enough, the career of this young naturalist was cut short by tuberculosis.

From Tulsa Albert J. Kirn gave us a wealth of information on the birds of that region and also of Washington County to the north. A keen oologist, he had learned a great deal about the nesting birds and had published seven short notes in "Brother Barnes" journal, *The Oologist*; these notes were on Oklahoma hawks and owls and the Kentucky[1] and Swainson's Warblers[2].

Walter E. Lewis, Quaker farmer and school teacher, sent us an annotated list of all the birds he had met in his interesting locality — Gate — on the 100th meridian, at the east end of the Oklahoma Panhandle.

I urged these naturalists to publish their observations in journals to stimulate interest in birds. Mr. Kirn shortly moved to Texas where he was too busy with his oil activities ever to write a long article. Mr. Lewis, however, did publish five short papers in the *Wilson Bulletin* and *Auk* from 1925 to 1930.

Mr. Shannon, home from his trip that had proved singularly unproductive so far as bird records went, asked us for a mimeographed list of the summer birds of Oklahoma to be distributed at the State Fair in Oklahoma City in September. Accordingly we prepared an unannotated list of 131 species and subspecies with both common and scientific names. It proved useful to send out to collaborators for their comments.

My absorbing occupation was the preparation of the bulletin. With state lists of Arkansas, Louisiana, Kansas, and Texas, all my books and government bulletins, some of them dating back to Clark University days and with my pile of *Bird-Lores*, we set to work. We pointed out the most glaring gaps in our knowledge of the breeding birds and encouraged readers to keep records of transients and winter residents. Each bird was briefly described, its status and known range given, its notes and nest mentioned; then followed a leisurely discussion of characteristics and life history anecdotes, largely gleaned from *Bird-Lore*. In short, we were trying to give a maximum of useful information to beginners.

We had achieved accounts of 92 species when a notice of the A.O.U. meeting to be held in early November in Washington, D.C.* arrived with an invitation to all classes of members to read papers.

[1]*Oporornis formosus.* [2]*Limnothlypis swainsonii.*

*The 38th Stated Meeting of the American Ornithologists' Union held in Washington, D.C. November 8-11, 1920.

Here was my chance; if only I could make Mr. Shannon see the necessity of consulting with Dr. Oberholser in person as to our "Summer Birds," then I could go to the meeting, give a paper on our Mourning Dove study and incidentally see something of the Morse family. Mr. Shannon was agreeable and promised to pay half my expenses. I invited my mother to be my guest at Washington, and I dropped "Summer Birds" and turned feverishly to dove problems. This trip proved to be of crucial influence in making me into an ornithologist.

I found Dr. Oberholser at the end of a large room housing a number of workers in the Biological Survey; he welcomed me and sent me to the meetings in the National Museum in charge of Miss May T. Cooke of the Biological Survey. She was the daughter of the eminent student of migration, the late Wells W. Cooke. There were 35 papers scheduled for the three days, only one of them by a woman.

The President was kindly Witmer Stone, editor of the *Auk*; the Secretary, affable, dominating Theodore S. Palmer, and the Treasurer, W. L. McAtee. Many of the papers lasted half an hour or longer and there was plenty of time for discussion. Prentis S. Baldwin, originator of bird-banding through systematic trapping, gave two interesting papers: "Marriage Relations of the House Wren" and "Recent Returns from Trapping and Banding." Wednesday afternoon was devoted to five papers illustrated with motion pictures, all in black and white, and far more ambitious than those I had admired 12 years earlier. They were a wonderful experience for my mother and me.

At the exhibition of paintings in the Library of Congress I was intrigued with pictures by Althea Sherman (1952), particularly of a cat creeping up on a nestful of Robins. I asked Dr. Palmer about Miss Sherman and he said she wrote a good deal for the *Wilson Bulletin*. This was the first time I had heard of this journal and of the Wilson Ornithological Club.

My own speech, "The Nesting of Mourning Doves at Norman, Oklahoma", came on the last afternoon when there was no time left for discussion. Mr. McAtee and Dr. Palmer hung up my charts on the blackboard, but the colours did not show up well. I was so over-awed that I read rapidly in a faint voice, and I fear the A.O.U. benefited little from my discoveries.

The next week Dr. Oberholser generously spent a whole day helping me with my problems, and this proved the most important part of the entire trip to me. He showed me the bibliography which the Survey had on Oklahoma birds; this was a revelation to me, particularly in the matter of early explorers. He gave me the names of Oklahoma collaborators, and had books and maps brought me to study. He showed me portions of his great manuscript on *The Birds of Texas* (1974) with splendid maps indicating the range of each species in the state. Through him I purchased a complete set of the *Nuttall Bulletin* and *Auk* (1876-1919) that had belonged to Henry W. Henshaw, one of the Founders of the Nuttall Ornithological Club, the parent of the A.O.U. Dr. Henshaw had been a naturalist on the Wheeler Survey, and later Chief of the United States Biological Survey; he was a notable worker for conservation.

Carefully, we went through our State Fair List of *Summer Birds*, and what a field day Dr. Oberholser did have in changing scientific names and adding subspecific labels! Seven of our birds he rejected but later all but one were reinstated. As the day wore on I grew more and more conscious of our appalling ignorance and of our presumption in attempting to treat of the "Summer Birds of Oklahoma." I resolved then and there that no bulletin would be written by us without a great deal more field work.

I owe a great debt to Dr. Oberholser for starting me on the straight and narrow path in ornithology and in giving me a different viewpoint from that which I had acquired from *Bird-Lore*. But his magnification of the importance of the subspecies was unfortunate for us and for those who followed us, for it diverted attention from the species and made matters unduly confusing for the field student.

VIII

The Oklahoma Panhandle

Deeply impressed with my heavy responsibility in attempting a book on the breeding birds of Oklahoma, I devoted my energies to studying ornithology.

I joined the Wilson Ornithological Club, the association primarily of middlewestern bird watchers and purchased the volumes of the *Wilson Bulletin*, beginning with 1912. These contained many life history studies which I eagerly read. J. R. Pemberton, Tulsa oologist, proposed my name for membership in the Cooper Ornithological Club, founded in 1889. In March 1921 I purchased a complete set of the *Condor* – the last set possessed by the Club. "This file of the *Condor*," wrote the business manager, W. Lee Chambers from Eagle Rock, California, "will give you the best working library on western birds obtainable." I also invested in a set of the *Oologist*, edited by R. M. Barnes of Lacon, Illinois, not for its ornithology, but to go through it page by page for references to Oklahoma birds. The money earned in girlhood by labours on the hens had now been put to worthy use.

I settled down to study the *Auk* and the *Condor*, going through them from beginning to end, reading the articles that most interested me and paying special attention to the editorials, correspondence, and book reviews. In the early days there had been real reviews by those great ornithologists Elliot Coues and J. A. Allen. Of the latter, Chapman (1922:12) wrote, "I do not recall ever hearing him speak ill of another, but he was unsparing in his condemnation of careless work, and particularly of generalizations based on insufficient data."

I absorbed techniques and standards besides learning much about birds and ornithologists.

The University Library subscribed to no ornithological journal, nor do I remember that it had any bird books. I built up my own library by sending for all the paper-bound State lists I could procure and many Biological Survey bulletins on migration and on the food of birds. Dr. Oberholser had my name placed on the list of the National Museum so that I would receive the current volumes of Arthur Bent's *Life Histories of North American Birds*. Fortunately, I was able to buy the early numbers of this notable set.

On December 26, 1920, on our Christmas census over the same areas as in 1919, we found 32 species and about 800 individuals (1921). On the 30th, a bright and sunny day, Constance and I took a memorable hike south to the Canadian River. Here the exquisite songs of Fox Sparrows rose on all sides. Suddenly there came a different sound — an extraordinary clanking, honking, deafening clamour, — and there was a flock of some 50 Canada Geese[1] sweeping down the river bed.

In the spring of 1921 Mourning Doves on the campus were again the family's chief project. Constance's discovery of two nests with three eggs apiece started me on a round of correspondence with observers all over the country, some of whom later became friends. Miss Sherman wrote me: "I am glad to welcome another woman to our ranks. Too many women are dabblers."

My avid perusal of journals stirred my ambitions to have something published myself. To the *Condor* I sent a note, illustrated with two photographs on "Nests of Mourning Doves with Three Young" (1921). In his note of acceptance, Joseph Grinnell, the editor, wrote: "There is always plenty of room for faithful descriptions of the actions of living birds, in other words, life history material. Even the commonest species are very little known, relatively."

"The Roadside Census" appeared under joint authorship of Blaine and myself in the *Wilson Bulletin* (1920). Miss Sherman commented, "I am glad that someone is making use of such drives, for the motor car is an abomination to me."

The meetings of the Oklahoma Academy of Science, founded in 1909, had proved pleasant and stimulating to us. In 1916 we were both elected Fellows and Blaine was made Secretary, an office he faithfully fulfilled for six years. At the 9th annual meeting in February 1921, the Academy appointed Blaine and Mr. Shannon

[1] *Branta canadensis.*

to superintend the publication of the first volume of Proceedings as a University Bulletin. Mr. Shannon wrote a historical sketch of the Academy and collected abstracts of geological papers. Blaine wrote to former members, trying to locate programs of the early meetings, but he was never able to find those of the third and fourth meetings. We published seven programs and 39 papers, 20 of them abstracts.

In the seven programs there are 15 titles on birds: one each by the geologists, Drs. D. W. Ohern and Charles N. Gould, and one by Blaine; two each by Drs. G. W. Stevens and Edward Crabb; three by Mr. Shannon and five by myself. No paper was given by a woman in the first three programs that we have; in 1916 I gave one on the vocabularies of my eldest daughter. After that I am happy to say that four women participated in 1917 and in the next two years; five in 1920 and seven in 1921; subsequently they have always been present.

The U.S. Biological Survey continued to be most helpful by copying for us further nesting censuses and even the reports of all their investigators in Oklahoma from 1892 to 1906. Dr. Oberholser identified many specimens sent him by me from the University Museum.

In order to increase our knowledge of the distribution of breeding species in the state, Blaine journeyed by train and on foot in the Spavinaw region in northeastern Oklahoma; here he enjoyed seeing the Cherokee Indians as well as the abundant birds.

In the meantime, the children and I travelled by train to Massachusetts. In former years I delighted in the birds at Grey Rocks; this summer I was amazed to discover what treasures I had missed. Each new nesting species was yet another wonder — Chestnut-sided[1], Nashville[2], Black-throated Blue[3], Canada[4], Magnolia, Myrtle[5], Blackburnian Warblers[6] — what a paradise we lived in! Night and morning we listened to the exquisite songs of the Wood and Hermit[7] Thrushes.

The longest hike we took that summer was what we called the "Fifty-bird Walk." On the morning of July 16 my brother Will drove Blaine and me to the Notch in the Mount Holyoke range; we turned east and climbed Mount Norwottuck, finding warblers and a pair of Peregrine Falcons[8] . From the summit we looked northeast

---

[1]*Dendroica pensylvanica.* [2] *Vermivora ruficapilla.* [3] *Dendroica caerulescens.* [4] *Wilsonia canadensis.* [5] Yellow-rumped Warbler, *Dendroica coronata.* [6]*Dendroica fusca.* [7] *Catharus guttata.* [8]*Falco peregrinus.*

to the Pelham Hills, and Grey Rocks did not look so very far away, so we decided to walk home cross-country. It was a memorable trip, especially for the Short-billed Marsh Wrens[1] we met in South Amherst (not included in Hubert Clark's *Birds of Amherst*) and for our long struggle in the growing darkness through the South Amherst Swamp. How tired we grew of hearing the Swamp Sparrow's[2] trill always in front of us when we were longing for dry land!

Back in Norman by September 9, we found only eight pairs of Mourning Doves still nesting; the last brood left on the 27th. One day I was astonished to watch *four* young doves, recently out of the nest, all begging from one adult. I wondered whether by any chance there had been an adoption of fledgelings, for I have found no record of Mourning Doves raising four young in one brood, and only one, so far as I know, of a pair raising three. This was on our campus in 1921.

Our plans for 1922 centred upon a camping trip through north-western Oklahoma, out through the Panhandle and into New Mexico. Through the Biological Survey we had come into contact with an ardent naturalist, Ralph Crompton Tate, whose home in Kenton, at the western tip of the Panhandle, was in an exciting region so far as birds were concerned.

Unfortunately, Blaine had become engrossed in remodeling two business buildings we had bought in Norman, and in the course of this activity he had broken a rib. So we decided that Constance and I should make the Panhandle trip as best we could by train.

On the 26th of May Constance and I started by train. The prairie flowers were not as splendid as they had been eight years earlier, for during the War much of the railroad right-of-way had been plowed to raise food. At the Northwestern Normal School at Alva we had a rewarding conference with Dr. T. C. Carter, Professor of Zoology. He gave me a copy of "Thesis on Oklahoma Birds" by O. J. Trenton and himself, published in *The Northwestern*, in April 1908; 162 species are mentioned with brief notes on their occurrence. It gave us the only records at that time for the Marbled Godwit[3] and Band-tailed Pigeon. Professor Carter showed us the bird collection, which unfortunately was inadequately labelled as to dates and localities.

The next day Constance and I spent an unforgettable morning along the Cimarron River, the chief glory being the Mississippi

---

[1] *Cistothorus platensis.* [2] *Melospiza georgiana.* [3] *Limosa fedoa.*

Kites[1]. We found two of their nests, and when Constance climbed up to see what they contained, the parents swooped at us. Other nests were two of Mourning Doves, two of flickers, two of Blue Jays, and one of a nighthawk[2].

Then began a zig-zag journey. One train took us southwest to Woodward, another went northwest to Forgan in Beaver County where we took a bus to Liberal, Kansas. This town was a great haunt of House Sparrows, the next most abundant bird being the Western Kingbird. A fourth train took us southwest to Texhoma on the Texas border. Early the next morning there was a great chorus of Western Kingbirds, followed by an even greater one of House Sparrows. At 7:00 a.m. we left with the mail carrier who took us 57 miles northwest to Boise City. The most abundant birds on the short-grass plains were Horned Larks[3] (parents accompanied by speckled young), Western Kingbirds, Western Meadowlarks, Burrowing Owls and nighthawks. Two new birds delighted us: spectacular black and white Lark Buntings[4] in small flocks and a pair of amazing Long-billed Curlews[5]. After travelling on four railroads, a bus and in a mail auto, at Boise City we were still 42 miles from our goal. The obliging mailman found a young man whose home lay on our route and who agreed to take us to Kenton.

For some time we drove over high treeless pairie, much of it an immense pasture dotted with sage brush and yucca, and inhabited by white-faced cattle and jack rabbits, Horned Larks, and Western Meadowlarks. Abruptly this changed into the "Breaks" — wild and picturesque country of canyons and sandstone mesas, wonderful scenery to us from central Oklahoma. Mesquite, yucca, cat's claw, devil's claw and cholla cactus on the plains, and pinyons, junipers and scrub oaks on the mesas — these formed the characteristic vegetation. Kenton itself was a village of a hundred inhabitants with two churches and no doctor. We found a pleasant room with a private family and were called to hearty meals at the Kenton Hotel by the landlady's beating on an iron triangle, the sound of which could be heard all over town.

That afternoon we visited Mr. Tate. We found him, who a dozen years before had ridden range over the Panhandle, confined to his home, a victim of polio. Isolated from other naturalists, and his only bird book Chester K. Reed's *Land Birds East of the Rockies* (1906), he had laboured under many difficulties. His collection of bird skins and eggs had been destroyed by a tenant. It was his

---

[1]*Ictinia mississippiensis.* [2]Common Nighthawk, *Chordeiles minor.*
[3]*Eremophila alpestris.* [4]*Calamospiza melanocorys.* [5]*Numenius americanus.*

interest in plants that had brought him into contact with Professor Stevens.

Mr. Tate told us of nesting Ravens[1] and Golden Eagles[2], and of how Great Blue Herons[3] used to nest in tall cottonwoods along the Cimarron, as many as 56 nests in one dead tree; unfortunately, however, these trees had been carried away in a great flood in 1912. I lent him a guide to western flowers and Mrs. Bailey's book on western birds. From this he was able to identify a number of birds whose names had been unknown to him.

Along the Cimarron, here nothing but a large brook across which we waded many times, we found exciting birds. The little Texas Woodpecker[4] or "Ladderback" was new to us, but not to the Oklahoma list. A large grey-brown comfortable-looking bird of towhee size with a reddish brown cap, was, according to Mrs. Bailey the Canyon Towhee (now dubbed Brown Towhee[5]). A pair of wonderful Lewis' Woodpeckers[6] — great black birds with rosy bellies and cheeks — were busy at their nest hole; to her disappointment Constance could not climb it.

One of the choicest of our new birds we discovered in alfalfa fields near town. Here a little sand-coloured sparrow would spring into the air and float down again, uttering one of the most touching and hauntingly lovely songs I have ever heard. The Cassin's Sparrows[7] won our hearts completely. We wished it would increase and spread over the country instead of confining itself to the arid Southwest.

I was happy to find that Henry Henshaw, whose set of the *Auk* I possessed, had also loved the Cassin's Sparrow. Fifty years before our discovery of the bird he had written of its song (1875):

It possesses an indescribable sweetness and pathos, especially when heard, as is often the case, during the still hours of the night. During a night's march (in Southern Arizona in late summer) from Camp Grant to Camp Bowie, I do not think of an interval of five minutes passed unbroken by the sound of one of these Sparrows; ere fairly out of the hearing of the notes of one performer, the same plaintive strain was taken up by another invisible musician a little farther on, and so it continued until just before dawn.

So far, most of our work had been done on the Flats; it was high time to climb the mesas with their fantastic wind-carved pinnacles. Here again we found ourselves in another world — that of the pigmy conifers. Our first Say's Phoebe[8] called *pee dur* from

---

[1]Common Raven, *Corvus corax*. [2]*Aquila chrysaetos*. [3]*Ardea herodias*. [4]*Picoides scalaris*. [5]*Pipilo fuscus*. [6]*Melanerpes lewis*. [7]*Aimophila cassinii*. [8]*Sayornis saya*.

the cliffs. Canyon Towhees were nesting — eggs in juniper and pinyon, young in a cholla. A Red-tailed Hawk[1] screamed. During a shower we retired to a cave and watched a Rock Wren carry grubs to its young, while a baby wood rat peeped out of its hole.

As we explored the mesa top we heard harsh, piercing cries *wee-ahk, wee-ahk* and soon came upon handsome Woodhouse's Jays[6] (now lumped in the 1957 A.O.U. *Checklist* with 12 other sub-species under the discouraging name of "Scrub Jay"). In the conifers were plenty of old nests that appeared to have belonged to these birds, but we could not find a new one. Another noisy bird was the Piñon Jay[2], and here we had better luck for Constance discivered a deep, well-built nest, 10 feet up in a juniper; in it were two small young and an egg. This was the first nesting record of this species for Oklahoma. Finally, we met three very small grey birds which consultation with Mrs. Bailey's book proved to be Lead-coloured Bush Tits[3] — new birds both for us and for Oklahoma.

We said goodby to Mr. Tate, promising to send him bird litera-ture and addresses of natural history bulletins to be had for the asking, while he promised to lend me his old notebooks and keep me informed of bird news. Thus started a warm friendship of much benefit to us both. I helped him with viewpoint, principles, and information so that he was able to get his observations into shape for publication, and he helped me with data on the wild life of the region.

A 54 mile drive with another mailman through a region abounding in prairie dogs and jack rabbits, yuccas and Horned Larks brought us to Clayton, New Mexico. From here we took a train to Oklahoma City and a trolley car home.

Coming into contact with a new avifauna, and *in Oklahoma*, had been a wonderfully stimulating event. We had met birds that were entirely new to me; indeed, I had not dreamt that such existed: The absurd little Bush Tit, the sedate Canyon Towhee, the astonishing Lewis' Woodpecker, the Cassin's Sparrow with its exquisite refrain. All these birds were *mine*. For Oklahoma belonged to me in a way it could belong to few others — only those who studied nature in the state. It was mine, for I loved it passionately — its pine forests, its flower-studded prairies, its rock-jumbled mountains, its great plains and cedar-topped mesas. I was

---

[1] *Buteo jamaicensis.* [2] Piñon Jay, *Gymnorhinus cyanocephalus.*
[3] Common Bushtit, *Psaltriparus minimus.*

keenly aware of its soil, and its weather, its contours and rivers, its plants, and most of all, its birds.

The strangeness and wildness around Kenton had given us deep satisfaction. Humanity has a spiritual need of wilderness. "In wildness is the preservation of the world," wrote Thoreau (1912).

IX

The First 'Birds of Oklahoma'

One day in July 1922, it suddenly occured to me: Why not write a bulletin on "Birds of Oklahoma" instead of Summer Birds? By this time we had learned much about the winter birds and transients in our region, and we had splendid collaborators ready to tell us what they knew, while the published lists, to which was now added Carter and Trenton's paper (1908) gave further information. Our friends — Messrs. Kirn, Lewis, Beard and Tate — responded generously as always.

Jean Linsdale, then a student at the University of Kansas, sent us information on birds observed near Sapulpa during three Christmas vacations; some of these had been collected and sent to Washington for subspecific identification.

Professor Stevens answered questions on 12 species he had listed for Mr. Beard.

Our best bird haunt readily reached by car was the Dump directly south of Norman on the Canadian River. Here among great elms and cottonwoods, the only place suitable for a park, the town emptied its sewer and scattered its tin cans. The birds did not mind, and we, despite our repugnance for man-made hideousness, followed them.

On July 2 I drove Mr. Crabb and his bird class there — a treat for the students, who until then had explored only the campus, which at that time with its extensive osage orange hedges attracted a rich nesting population. Mr. Crabb collected a Downy Woodpecker for himself and a Screech Owl for me. The chief reward of the expedition was finding the Sycamore Warbler (now called

Yellow-throated Warbler[1]) feeding young; until then I had seen these beautiful birds only in eastern Oklahoma, and here it was nesting on our doorstep.

Snail Brook, the half mile between West Boyd and Lindsey Streets, had been my laboratory, the chief place to watch the spring and fall migrations, and a good place to study winter birds. In summer it became too tangled for me to learn much of nesting success or failure. For three years I had made almost weekly censuses, laying the foundation of my knowledge of local birds and gaining inspiration from this wilderness in miniature.

Now, alas, Snail Brook was suffering cruel blows from Philistines who saw no beauty in unspoiled nature. Most of the trees were hacked down and all the undergrowth cut out. In August a man told me he planned to cut down the last fine grove of cottonwoods so as to plant crops; I tried to dissuade him by telling him how badly flooded the land became each spring. Whether my advice influenced him, I do not know, but the trees were left in peace. After this trip, Snail Brook was still valuable during fall migration, largely due to its masses of giant ragweed; but my visits at other times of the year ceased almost entirely.

The joint A.O.U.* and Wilson Club** meeting in October 1922 in Chicago was extremely fruitful, both in scientific and social values. The same officers officiated as in 1920: Dr. Stone, President; Dr. Palmer, Secretary; Mr. McAtee, Treasurer. This time everyone wore his or her name, and no one waited for introductions. I knew many of the men from their writings and many people knew me, for the first part of *A Study of the Nesting of Mourning Doves* had just appeared in the October *Auk* (1922). Moreover, I gave my talk on "The 'Broken-wing' Ruse in Mourning Doves" the first morning. Afterwards Dr. Palmer told me I had not spoken loud enough. "Throw your voice," he said. After that my talks could be heard. It was some years before microphones were used.

The papers appealed to me much more than those given in 1920. Miss Sherman's on "Habits of the Short-billed Marsh Wren" was outstanding. Others of special interest to me were Francis Herrick's notable studies on the nesting of the Bald Eagle; R. M. Strong's on

---

[1]*Dendroica dominica.*

---

*The 40th Stated Meeting of the American Ornithologists' Union, Chicago, Illinois, October 23-27, 1922.

**The 9th Stated Meeting of the Wilson Ornithological Club, Chicago, Illinois, October 23-27, 1922.

the behaviour of the Herring Gull[1]; Arthur Allen's (of Cornell University) account of the inroads by a pair of Screech Owls on the song bird population; and Dr. Oberholser's speech on "The Great Plains as a Breeding Ground for Waterfowl." There were also five excellent motion picture films, all in black and white.

It was indeed a privilege to have leisurely talks with Miss Sherman. She told me of the great increase of House Wrens in response to the putting up of Wren boxes; this species destroys eggs of all kinds of small birds, vireos, warblers, bluebirds, and native sparrows.

At the A.O.U. dinner, the distinguished bird artist Louis Agassiz Fuertes spoke, and Frank Chapman told of the first A.O.U. meeting he had attended (in 1886) and of his disappointment at the entire lack of social features for associate members. I was enchanted with my first *Auklet* (1922), a humorous booklet written by the local committee; in my opinion the most absurd contributions were O.G. Dix Cissell's "Evolution of Deecnomialism" and the thousand subspecies of the "Song Sparrows of the Thousand Islands."

The next evening there was a Wilson Club dinner and after that a meeting of bird banders at which the Inland Bird Banding Association was organized and all interested invited to give in their names and a dollar. Unfortunately, I failed to follow this suggestion. If I had started seriously with banding then it would have been of great advantage to my life history studies.

On the field trip to the William H. Richardsons' cottage in the Indiana Dunes on October 22 we walked through jack pine and white pine woods, over cranberries and between prickly pears, with oaks in full colour, and with witch hazel, harebells and bird's-foot violets in bloom. It was a triumph to show Harris' Sparrows[2] to the Percival Coffins of Chicago — their first sight of this notable bird — and it was fun to visit with that genial Canadian and fine friend, W. E. Saunders.

In my chief aim in coming to Chicago, I was well rewarded. The decision to cover all the birds in our state list had brought up many problems as to which records to include from the published lists and from our collaborators. Dr. Oberholser was so busy in Washington that my letters were answered only after long, long intervals. In our conference at the meeting he was his kind and omniscient self. Despite all my labours and studies, he ruled out a goodly number of species I had thought safe. For people as new to

---

[1]*Larus argentatus.* [2] *Zonotrichia querula.*

the game of ornithology as the Nices, the guidance of Dr. Oberholser was of inestimable value in getting out a trustworthy publication on birds of Oklahoma.

The second part of the Mourning Dove study came out in January 1923, my first major ornithological paper since *The Food of the Bobwhite* published in 1910, thirteen years earlier. It is a population study of an abundant species whose nests were easy to find and, with the children's help, easy to investigate. It received compliments from a number of people, among them Miss Sherman; Otto Widmann, author of *Birds of Missouri* (1907), and Eugene Law, eminent member of the Cooper Ornithological Club and zealous birdbander, who wrote me, "An exceedingly valuable contribution to life history, based on quantitative observation." And he encouraged me to continue the work "for 10 or 20 years!"

The two bird papers on the Academy program in February 1923 were published in the third volume of the Proceedings in 1924. R. C. Tate's "Some Birds of the Oklahoma Panhandle" is a valuable annotated list of 124 species, nine of them recorded for the first time for the state. My article on *Nesting Records from 1920 to 1922 at Norman, Oklahoma* lists 612 nests of 37 species found by us, with brief notes on dates, size of sets, and so on.

In hopes of seeing a good warbler migration, on May 4 I took a sleeper to Muskogee and from there another train carried me to Tahlequah in northeastern Oklahoma. How I grieved that the University had been established on the prairie in Norman instead of in this idyllic spot, with its hills, its clear streams and oak woods on every side. The birds and plants were much like those of Kentucky and Tennessee.

Sunday, May 6, was a day long to be remembered. Fortified by a very early and delicious breakfast of T-bone steak, hot cakes, and coffee — all for 40 cents — I walked east until I reached the Illinois River and near noon climbed the high bluff above it to Sycamore Inn. Flowering dogwood, huckleberry, bird's-foot violet, wild geranium, wind anemones and bloodroot were all in bloom. I rejoiced in all these friends of my childhood, and in the birds — 66 species in one day — my best record for Oklahoma.

There were migrating Rose-breasted Grosbeaks, the first I had seen since Massachusetts. A singing Solitary Vireo[1] gave us a new bird for the state. Warblers were the chief glory of the day: 14 species, several of them being the first definite records for Oklahoma with date and locality, and one — the Tennessee[2] — the only

---

[1] *Vireo solitarius.* [2] *Vermivora peregrina.*

record. Nashville, Blackpoll[1], Black-throated Green[2], and Wilson's[3] – all these were important finds. Most exciting to me, an entirely new acquaintance, was a pair of Worm-eating Warblers[4]. I wondered whether they might be preparing to nest; 14 years later George Sutton discovered a breeding pair just to the north in Delaware County (1938).

Red-headed Woodpeckers were excavating homes; Blue Jays, Tufted Tits, Carolina Wrens, and Wood Thrushes were building. A Robin nest 18 inches from the ground in an oak grove held four callow chicks and – best prize of all – a Pine Warbler[5] was fitfully incubating her eggs 25 feet up in a scraggly yellow pine. At night I was happy to hear our friends – the Chuck-will's-widows.

In the Museum of the Northeastern Normal School I found something unique in Oklahoma – a collection fully labelled as to time and place of capture! Between 1906 and 1914, Professor C. W. Prier had collected and mounted 76 birds, several of which proved to be of importance: a Mourning Warbler[6] taken September 13, 1912, the second record for the state; a Pigeon Hawk[7], September 22, 1912, the only specimen recorded for the state; two Woodcocks[8], November 6, 1913, the only known specimens at that time; and a female Swallow-tailed Kite[9], June 18, 1910, the only specimen of this splendid and once numerous species preserved in an Oklahoma Museum; it was also our last record of its occurrence in the state.

A change of political administration had thrown our friend Mr. Shannon out of the directorship of the Oklahoma Geological Survey. We turned to the University and the authorities agreed to publish our report as a University Study. We bought camping equipment – cots and a manageable tent – and on June 24, the whole family started out once more.

In the Arbuckles we camped by the Devils' Punch Bowl on Price's Creek; here we swam and the children tried to catch the vocal little cricket frogs. Birds we had not found three years earlier were a pair of Acadian Flycatchers, a pair of Chipping Sparrows and many Kentucky Warblers. Our most exciting discovery was a family of Black Vultures[10], well down in a crevice in the rocks; two half-grown, buffy, downy young were watched over by a parent.

We travelled east to McCurtain County in the southeastern

---

[1] *Dendroica striata.* [2] *Dendroica virens.* [3] *Wilsonia pusilla.* [4] *Helmitheros vermivorus.* [5] *Dendroica pinus.* [6] *Oporornis philadelphia.* [7] Merlin, *Falco columbarius.* [8] *Philohela minor.* [9] *Elanoides forficatus.* [10] *Coragyps atratus.*

corner of the state and camped under primeval yellow pines and white oaks by rushing Mountain Fork. Here there was much the same wealth of bird life as we had met three years earlier in Pushmataha County — Scarlet[1] and Summer Tanagers and Cardinals; Red-eyed, White-eyed, and Yellow-throated Vireos[2]; Wood Thrushes; and many, many other lovely species. Warblers were abundant — Pine, Parula[3], Cerulean[4], and Kentucky, as well as Redstarts[5] and Yellow-breasted Chats. And here for the first time I met the beautiful Hooded Warbler and, indeed, he looked very different from those Maryland Yellow-throats I had mistaken for him in my childhood. The ringing *teacher-teacher-teacher* of an Ovenbird[6] and the sight of two well-grown chicks gave us another nesting warbler for the state. A dozen American Egrets[7] on the river were a thrilling sight; little did we imagine that one day we would find them nesting lower, near Mountain Fork.

Turning westward, we drove to the southwestern corner of Oklahoma, camping one night in tiny Platt National Park and three nights at different spots along the Red River. Wild and desolate country of sand dunes and sage brush, of mesquite, cactus and yucca. Prairie dogs were seen here and there and a few Burrowing Owls. Other notable birds were a Prairie Falcon[8], a Mississippi Kit, a Roadrunner[9], a number of Bullock Orioles[10], and, in Jackson and Harmon Counties, our beloved Cassin's Sparrows.

On this trip the children gathered up five horned toads as our companions; they named them Pancake, Griddlecake, Flapjack, Puffball, and Cocklebur.

We had now visited all four corners of the state.

In August the rains started and for two months they descended. Overgrazing and plowing of the high plains at the headwaters and along the courses of the rivers — this abuse of the land was revenged.

The South Canadian became a raging flood and devoured the countryside. At the Dump the sand dunes crumbled away and fell into the torrent with great thuds. Saddest of all for us was the carrying away of our loved haunts to the west. Low Brook — the great pastures and alfalfa fields, expanses of sand where the children had so often played, and the mighty elms and cottonwoods by the bank where I had taken my walk so full of vision four years earlier. It was a grief to think that this wild and splendid landscape existed now only in our memories.

---

[1] *Piranga olivacea.*   [2] *Vireo flavifrons.*   [3] *Parula americana.*   [4] *Dendroica cerulea.*   [5] *Setophaga ruticilla.*   [6] *Seiurus aurocapillus.*
[7] Great Egret, *Casmerodius albus*   [8] *Falco mexicanus* [9] [3] *Geococcyx califorianus.*
[10] *Icterus galbula bullockii.*

We followed the fall migration as usual with trips to Snail Brook and the Dump. Here one day we met a hunter carrying three Franklin's Gulls[1]; when remonstrated with he explained he had thought they were ducks! "I have to shoot things to find out whether or not they are game birds," he said. After reproving this ignoramus I wrote a clear and concise letter to the *Daily Oklahoman* on "What is a Game Bird?"

Our new baby kindly timed her arrival after the fall migration and before the Christmas census. On December 23, leaving Janet with her sisters, Blaine and I spent an afternoon looking for birds, incidentally getting our only winter records for the county for Belted Kingfisher[2] and White-throated Sparrow[3].

April 24, 1924, marked the attainment of the goal for which we had been striving for nearly four years. *The Birds of Oklahoma* by Margaret Morse Nice and Leonard Blaine Nice appeared as a University of Oklahoma Bulletin; University Study, No. 286. It is a small, paper-bound publication of 124 pages, starting with a physiographic map which shows the 77 counties in the state and ending with four of our photographs of scenes from the southeastern, southwestern, and northwestern corners of Oklahoma.

In the Introduction we had tried to fire the reader's imagination and to arouse enthusiasm for the protection of birds. An historical sketch gives vivid quotations from the early explorers – Long in 1820 (see James, 1823), Washington Irving in 1832 (see 1835), and Abert in 1845 (1846). Others also described the incredible wealth of wild life they found – the Passenger Pigeons, Carolina Parakeets[4], Ivory-billed Woodpeckers[5], Whooping Cranes[6], and Swallow-tailed Kites. Brief sections are concerned with physical features and faunal areas of the state, with the game laws, the economic value of birds, and the attraction and protection of birds. The main body of the bulletin is devoted to the 361 species and subspecies we accepted; here we gave what we knew about the occurrence of each form – its status and its range with records according to counties, with dates and authorities. Errata were minimal: four misspellings of names.

The University printed 2,500 copies and distributed them widely without cost, sending up to 100 copies to the Zoology Departments of the numerous colleges in the state. Mr. Kraettli, Secretary to the President of the University, told me there had

[1]*Larus pipixcan.*   [2]*Megaceryle alcyon.*   [3]*Zonotrichia albicollis.*
[4]*Conuropsis carolinensis.* [5]*Campephilus principalis principalis.*
[6]*Grus americana.*

been more demand for our bulletin than for any other they had published.

Witmer Stone, editor of the *Auk*, spoke of this "excellent state list . . . thoroughly up-to-date . . . carefully compiled." Joseph Grinnell in the May 24 *Condor*, said it "bears the stamp of good workmanship throughout."

We had letters from twenty-six appreciative ornithologists; three of these especially pleased us. Charles N. Gould, Director of the Oklahoma Geological Survey called our bulletin "something from which to date Oklahoma ornithology." Ed Crabb, then at the Public Museum in Milwaukee, wrote: "You certainly exhausted about every possible bit of source material that is to be had and condensed it into the minimum amount of space. I consider your book the first important step that has been taken in putting Oklahoma in the ornithological world." And finally a postcard from W. L. McAtee gave his approval to this piece of work: "It seems *sound* and well done."

Rain in the fall had brought destruction to some of our best bird haunts, but rain in the winter and spring formed "Shorebird Pond" in a low spot a half mile south of Norman where in other years we had found Wilson Snipe[1] and brightly coloured LeConte's Sparrows[2]. Hardly was our bulletin out before we began making exciting discoveries as to shorebirds. Day after day we saw species we had included on the basis of one or two reports — White-rumped[3] and Stilt Sandpipers[4] and Long-billed Dowitchers[5]. Semipalmated Sandpipers[6] of which we had found records of two specimens were amazingly abundant for two months. The Semi-palmated Plover[7], included on a sight record, became substantiated by a specimen. Two species were additions to the state list — the spectacular Hudsonian Godwit[8] and the handsome Dunlin[9].

It was clear we would have to write a second *Birds of Oklahoma*. Although we had worked faithfully to learn all we could about the birds of this great state, Shorebird Pond had shown us we had only made a beginning on this happy, wonderful enterprise.

---

[1]Common Snipe, *Capella gallinago*. [2]Le Conte's Sparrow, *Ammospiza leconteii*. [3]*Calidris fuscicollis*. [4]*Micropalama himantopus*. [5]*Limnodromus scolopaceus*. [6]*Calidris pusilla*. [7] *Charadrius semipalmatus*. [8] *Limosa haemastica*. [9]*Calidris alpina*.

Eleanor with her father, mother Margaret with baby Janet.
Summer, 1924

X

The Year in Massachusetts

Blaine was planning to spend his sabbatical leave in Europe, while the children and I were to stay in Amherst near my mother and my sister, Sarah. In late June of 1924 we packed ourselves into our car and started east. It was the initial camping trip for the baby and she throve on it. At our first camp — on Spavinaw Creek in Delaware County in Oklahoma — we were delighted to find among the roots of an overturned tree our first nest of a Louisiana Waterthrush[1]; it held three chicks.

After a happy summer at Grey Rocks in Pelham, Blaine established the children and me in a roomy flat not far from my mother, and Will's three children and Sarah and her three children in our old home at 28 Northampton Road. (Unfortunately Will's wife had died and the same was true of Sarah's husband.) Blaine left us for eight months. This was his first trip abroad and he greatly benefited from contacts with physiologists at Cambridge, at the Sorbonne and in Vienna, besides taking full advantage of concerts, operas, the theatre, museums, and churches in England and on the Continent.

What a boon to us prairie dwellers — the year in Amherst and Pelham proved to be — the fall, winter, spring, and summer in this fascinating countryside. In the perfect fall weather I drove our children and some of their cousins, as well as my mother, to the hill towns of Leverett and Shutesbury, to Roaring Hill, Mount Lincoln, and Rattlesnake Gutter. The colours of oaks and maples

[1] *Seiurus motacilla.*

were a splendour to us who saw but little of this in central Oklahoma. In winter we journeyed south, north, and east on trolley lines; we climbed Mounts Toby and Norwottuck and explored Grey Rocks when its hemlocks and white pines were heavy with snow. Very early on the morning of January 24, 1925, we travelled by train to Connecticut to see the total eclipse of the sun, a notable and unique experience. Although in Amherst there were few birds but Starlings[1], on our Christmas census in Pelham, Constance, her cousin Duncan Morse, and I found 15 species and 137 individuals.

All the children but the baby were enjoying the public schools of Amherst. The two older daughters did much of the cooking, dishes, and cleaning. As for Janet, she accompanied us on many trips, but in winter Constance, Marjorie, and I took turns staying at home with her, while the others with some of their cousins went on day-long expeditions. When I went on two longer trips, a practical nurse looked after the family.

To my disappointment, the A.O.U. met this fall in Pittsburgh rather than in the East, but I went to two other bird meetings.

In Boston, it was a treat to stay with my college roommate, Lucy Day, and her husband — both psychologists with Ph.D.'s from Cornell University. Gary Boring was a distinguished professor at Harvard University. They had two small sons and a daughter. At the meeting of the Federation of New England Bird Societies, Winthrop Packard, Secretary of the Massachusetts Audubon Society, urged the abolition of the shooting of Bobolinks[2] in the South; and Alfred Gross of Bowdoin College, Brunswick, Maine, spoke on the almost extinct Heath Hen[3] on the island of Martha's Vineyard.

In New York City, I visited my friend of Clark University days, Edith Wallace, assistant to the noted geneticist, Professor T. H. Morgan of Columbia University. I went to museums and attended the annual meeting of the National Association of Audubon Societies*. Here Dr. Arthur A. Allen told us of his great joy in finding a pair of Ivory-billed Woodpeckers in Florida in March 1924 and showed us his pictures of them. Shortly thereafter they were killed by a taxidermist. Dr. Jonathan Dwight told me how years ago William Dutcher, organizer and first President of the National Association of Audubon Societies, secured the conviction

[1]*Sturnus vulgaris.* [2]*Dolichonyx oryzivorus.* [3]*Tympanuchus cupido cupido.*

*The 42nd Stated Meeting of the National Association of Audubon Societies, New York City, November 9-12, 1925.

of a Florida taxidermist of a similar illegal act with the result that the judge fined the miscreant *six cents* for each!

At this meeting Mr. Forbush nominated me as the Oklahoma representative on the Advisory Board of the Association and the motion was passed. I was pleased, but when the next *Bird-Lore* appeared, Dr. A. K. Fisher was still listed as the advisor for Oklahoma.

For research this winter I returned to speech development. Strange as it seems, child psychology continued to be a major interest with me for years after I had found out that the study of birds was my true vocation. It was the challenge of the problem — how did the child acquire his language? The more I observed and recorded and the more I worked over my results, the more questions presented themselves. My small subjects were always with me and each showed a different picture. Doggedly I went ahead, despite the fact that my articles brought me almost no response.

Almost two years earlier I had finished the manuscript of a book on "The Speech Development of Children." It was typed by a college girl and sent to Dr. Hall for the Introduction he had promised to write for it. It represented an appalling amount of labour — years and years of collecting the four children's vocabularies, classifying them at each age by parts of speech and by interests, analysing and computing proportions and averages, pondering over relationships. Moreover, it involved a great deal of reading of the pertinent literature in English, French, and German, and this had largely to be done on trips to Alva, Chicago, and Massachusetts. The first seven chapters of my book are devoted to detailed studies of my children whose vocabularies had been recorded until they were six, four, four, and three years of age. Thirteen chapters are concerned with the subject in general; there are 60 tables, a bibliography of 262 titles, four appendices, and a full index.

Dr. Hall had kindly forwarded the manuscript to one publisher after another, but it always came back. As I look at the book after a lapse of forty years, I believe it would have been a useful reference work for college courses containing, as it does, much first hand information and a wide survey of the pertinent literature. Publishers, however, do not necessarily judge a book on its merits, and my lack of a Ph.D. and of professional status was far more of a handicap in this field than it was in ornithology. Dr. Hall was failing in health, and despite my pleadings, never wrote the hoped-for Introduction. With his death in 1924 I lost a friend, the man who had stimulated me to start these researches and who had constantly encouraged me with his interest and appreciation.

Surrounded as I now was with good libraries — in Amherst, Mount Holyoke and Smith Colleges — as well as in Worcester, I fell busily to work reading multitudes of books and articles with the view of enlarging and improving my book. At a conference at Clark University on Genetic Psychology in memory of Dr. Hall I consulted with Dr. Arnold Gesell, the well-known author of books on child development. He encouraged me to continue my studies although he had few suggestions as to publishing possibilities. I finished two articles — *A Child Who Would Not Talk* (1925) and *Length of Sentences as a Criterion of a Child's Progress in Speech* (1926).

I realized that I could not do exhaustive work in such different fields. In view of the uncertainties of publication I did nothing more with my book except some years later to give a copy of the manuscript to Madeline Horn, a friend working on speech development at the University of Iowa. Marjorie's and Eleanor's vocabularies were published in the Proceedings of the Oklahoma Academy of Sciences (1927).

In response to a request from the editor of *American Speech* I wrote a paper on *The Size of Vocabularies* for that journal (1926 c). Over a hundred years ago two clergymen asserted that the labourer had less than 300 words in his vocabulary. This was quoted by many learned men. In reality, 19 children of three years of age averaged vocabularies of 910 words, three of six years averaged 3,000 words. "Refutation," I concluded, "never overtakes a well-launched error. Let us be very, very careful about publishing unverified statements." Twenty-five years later I was to trace down errors concerning incubation periods of birds that had been repeated for 20 centuries.

With all the problems fresh in my mind, I kept voluminous notes on Janet's speech development, but eventually wrote what was largely a summary of one aspect — her attainment of the sentence. I sent this to my professor of psychology at Mount Holyoke College, Dr. Helen Thompson Wooley, an assistant editor of the *Pedagogical Seminary and Journal of Genetic Psychology*. She recommended my paper to Dr. Carl Murchison, editor-in-chief of the journal "with great cordiality. It is distinctly good work of a kind very rare in the world, and very much needed." This was the last of my 15 papers on child psychology (1933 b).

Although my studies are mentioned in books on child psychology, I often wish I had never been led astray into this blind alley.

Nevertheless, the speech development studies were valuable training in evaluation of the literature in English, German, and French and, what was more important, in close observation, clear thinking, powers of organization, and initiative.

To return to birds, our old haunts around Amherst seemed much the same as they had been 20 years earlier, but changes had taken place in the bird life (1925). Least Flycatchers, Bobolinks, and House Sparrows had decreased in numbers; House Wrens had increased. The Starling was a newcomer, having first appeared in 1910. To my delight Song Sparrows had moved into town, as well as Yellowthroats, and best of all, Wood Thrushes. On the two acres of 28 Northampton Road four species had nested regularly during my childhood: Least Flycatcher, Chipping Sparrow, House Sparrow, and Robin. In 1925 the first had disappeared but, in addition to the last three, there were in 1925 a pair each of Phoebes[1], Song Sparrows, Yellowthroats and Catbirds.

Inspired by some articles in the *Atlantic Monthly* by William Beebe, I decided to try to become a more all-round naturalist. The study of ferns seemed to be a good choice. These plants have a fascination with their ancient lineage and the wide distribution of many species over the world. In the fall of 1924 and the following summer we identified and mounted 21 species from Grey Rocks, three from east of Grey Rocks, yet still in Hampshire County, and six to the north from Mount Toby in Franklin County.

At Grey Rocks there was solitude. Down Butter Hill our brook tumbled over rocks under yellow and grey birches, hickories, maples, oaks and elders, past arbutus, ferns, hepaticas and violets. To the west stood the Sabine Woods, their white pines and hemlocks towering over ground pine, partridge berry and pink lady slippers. On the hilltop near the house, pitch pines, red cedars, junipers, and white oaks predominated. On May 30 we found a Red-shouldered Hawk's[2] nest in the valley; Constance borrowed climbing irons and ascended the tree to view the three downy young, which fledged four weeks later. On July 19 we discovered a Broad-winged Hawk's[3] nest and banded the one well-grown youngster.

We became so fascinated with birds that I thought of writing a paper on "Summer Birds of Pelham, Massachusetts" and this project gave an added incentive to explorations. It was exciting to hear White-throated Sparrows singing on Pine Hill at 1220 feet elevation and to have them scold when we approached. On a

[1]Eastern Phoebe, *Sayornis phoebe.* [2]*Buteo lineatus.* [3]*Buteo platypterus.*

swimming trip to Swift River Valley we saw pitcher plants, a Pileated Woodpecker, and an Alder Flycatcher[1].

All my discoveries I promptly reported to my friend Edward H. Forbush, State Ornithologist. He was particularly curious as to the presence of Magnolia Warblers on Grey Rocks, for typically they nest in spruce. It was a special triumph when I discovered the little lady building in a juniper and when the eggs hatched, I resolved to make my first nest study (1926).

For 26 hours in 17 sessions on 9 days, I watched the little family at distances from five to fifteen feet. Mother fed the three chicks 91 times; Father fed them 118 times and sang 1,178 songs. I will quote from my chapter on "The Nest in the Juniper" in *The Watcher at the Nest* (1939).

It had been a never-to-be-forgotten experience — these hours watching the exquisite little birds and listening to many bird songs, the loveliest of which was that of the Hermit Thrush. The Magnolia Warblers gave me my initiation into bird watching, and, although later I was to spend far more time at Warbler nests, yet none of them held quite the same enchantment for me as this little family nesting in the juniper.

---

[1] *Empidonax alnorum.*

XI

I Wonder
as I Wander
Out Under the Sky

We were happy to return in early September to our own small house in Norman and to our Oklahoma birds. On the campus we discovered the largest number of occupied Mourning Dove nests in all our seven years of fall observations: forty-four in contrast to the eight to twenty-eight in other years (1926 d). Thirty-two of thirty-nine nests succeeded in fledging young — 88 per cent!

During the next 21 months I spent my best energies on bird study. I will quote from my journal:

Oct. 16, '25. To many people a clump of weeds is undoubtedly an abomination. To me, on the contrary, they are the most eagerly sought features of a central Oklahoma landscape. They are places of mystery, full of little voices that tantalize me. Today there are a great many Sparrows — Lincoln's and White-crowns, and a few Chippings.

Oct. 28. We go to Snail Brook and see two beautiful Harris' Sparrows. It seems as if the crown of the Fall migration has been reached when these distinguished birds make their appearance; they are our most abundant winter bird and also our sweetest songsters. They give the finishing touch to the delights of the winter bird life. "The Great Weed Patch" (our new name for the "Dump") seemed like itself once more when the metallic chirps of the Song Sparrows were to be heard on every hand.

Several of these lovely birds sang their fine songs. The full moon rising in the east and the sunset flame in the west transformed this prosaic spot into a place of rare and strange beauty.

Nov. 8. A Cooper's Hawk[1] swooped at a company of little birds but failed

---

[1] *Accipiter cooperii.*

to capture any. What a sudden silence in the place, but now full of life! Soon we hear again the sweet strains of the Harris' Sparrows. So far not a single one has had a black hood indicating maturity.

Nov. 11. Mr. Albert J. Kirn spends the day with us. He shows us a Roadrunner's nest — 8 feet from the ground; a large, flat structure with some bits of egg shells in it. He also pointed out to us some hawk nests and, excitingly enough, two platforms that must have been Black-crowned[1] or Yellow-crowned Night Heron's[2] nests!

Dec. 23. The feature of our sixth Christmas census in Cleveland County was the presence of four new birds: two Roadrunners, a Goshawk[3], a *Pileated Woodpecker*, and a Hermit Thrush, as well as a Barred Owl and Rusty Blackbirds[4], great numbers of Tree Sparrows and Robins, abundance of Red-tailed Hawks (nine of them) and of Blue Jays. Cardinals and most Blackbirds were present in small numbers; White-throats, White-crowns and Bluebirds were absent (1926 a).

From 1920 through 1922 I had taken 128 censuses of the first half mile of Snail Brook and had obtained consistent results year by year as to numbers of species and individuals throughout the seasons. It now occurred to me that it would be of interest to check these findings by monthly all-day censuses over varying kinds of habitats: two miles of Snail Brook, then woods, prairie and the river. Kind Blaine met me at the bridge late in the afternoon and drove me home.

On March 22, 1926, I wrote:

Two days ago I took my all-day walk. It is an inspiring experience to have "a day for wandering" — to be free and alone with nature for a whole long day; to feel unhurried, to be able to search carefully for birds, to be unmolested by considerations for other people. All day I wandered alone letting the marvelous beauty of this early spring day sink into my being. I welcomed some of the gentle little wild things as they tarried on their stupendous journey from south to north. I view them with love and admiration. When out in the wilds I efface my own big alien self as much as I can; I am all ears and eyes for sound and movement.

This is one of the loveliest times of the whole year: the cultivated fruit trees gloriously pink or white, the wild plums all in bloom and redbud also. The Carolina anemone is one of the most beautiful flowers I have ever seen — holding its deep blue chalice to the sun. The large purple woods violets are in bloom. Parts of the prairie are an enchanting blue with masses of tiny bluets.

This spring I had high ambitions of making nesting studies, but all the nests came to untimely ends, those of Tufted Tits, Blue

---

[1]*Nycticorax nycticorax.* [2]*Nyctanassa violacea.* [3]*Accipiter gentilis.* [4]*Euphagus carolinus.*

Grosbeaks, Wood Pewee, and Blue-gray Gnatcatcher. Our hand-raised Mourning Doves, Lionel and Artemise, failed to incubate any of the 15 eggs in the nine sets laid in 69 days due to Lionel's removal of all nesting material and his persecution of his unfortunate mate whenever she tried to incubate. The pair of Bell's Vireos on the campus lost three nests to a cat, whereupon they left their territory.

A flying trip to the Arbuckles May 15 to 16 was a joy. The flowers were nearly all different from those we had seen in June 1920 and 1923. It was exciting to identify the ferns, among them the choice Venus-hair, and on a limestone cliff the exquisite little powdery cloak fern (*Notholaena dealbata*). Two White-eyed Vireos were new inhabitants in our experience. The greatest discovery was a Rock Sparrow's nest with four eggs that Constance found between two rocks on the slope opposite Turner's Falls; this was the first nest of this species to be recorded in Oklahoma.

At a Wild Life Conference in June at the Wichitas, we identified 11 species of ferns including hairy and woolly lip ferns as well as two other species of *Cheilanthes*. The curious adder's tongue (*Ophioglossum Englemanni*) was found by Constance on top of Eagle Mountain. We sent samples of all our finds for identification to the President of the American Fern Society, Dr. William A. Maxon of the Smithsonian Institution in Washington. We came to the conclusion that many ferns in western Oklahoma are subjects for specialists, so difficult is their identification.

On August 21, we headed for the Oklahoma Panhandle. From our first camp 16 miles west of Alva we hastened away from great menacing clouds at 4:00 in the morning, driving through darkness past rocks and trees that dimly gave a picturesque impression. At last we reached the valley of the Cimarron where we were rejoiced by a most welcome sunrise. In the still uncertain light we noticed that the tops of the telegraph poles had a strange appearance; each of eight was crowned by a Sparrow Hawk[1]! Since there were no trees about, the poles were the only available perches for watching for grasshoppers.

It was a great pleasure to make the personal acquaintance of Mr. and Mrs. Walter E. Lewis and their fine family. They took us to their best bird haunts, but due to the exceptionally dry weather they could show us no gulls or shorebirds.

We crossed the Hundredth Meridian into the Great American Desert and there we found a ranch surrounded by trees enlivened

---

[1] American Kestrel, *Falco sparverius*.

by peacocks, goats, and Mallard Ducks, besides the usual farm animals. The owner, Dr. Archibald Dugans, told us how originally this region had been fine cattle country but it had been ruined by people trying to farm it; when the prairie was plowed, erosion followed, consequently the streams are being choked and the country is becoming dryer and dryer. Thirty-five years earlier Upland Plover[1] covered the prairie; near Ponca City they nested by thousands. Chapparals (Roadrunners), however, were formerly rare, but now were fairly common.

"Do they do harm?" I asked.

"Only to grasshoppers," said Dr. Dugans.

During the long trip from one end to the other of the Oklahoma Panhandle, Horned Larks and Lark Buntings were the commonest birds. Two hundred and fourteen of the former were counted during the 200 mile drive; during the heat of the day we learned to watch for them in the shade of the fence posts. Lark Buntings became numerous west of Guymon; they were all in flocks and only one of the 200 seen was in the black and white plumage of the summer male, all the others being brown with white wing bands.

Constance and I proudly exhibited to the rest of the family the wild and rugged country around Kenton with its Scaled Quail[2], its noisy Piñon and Woodhouse's Jays, its Canyon Towhees and other birds of the Rocky Mountains. To our great joy we heard Canyon Wrens[3] singing in two different valleys.

We were happy to find Mr. Tate much improved in health and able to accompany us in the car. He found us a shaded camping spot on the Texakite where the children revelled in swimming. He showed us petrified trees and pointed out the Robbers' Roost where bandits had built a fort and from which they were finally routed by a cannon. One day we drove north of the Black Mesa to the spot where three states join; in hills south of here Mountain Bluebirds nested. On August 17 we all drove across ranches (from which all the prairie dogs had been exterminated by poison) to the fruit ranch of the Dalharts. Here we found seven pairs of Mourning Doves still nesting and saw to the north the canyon where Magpies nest. Fern Canyon was one of the most alluring places of all; as we climbed, it grew narrower and narrower, the great rocks standing opposite each other with only the brook bed between them. Here we came upon the rare and beautiful male fern, while a Great Horned Owl with a rabbit in its claws gave the last touch of

---

[1]Upland Sandpiper, *Bartramia americana.* [2] *Callipepla squamata.* [3] *Catherpes mexicanus.*

wildness to the scene.

We found ten species of ferns in Cimarron County, specimens of all of which were identified by Dr. Maxon. Four were new records for us. There was Standly's star fern (*Notholaena Standleyi*) whose fronds during droughts contract into white balls but after a rain expand into triangular shape. Fee's lip-fern (*Cheilanthes Feei*) made our sixth *Cheilanthese* in Oklahoma. One tiny plant, curly grass (*Asplenium septentrionalis*), found by Constance, did not look like a fern at all, whereas the male fern (*Dryopteris filix-mas*) was the handsomest, most conspicuous inhabitant of Fern Canyon.

I planned to write a little article for the *American Fern Journal*, telling of our exciting finds among the rocks of central and western Oklahoma. I changed my mind, however, when I heard that Frank C. Greene, a Tulsa oil man, was also a fern enthusiast and was planning a paper on the ferns of the whole state. So I sent him the names and localities of the 23 species we had found in Oklahoma. In 1927 he published his paper (see Greene, 1927) which listed 33 species on 11 of which he quoted Constance and myself. Two of these — curly grass and male fern — were the only records noted for the state, although Mr. Greene had found curly grass just over the Oklahoma line in Baca County, Colorado.

Eleven days in New Mexico were full of new and happy experiences: camping among the spruces on the Sangre de Cristo Mountains and among junipers above Taos; enjoying the quaint charm of Santa Fe and its delightful celebration El Paso-tiempo, visiting ruins of cliff dwellers, and a number of pueblos in one of which, San Ildefonso, we happened upon a spectacular harvest dance.

New Mexico was a joy because of its loneliness — its great unpeopled stretches — and also because of its beauty, beauty of nature and, strange thing to find in the United States, beauty of architecture. The simple adobe houses of the Indians and Mexicans blend with the landscape, while the buildings in Santa Fe were an inspiration.

At home once more, we found 28 occupied Mourning Dove nests; one of these was still active on October 3.

The first *Birds of Oklahoma* was arousing more and more interest. Tulsa became a focus of activity, the leader being Miss Edith Force, dynamic teacher of Science at the Woodrow Wilson Junior High School. She organized the efforts of W. H. Koons, the E. A. Gilmores and George W. Morse. This last gentleman was an ardent egg collector. He used to write to me as "Dear Sister

Oologist" until at length becoming convinced that I had no flair in that direction, he switched to "Dear Sister Naturalist." He regularly signed himself "Oologically yours."

It was a rich experience to meet and talk with Charlotte Perkins Stetson Gilman who came to the University at the invitation of President William Bizzell. She gave an impressive lecture on "The Fundamental Falsity of Freud," saying that he had "blackened the face of America." "Sex is not the life force," she said. "It is only part of life. It is not essential to individual life but to the race. Its purpose is the improvement of the species — to help it to vary."

Mrs. Gilman was a remarkable woman, brilliant and original, a clear and logical thinker in many fields. Her first book *Woman and Economics*, published in 1898 was translated into many foreign languages, including Hungarian and Japanese. She wrote at least 15 other books, as well as writing and publishing her unique little magazine *The Forerunner* from 1909 to 1916. Yet, sadly enough, it seems as if she had been a voice crying in the wilderness, for now she appears to be forgotten.

At home we had the treat of hearing a migrating Olive-backed Thrush (now Swainson's Thrush[1]) singing each morning from May 11 to 22. Janet, her pet bunny, and I went on many bird trips in the car. Once I pointed out a Horned Lark by the roadside, then showed her its picture in Reed's *Guide*. "Dis one bunt people?" she inquired.

My most interesting ornithological experience this spring came from watching a family of Yellow-crowned Night Herons in the Olivers' woods (1929), a primeval grove just west of the Great Weed Patch. Its ancient trees and wild life were jealously guarded by its owner, Fred Oliver, who later deeded it to the University as a sanctuary.

I had taken my all-day censuses throughout 1926 and during the first five months of 1927; they corresponded well with the findings on the earlier censuses which were confined to Snail Brook. These experiences had provided me with an over-all picture of the bird population throughout the year. From my day-long wanderings through the woods and prairies, along the brook and the river, I had gained a deep sense of belonging, of kinship with the wild life of this region.

---

[1] *Catharus ustulata.*

XII

We Find
Interpont

After a happy summer at Grey Rocks, where I watched both a Myrtle Warbler's and an Ovenbird's nest, we started west again in the fall of 1927. In Columbus, Ohio we made a decision that changed our lives and that also proved to be significant for ornithology. Blaine accepted a Professorship in the Ohio State University Medical School.

It was a blow to all of us to leave our beloved Oklahoma, our birds and our prairie flowers. Most of all it was a blow to me. It seemed as if I were being wrenched up by the roots. My walks and my birds around Norman had grown to be such a part of me that I did not see how I could be happy or function properly without them, that rather I might become a maimed and stunted creature. I was suddenly snatched from my rich field of activities where every walk offered possibilities of discovery, of additions to our knowledge of Oklahoma birds.

We were most fortunate, however, in finding a house on a bluff above the flood plain of the Olentangy River. Here were another "Great Weed Patch" and a new "Snail Brook" for me, with a larger stream, bordered by primeval trees: cottonwoods, sycamores, elms, silver maples, hackberries, box elders. The masses of giant ragweeds, towering above our heads, were brightened with sunflowers, purple asters and goldenrod. Our home at 156 West Patterson Avenue stood a quarter of a mile east of the Olentangy, a half-mile south of the bridge at Dodridge Street and a half mile north of the bridge at Lane Avenue. I called this wild, neglected piece of flood plain "Interpont", that is, "Between the Bridges."

The richness of the bird life at our doorstep charmed us — the abundance of migrating warblers, sparrows, and many, many others. On November 11 I wrote:

When we chose to settle next to this great weed patch it was largely for the sake of the birds we expected as neighbors. But the weed patch has outdone our hopes. It was no part of the contract that we should be treated to the rich songs of the Fox Sparrows this fall! The ethereal strains of the White-throats rejoiced us for weeks, while the fine singing of the Song Sparrows still delights us.

One advantage of Ohio over Oklahoma was its proximity to bird meetings. The A.O.U. this year in Washington* was notable for renewing old friendships, for making new ones, for good papers, and a fine excursion on the Potomac River, as well as for discoveries of Oklahoma specimens and records in the National Museum. The Secretary and Treasurer were the same as seven and five years previously, but the President was Alexander Wetmore, Assistant Secretary of the Smithsonian Institution. Florence Merriam Bailey greeted me as "Mrs. Mourning Dove Nice". She and her husband, Vernon Bailey, invited me to their home for dinner, where I heard about their pet bats. My paper at the meeting was on the nesting of the Yellow-crowned Night Herons I had watched that spring in the Olivers' woods (1929 a).

The joint meeting of the Wilson Club and Inland Bird-Banding Association at Cleveland, Ohio** was eminently satisfactory in the way of human contacts; there was a warm feeling of friendliness and royal entertainment at the hands of the Cleveland people. It was a pleasure to renew my friendship with the Coffins, to get to talk with George Sutton, then the Game Department at Harrisburg, Pennsylvania; to come to know the Lynds Jones of Oberlin College. Most of the papers were good while the pictures of shorebirds by Arthur Fuller of the Cleveland Museum were thrilling to me. I reported on the happenings at my Myrtle Warbler's nest (1930 a). An excursion to Prentiss S. Baldwin's Laboratory at Gates Mills was full of interest, as was his important paper on "Temperature Control in Nestling Birds." At a reception at the home of Herbert Brandt, a wealthy oologist, I saw for the first and only time William Leon Dawson, author of the sumptious volumes

---

*The 45th Stated Meeting of the American Ornithologists' Union, Washington, D.C., November 17-19, 1927.

**The 14th Stated Meeting of the Wilson Ornithological Club, Cleveland, Ohio, November 25-27, 1927.

on *The Birds of California* (1923). Poor man, he had just been robbed by two youths of his car, his watch, his green ring, his purse, and his lucky green fountain pen.

In Columbus the hearty welcome accorded us by the Audubon Society warmed our hearts. Charles Walker, assistant at the Ohio State Museum, invited us to lead a hike and to visit the museum; Mr. James C. Hableton, President of the Society, requested a speech from me. I talked on "The Home Life of Wild Birds," describing happenings at a variety of nests I had studied. It was indeed a pleasure to find a group of bird lovers, after being such solitary lights as we had been in Oklahoma.

A great sorrow came to us that winter in the loss of our daughter, Eleanor, a beautiful, courageous child of nine years. In her memory we gave a set of 50 children's books to the State University Hospital in Columbus, and 100 children's books to the Public Library in Norman. It was some solace in our grief to have done this thing which would bring joy and inspiration to many children, both in her home and in Columbus.

The richness of our bird life — the far from "Silent Spring" on Interpont in 1928 — is reflected in my journal for March 15:

The chorus of song is bewildering in its beauty and its sense of joy: the wistful sweetness of the Mourning Dove, the minor strain of the Eastern Meadowlark, the loveliness of the Song Sparrow; the courage and charm of the Cardinal and Robin. What a blessing it is to be alive this bright morning of early spring — to be able to go out by the Olentangy with my precious four-year-old.

On March 26 I had banded a very important individual — my first Song Sparrow — later called Uno. He owned the territory next to our house and on May 22 I found his nest with three eggs, two of which hatched on May 28 and 29. For five days I spent a total of 18 hours watching the family. Uno's mate was evidently an experienced bird for she fed more than he did during four hours on the 29th, but after that he outdid her record. They were easy to distinguish — he by his bands, she by a large dark crescent-shaped area on her breast, evidently the scar of some old injury. The two babies were carried off by some enemy the night of June 2. And so ended my observations on Song Sparrows in the spring of 1928 except for my becoming acquainted with Uno's spirited neighbour, later dubbed 4M, and my recording in words and symbols of four of his distinctive songs.

The bird trips of the Columbus Audubon Society acquainted us with promising areas in the vicinity. On an excursion to Black Lick

MARGARET MORSE NICE AND DAUGHTER ELEANOR
Truby Studio, Norman, Oklahoma, 1921

Woods, we discovered a pair of Blue-gray Gnatcatchers constructing a nest. My observations of this charming little bird in Oklahoma had been so fragmentary that I welcomed the opportunity of watching this nest, despite the fact that it was 17 miles from our home, seven of which miles were through the city. I drove out there six times, watching the birds for an hour during building, two hours during incubation, and from three to six hours on three days while they cared for their young (1932). Such unbounded energy, such tireless zeal in these little birds — what a rich experience were these hours in Black Lick Woods!

At Grey Rocks that summer it was a treat to watch a pair of Black-throated Blue Warblers with four chicks about three days old. There was never any doubt as to which parent was present; for the blue-gray back and black throat of the male are very different from the brownish plumage of his mate. For a week I watched the nest from three to nine and a half hours a day, seeing the male bring 201 meals and his mate 193. I recorded 1,285 songs from him; these were of four different types. It was a triumph on my last day of watching to witness the exit from the nest of one of the baby birds (1930).

The discovery of an Ovenbird's nest gave me a renewal of last summer's happy experience. It contrast to many song birds that bring small meals at short intervals, Ovenbirds bring large meals at long intervals. Consequently watching an Ovenbird's nest is a restful occupation, giving one a chance to enter into the life of the forest, to contemplate and to dream. Alas, some enemy killed both the mother and the five-day-old chicks. Of the seven nests of five species of warblers that I watched at Grey Rocks, this was the only one that suffered disaster.

Back on Interpont, the fall and winter were busy with writing up researches on birds in Oklahoma and Massachusetts. The Wilson Club met the end of November at the University of Michigan at Ann Arbor*; I noted:

Friends are the best part of a bird meeting. The Museum was an inspiration. It was pleasant to get acquainted with Dr. Josselyn Van Tyne, Curator of Birds at the University Museum. Mrs. Rose Taylor's sketch of Elliott Coues greatly interested me. My own talk was on "The Fortunes of a Pair of Bell's Vireos'." (1929)

As winter progressed, I worked steadily on the second edition of *Birds of Oklahoma*, but gradually Song Sparrows crept into the

---

*The 15th Stated Meeting of the Wilson Ornithological Club, University of Michigan, Ann Arbor, November 30-December 1, 1928.

picture. On February 19, 1929, a Song Sparrow was caught in the pull-string trap north of the house; we decorated him with a home-made green celluloid band as well as with the numbered aluminum band from the U.S. Biological Survey. Later we discovered him singing on his territory which included a pool in the southwest corner of our land. I called him 5M. On the 20th 4M was singing splendidly, and I recorded my versions of six different songs from him.

On March 7, I noted: "Thanks to the bleak, fierce wind, the Song Sparrows are silent and I can concentrate on *Birds of Oklahoma* this morning. (Since I've conditioned myself to Song Sparrows, I find them very distracting.)"

On March 9 I captured *Uno* — my first and only Song Sparrow banded in 1928 — 100 per cent return for this species! We gave him a pink celluloid band and later in the morning I went out to look for him.

To quote from my journal:

4M appears to be monopolizing entirely too large a territory — his own and Uno's. Uno is skulking about in his old favourite place — the southeast corner. I go to look for 5M and find him in the maple next to the ditch. When I return 4M is singing in a burdock where poor Uno had been 5 minutes before! 4M is spreading himself over two territories and seems to take special delight today in singing on Uno's last year's land. I don't know what Uno will do. He always was a mild-mannered Song Sparrow.

Early the next morning I found out. I quote from my notebook:

Uno and 4M are in Uno's southeast corner, down on the ground and in the weeds. Uno sings quite steadily from these low positions — rapidly and not loudly. They pay no attention to me, although I am very near. Both are very much puffed out, and even fly in this odd shape. 4M says nothing, but follows Uno, going for him or after him every minute or so, but not fiercely; Uno merely flies a few feet. This keeps up for perhaps 10 minutes. Then 4M grows more belligerent, chases Uno around and about, and at last they come to blows, falling to the ground and battling furiously. They separate and Uno sings in his Norway maple, while 4M goes to his own box elder. Each sings and sings and sings.

So Uno's battle was won and the territories apportioned.

Witnessing this territory establishment sealed my fate for the next 14 years. I was so fascinated by this glimpse behind the scenes with my Song Sparrows that I then and there determined to watch Uno for several hours every day, to find out the meaning of his notes and postures, in short, to discover exactly what he did and how he did it.

Despite the fact that the Song Sparrow is one of our most abundant, familiar and well-nigh universally distributed North American birds, at that time almost complete ignorance prevailed as to its life history. The books said that this species has two notes besides its song, and that incubation lasts ten to fourteen days and is performed by both sexes. I discovered that these birds had more than twenty-one utterances besides the many songs possessed by each male, and that incubation lasts twelve to thirteen days and is the function of the female alone.

At that time we believed that our nesting Song Sparrows in Ohio all wintered to the south and our winter Song Sparrows wintered to the north, whereas it developed that this was true of only a part of our birds in Interpont; for some of these proved to be permanent residents. I talked over my problems with Mr. James S. Hine, all-around naturalist and father of the Wheaton Club, and with his assistant, Charles Walker at the State Museum; they knew nothing of the status of individual Song Sparrows in this region. Indeed, they tried to discourage me from studying such a common bird, saying that the Blue-gray Gnatcatcher would be more rewarding. Dr. Grinnell, however, wrote me: "I note that you are studying Song Sparrows. Almost anything you find out will be new to our literature!"

Pursuing my plan of daily watching Uno and 4M, I wondered what form courtship would take, what special displays and songs would occur. The males sang splendidly hour after hour and chased the migrating Song Sparrows and other visitors from their territories. Suddenly Uno and 4M stopped singing. Instead of 260 songs an hour they might give three! I was greatly puzzled; it seemed that Uno *must* sing as he alighted on one favourite singing perch after another.

On March 15 I noted:

Uno, 4M and another Song Sparrow are on the border of Uno's land. 4M is puffed out and hunched up. He is furthest west, then Uno (very little puffed), then the new bird. Uno keeps between 4M and the unbanded bird. 4M finally leaves. Uno approaches Stranger; it flips its wings, then opens its bill and says *eee eee eee*. Uno retires; it flies into a small tree, Uno dashes for it and attacks it.

Uno has a short, fierce battle with a stranger. Afterwards his crest is raised and his bill open. Stranger doesn't leave.

Three days later I wrote:

Uno hops on the lawn. He goes up the road a ways, is chased by another Song Sparrow. He tries to return to his land, but is driven off by a cross scold from Stranger who is perched on the corner burdock. (Think this must have been a migrating male of considerable courage.) If Uno and 4M were not color-banded, I should be perfectly distracted by the multiplicity of birds that all look practically alike.

The next day the truth began to dawn on me. I noted: "Stranger starts working up the bank as if searching for a nesting site; at one hollow 'she' twitches her wings. *So Stranger must be Uno's mate!*"

But still I had seen no courtship. Uno continued to fly at his mate, hit her, then fly off with a loud song! This pouncing, as I called it, proved to be an integral part of Song Sparrow courtship. The male may also pounce upon his neighbour's mate, whereupon neighbour male rushes to the rescue and a fight ensues. Pouncing has no connection with copulation which appears later in the cycle.

The "engagement" period with Song Sparrows is characterized by the almost total suppression of song in the male, by his concern in keeping and guarding his mate, by their attachment to each other, and by this rather curious pouncing. Uno and Una carried on symbolic building, each bird carrying nesting material hither and yon to different parts of the territory, but only once did Una actually use one of her chosen spots; in May she built her third nest in one of the places favoured in March.

When the female starts to build the nest, the male begins to sing once more. Usually she works quietly and stealthily, but Una, with what was evidently her first nest, was a delightful exception. On April 6 with a large load in her bill she flew chattering to the burdock above the site, dropped down out of sight for less than a minute and left again with a chatter. Uno never accompanied her on her trips as the males of some other species do, but sat quietly on a tree watching her. In two and a quarter hours on this day she carried 25 loads.

On April 10 Una laid her first egg, but on the morning of the 12th, I found that some enemy had despoiled the nest. The pair, undiscouraged, began again to hunt nesting sites, flipping their wings, making soft little noises and carrying dead grass about.

This time Una built a flimsy nest, well hidden under sweet clover, ten yards from her first substantial nest. Here she incubated four eggs, while Uno stood guard, occupying himself with singing and other activities. I wrote:

Uno suddenly flies directly west over 4M's rose hedge and swings back home with 4M and Quarta in hot pursuit. He sings as he lands in safety, puffed out and tail spread. Una hurries off the nest, exclaiming in disapproval *zhee zhee*. Uno and 4M have a real fight while their mates expostulate with vehement *zhees*."

Another time:

Una came flying out from the nest, scolding *tchunk tchunk*. 4M attacks her, knocking her off her perch. Uno speeds to the rescue and the two males have a rough and tumble battle, while Quarta hurries near, chattering and scolding. Uno returns, singing, and Una greets him with her note of welcome *eee eee eee*."

The babies hatched May 5 and 6; Uno fed them faithfully but foolish Una continued to treat them as eggs, merely keeping them warm. It was not until four days later that Una really began to help feed her chicks, bringing a third as many meals as did Uno, and the next day half as many. During the ten days the young were in the nest, I watched it for 39 hours; I recorded Uno as bringing 367 meals and Una 113.

A week after these young fledged Una started her third nest and when she began to incubate this set, I took the opportunity to slip away for 12 days to Oklahoma.

XIII

Again
'The Birds
of Oklahoma'

It was in November 1927 that I had made exciting discoveries at the National Museum in Washington, D.C. When I asked Dr. Oberholser on the Monday (the day before the A.O.U. started for Associates) how I could find out what specimens of Oklahoma birds there were in the larger museums, he said the only way was to go to the museums and inquire about each species. So I went to the National Museum; I showed my list to Joseph H. Riley, Assistant Curator in the Division of Birds, and asked him to find out what there were of each species in their collections. He cheerfully answered that he was sure there weren't any of them, but he would look.

At first the search was fruitless, but at last a Lesser Prairie Chicken[1], without much data, came to light. On checking on it in the catalogue, lo and behold, 44 entries from Camp Supply (Woodward County in northwestern Oklahoma) were discovered; they came from Dr. S. Kitching from January to March 1878. The most important item listed was that of two Eskimo Curlews[2] — the only instance we have of specimens taken in Oklahoma. Other noteworthy records were a Richardson's Pigeon Hawk[3], an Avocet[4], a Northern Shrike, a Gambel's Sparrow[5] and a Lark Bunting, this last collected February 7.

The next key bird was a Swallow-tailed Kite that led me to Dr. Edward Palmer's collection of 80 skins from Kiowa Agency

[1]*Tympanuchus pallidicinctus.* [2]*Numenius borealis.* [3]*Falco columbarius richardsonii.* [4]American Avocet, *Recurvirostra americana.* [5]*Zonotrichia leucophrys gambelli.*

(Caddo County in central Oklahoma) in 1867. Other interesting records were a Townsend's Solitaire[1], taken March 19; two Road-runners, the first record for the state; Black-and-White[2], Protho-notary[3] and Kentucky Warblers; as well as a Bald Eagle.

After some difficulty Mr. Riley found the famous specimen of the White-tailed Kite[4] — the only record of the species from Oklahoma — and so we discovered the extensive collection of Charles S. McCarthy and John H. Clark, the latter having been Commissioner of the Survey of the Northern Boundary of Texas. These men collected from southeastern to southwestern Oklahoma from April 16 to July 9, 1860. Among the 57 skins listed was the first example of the Western Kingbird for the state as well as four specimens of Carolina Parakeets.

Thanks to a suggestion by Dr. Charles H. Richmond, Curator of Birds at the Museum, I found the list of 139 sets of eggs of White-tailed Kite and Lesser Prairie Chicken, and sets of Western Kingbird, Mountain Plover[5], Virginia Rail[6], Chuck-will's-widow, Cassin's Sparrow, White-necked Raven[7], and many others.

I started to go through the mighty catalogue page by page, volume by volume, and very interesting it was to come upon collections by W. H. Hudson, Robert Ridgway, Elliott Coues, and other notables. There were four very small collections from Oklahoma from 1877 to 1890, as well as one of 14 sets of eggs. Most exciting was the discovery of records of 47 birds taken by Dr. S. W. Woodhouse from 1849 to 1850; the most important of his specimens was a Bonaparte's Gull[8], the only record at that time from the state.

Instead of nothing from Oklahoma as Mr. Riley had predicted, 13 hours of work brought to light records of 242 skins in eight collections and 153 sets of eggs in two collections. From 37 to 78 years previously, zestful ornithologists had been searching for birds in Oklahoma; hardships, disappointments, trials in that wild country were more than compensated for by the triumphs of success in collecting these specimens. With the exception of Wood-house, none of these men seems to have published a word on their findings. Clark's and McCarthy's records of the White-tailed Kite, Lesser Prairie Chicken and White-necked Raven had found their way into ornithological literature, as well as a set of Prairie Chicken

---

[1]*Myadestes townsendi.* [2]Black-and-White Warbler, *Mniotilta varia.* [3]*Protono-taria citrea.* [4]*Elanus leucurus.* [5]*Charadrius montanus.* [6]*Rallus limicola.* [7] *Corvus cryptoleucus.* [8]*Larus philadelphia.*

eggs taken by Dr. J. C. Merrill, a Fellow of the A.O.U. But all the rest of Clark's and McCarthy's finds and all the labours of Palmer and Kitching had remained unknown until November 1927 when I joyfully copied them for inclusion in the second edition of *Birds of Oklahoma.*

On May 26, 1929, I left Columbus on the train for a brief visit to Oklahoma. I wrote to Constance who was then a junior at Oberlin College in northern Ohio:

It is a great joy to be back in this beautiful country once more and see my beloved flowers and birds. It is really a revelation to me to find how delighted people are to see me. Friends add a great wealth of happiness to life. The memorial for Eleanor of the children's books had made a link that has touched people hearts.

In Norman I found a new friend, a young Canadian Zoologist, Dr. Ralph D. Bird, who had become engaged to Lois Gould, botanist and artist, daughter of our friend, Dr. Charles Gould. Ralph and Lois took me on trips to my old haunts where I was happy to meet old friends in the way of flowers and birds. Very early one rainy morning at Snail Brook, I recorded the twilight song of a Crested Flycatcher, and on another morning on the farm of Blaine's older brother near Kingfisher, I took notes on the twilight song of the Scissor-tailed Flycatcher. Four days at the Wild Life Conference at the Wichitas were rewarding, for here I recorded twilight songs of three more Crested Flycatchers; I watched Rock Sparrows, a Red-tailed Hawk's nest and two singing Black-capped Vireos — our first record for this rare species in these mountains.

The A.O.U. met in Philadelphia in October*. Two papers were given on Song Sparrows: Doris Haldeman, a student of Dr. Arthur Allen, reported on the nesting of a pair for two years in succession, and I told of the troubles of Uno, Una, 4M, and Quarta when Una built her fourth nest in 4M's territory. Other papers that especially interested me were Miss Teddy Nelson's (1930) (of Hunter College, New York City) on Spotted Sandpiper[1] chicks and that of J. Dewey Soper (1930) (of the Department of the Interior, Ottawa, Canada) on "Discovery of the Breeding Grounds of the Blue Goose." *(Chen caerulescens)*

At home, my chief occupation was the second *Birds of Oklahoma.* Some quotations from my journals will give a picture of my progress in this enterprise:

*The 47th Stated Meeting of the American Ornithologists' Union, Philadelphia, Pennsylvania, October 21-24, 1929.

[1] *Actitis macularia.*

Feb. 13, 1929. I have had a glorious morning for I achieved all of 'Past and Present in Oklahoma Bird Life.'

Although I miss some one to consult with and at times feel very much alone in this great undertaking, yet it is fun to be perfectly independent, to be able to do exactly what I want with this *Birds of Oklahoma*; for there is no one to direct, criticize, nor even make suggestions. Gradually, by means of various false starts and many different attempts, I am working out the kind of bulletin I want – the one that seems to me will have the most originality, the least copying from other works and that will be filled with original observations.

Three weeks later, however, I wrote:

As I looked at the mass of material this morning, my heart misgave me. It's such a task to tackle single-handed. I have done nothing on it for over a week – too busy with Song Sparrows.

Dec. 11, 1929. After waiting all summer and all fall, I finally learned that the Oklahoma Biological Survey will publish *Oklahoma Birds* after they have published four other bulletins, supposedly early in 1931. The date suits me.

At one time I was inclined to deal primarily with species, as P.A. Taverner, Chief, Division of Ornithology, National Museum of Canada at Ottawa, had done in his *Birds of Western Canada* (1926). Unfortunately, I rejected this eminently sensible plan.

Feb. 23, 1930. In a way it's a good combination – Song Sparrows and *Birds of Oklahoma*, for the former keep me outdoors an hour or two every day. If I didn't have *Birds of Oklahoma* I'd spend more time on Song Sparrows but I can do most of the essential things with them. I'm cutting out everything else I possibly can except Song Sparrows and *Birds of Oklahoma*; I work at the latter nearly all day after I'm through with the former.

Aug. 6. Song Sparrows monopolized my attention for several months in spring. I started again on *Birds of Oklahoma* in late June. Marjorie usually types for me in the morning. We've now done about 85 pages. Next week we are all going to Grey Rocks for a short vacation.

Under the accounts of the species and subspecies there are (1) some contributions to life histories from Oklahoma sources; (2) help in field identification when needed. I want to arouse people's interest, capture their imaginations, whet their curiosity, start them on problems.

Marjorie had typed 250 pages of the manuscript before October 2 when she started her freshman year at Ohio State University. I then planned to work at a more moderate pace with the expectation of finishing by the end of January. But word came from Oklahoma that the manuscript must be in by December 1. So I plunged in harder than ever and worked more steadily and unremittingly than I had ever done at anything before – morning, afternoon and evening, only taking off a little time for outdoor study of Song Sparrows (which served as necessary recreation) — besides the most essential housework. Two Sundays were devoted to trips to southern Ohio, but even then I achieved two hours or so of writing beforehand. When a second statement arrived about November 1 to the effect that the manuscript *must* be in by December 1, I determined to send it off the day before Thanksgiving and this I did. This manuscript was nearly twice as long as the first *Birds of Oklahoma* due to much fuller treatment as to migration dates, suggestions as to identification, and discussion of habits.

For the last five months *Birds of Oklahoma* had been almost my only thought, my chief occupation. Nothing else was done that could possibly be postponed or avoided. There was a simplicity, a deep satisfaction in such a life, but it was a relief to have achieved the end and to have escaped from under it. That great amorphous incubus I had moulded into a thing of sense and usefulness.

This volume was a tribute of my love and admiration for Oklahoma — the country, the birds, and many of the people; those early workers who before this had received almost no recognition; our contemporaries who had so generously shared their discoveries with us, and those people who, we trust, will in the future be inspired to love and cherish the wild life of that marvellous state.

Time passed but never a word came from Oklahoma.

At the end of December Blaine and I went to Cleveland, Ohio, to attend the Wilson Club which was meeting with the American Association for the Advancement of Science*. Here I saw the professor who was superintending the publication of *Birds· of Oklahoma.*

"Did you receive the manuscript?" I asked him. He looked a bit startled, but answered, "Yes." "How is it coming?" I inquired. "Oh, we haven't started on it yet."

Blaine and I had breakfast with him so as to discuss *Birds of Oklahoma.* He promised to have several batches of proof sent to me, including page proof.

I wrote to my mother:

The bird papers at the Meeting were all good, some very good; there were also some excellent reels of motion pictures. My paper — 'Survival and Reproduction in a Song Sparrow Population During One Season' illustrated with slides of a map and several tables, made a great impression. Dr. Van Tyne

---

*The 17th Stated Meeting of the Wilson Ornithological Club, Cleveland, Ohio, December 29-30, 1930.

gave a fine tribute to my talk — 'a very interesting, very important contribution representing much labour and patience.' Multitudes of people spoke to
me about it with praise and appreciation. Dr. T. C. Stephens asked for it for
the Wilson Bulletin. In short, I was never so admired before in my life. Somehow 30 territories and 79 nests seemed to have impressed the bird people.

It was not until February 19, 1931, that the first batch of proofs
arrived. This covered nearly half the manuscript and took five days
of solid work for correction. In March came the rest of the proofs
except for the bibliography. No page proof was ever sent to me.

My excitement was great when in mid April on returning from a
well-spent morning on Interpont I spied in our mail box what
looked like *Birds of Oklahoma*, Revised Edition. Eagerly I opened
it and was met by practically a full page of errata. These referred
mainly to the bibliography, the proof of which I had never seen.
From page 198, 24 references between Edith Force and Charles N.
Gould had been displaced to page 201 with the result that *27 of
my own 50 references were attributed to Dr. Gould*. I could well
echo Beethoven's distress over the proof of one of his compositions:
"Errors swarm in it like fish in the sea." It was particularly
disappointing to find out later that many of the copies were *not*
provided with a page of *errata* which called attention to some of
the most glaring mistakes.

I considered various sarcastic letters to the Publication Committee but finally decided to say nothing. I wrote to the University
Press inquiring what price they were asking for the book. Instead
of an answer, I received an elegant form letter announcing that the
University of Oklahoma Press had received an award for "The
most beautiful printing of the year!" Among the tens of thousands
of letters I have received in my long life, this was the only occasion
I can remember on which a wrong letter had been put into an
envelope for me.

The reviewers considerately made no mention of the inexcusable
negligence that marred the bulletin. They emphasized the good
features and one called it "a masterpiece of thoroughness."

Despite the mix-up in the bibliography, *Birds of Oklahoma*
(1931) carried its message. In 1967, on page ix of his monumental
Oklahoma Birds, George Sutton writes that my book "has been of
inestimable value not alone for the information it contains but for
the interest it has aroused in the conservation of wild life."

XIV

The Song Sparrow on Interpont

The foundation of my Song Sparrow studies lay in the banding technique which gave sure knowledge of the individual bird through season after season. Each bird was given a numbered aluminum band from the United States Biological Survey (now the Fish and Wildlife Service) in Washington, D.C., adults on the left leg, nestlings on the right. In addition, each trapped bird was supplied with a different combination of coloured celluloid bands so that its identity could be known in the field. I made these bands from brightly coloured toys, following the technique of Wilbur Butts (1930). Most of the nesting birds I had to bait and later trap on their territories, these endeavours taking place before the introduction into our country of mist nets for banders. Cold, snowy days in winter and early spring were the best times for trapping.

In Chapter XII, in 1929, I had left Una incubating her third set of eggs. Three of these hatched. Again she failed to feed the chicks until they were half grown, Uno, her mate, once more providing nourishment for the first four to five days. One of this brood returned the following spring and joined a mate within 300 yards of her birthplace. In 1931 one of this bird's sons, 50M, took up his territory next to the former home of his maternal grandparents.

In my book *The Watcher at the Nest* (1939) I tell of the adventures of Uno and Una, of 4M and Quarta, in their fourth nestings in 1929: how Una started to build her nest in 4M's rose hedge and, since Uno could not defend her there, how she became a very lion of defiance against 4M. Territory lines had broken down and the whole pattern of behaviour rested on personal relationships, 4M and Quarta dominating Uno, but being dominated by Una. Fortunately, by a series of territory establishment ceremonies and fights, Uno won his right to visit his own nest just before the babies hatched. At last Una had learned that infants differ from eggs and must be fed from the beginning. Uno also tended the brood faithfully, at times even singing softly while perched on the rim of the nest!

In the fall of 1929 Uno and Una, 5M and Quarta, left Columbus to winter further south, but 4M stayed on and on. In time I was to find out that about half the nesting male Song Sparrows were permanent residents in Interpont, and the same proved true for about a tenth of the females. In February (1930) came mild and sunny days and all the resident male Song Sparrows started to sing. On the 23rd to my great joy Uno returned. After a brief encounter with 4M he quickly won back his territory, *including the rose hedge*! Two days later 5M was back. On March 10 Uno stopped singing; his newly arrived mate was unbanded and I named her Een. On the 15th Una arrived. With Uno already mated, she joined their neighbour 5M.

This season Uno and Een raised seven young in their first two broods, but none in their third. 5M and Una, who fed these children from the start, lost their first brood, but raised seven young in their second and third attempts. 4M had bad luck; his first two mates disappeared, but he and his third mate raised four young.

During the season of 1930 I gradually extended my interests over some 30 acres of Interpont, trapping and banding the Song Sparrow territory owners and searching diligently for their nests. We stayed in Columbus until mid-August and I was able to band 47 of the breeding adults. I discovered no less than 61 of their nests and banded 102 nestlings that fledged in safety. During the next winter I found seven right-banded young males scattered all over Interpont and naturally I had to follow them.

Capturing these seven young males was an exciting occupation. Would they all prove to be sons of resident parents, thus indicating the presence of two *gentes* in the population — resident and migratory — as A. Landsborough Thomson (1926) had suggested for Lapwings[1] nesting in Aberdeenshire?

What I found was this: all the mothers had been summer residents and another had been present for only a short time, one father had been unbanded, so their status could not be determined. But the mate of the second one had been Uno's daughter and he, the

[1] *Vanellus vanellus.*

grandfather, had been a summer resident. Yet his grandson — 50M — had been a resident. One resident son had a resident father. But *four resident sons* had had *three summer resident fathers*, two of the sons having come from the same brood. So identification from banding did not support the theory of migratory and non-migratory strains in this Song Sparrow population.

As time went on I found that seven of my birds changed their status: one male migrated for two winters and remained the third; three males and a female remained one winter, migrated the next and returned the following spring; while two males remained two winters, migrated the third, and returned in the spring. Wherever the migrating Song Sparrows spent the winter, it was not in the outskirts of a city, for the plumage of all returning migrants was bright and clean in contrast to that of the soot-darkened permanent residents of Interpont. I came to the conclusion that the weather in October influenced some of my birds, mild temperatures tempting them to stay, bleak weather hastening them south.

The Song Sparrow is well named — *Melospiza melodia* — that is, "Melodious Song-finch." Each male has a repertoire of from six to 24 individual songs, which, with a very few exceptions, are possessed by him alone. This characteristic bestows an individuality on each of the birds unequalled by any other species known by me. By careful study and by recording songs in words and symbols I came to know by heart all of Uno's six songs and all of 4M's nine songs, besides one or more songs of practically all of my nesting males.

The second chief question on which the capture of these males, banded in the nest, was to shed light was that of the origin of their songs. Is the possession of like songs an indication of relationship, as suggested by Saunders (1924)? Might patterns have been innate or might they have been learned during the first four weeks of life while the young bird was in his parents' care?

This question of relationship was also answered in the negative. *No son had any song of his father.* Nor did 50M have any from his maternal grandfather, Uno. The two brothers had no song in common. 58M possessed a wild and lovely strain unlike any other Song Sparrow I have ever heard. Experience in later years showed me that young Song Sparrows learn their songs in late summer and perhaps early fall after they have left their natal territory, as discussed in my book *The Behavior of the Song Sparrow* (1943). In late winter they start singing a great variety of phrases, by early spring developing their favoured repertoire of definite songs.

I soon found that trying to keep track of so many Song Sparrows meant a great deal of home work. Gradually I evolved a number of different techniques. There were seven: the banding record in chronological order; a card catalogue with a card for each of the breeding birds; a summary of these in key tables; a daily record for presence and/or singing of all birds recorded; a set of field notebooks, 8 x 10 inches in size; an ample supply of mimeographed maps of Interpont on which I showed the location of each bird found; and finally a special Nest Record.

In the spring of 1931 several of my cherished Song Sparrows failed to return. Una, Een, 5M and, saddest of all Uno, all had perished. It was a deep disappointment to me to realize that never again could I welcome home this engaging personality who had started me on my study of his species and never again could rejoice in his special, lovely songs.

This season I had 38 banded nesting females and 30 banded males; I found 40 nests and banded 65 nestlings that fledged in safety. We left Interpont on June 6, so that I could attend my twenty-fifth reunion at Mount Holyoke College.

At Grey Rocks I was lucky enough to find two nests of the Black-throated Green Warbler, both while the females were incubating. This warbler has always held a warm place in my heart because of the charm of his chief song — *trees, trees, murmuring trees* — a delightful and unforgettable little message that seems to express the very spirit of a drowsy afternoon among the hemlocks.

The first nesting was cared for by an efficient mother, while father was absorbed in singing, apparently oblivious to the fact that his babies had hatched. In seven hours on July 15 I had recorded 1,680 songs from him, so Blaine and I decided to watch the family for a whole day, hoping to make a world's record for songs given by one bird in a day. So, on the 16th we spent 16 hours at the nest but recorded only 1,313 songs, apparently because part of the time the uncooperative little fellow had sung too far away for us to be sure it was he and not a neighbour. Mother, in the meantime, fed her charges a total of 46 meals.

Three days later two little birds left the nest to the accompaniment of much chipping by mother and calls from the youngsters. The excitement brought father to the scene; he left and quickly returned to the nest with a small caterpillar which he placed far down the baby's throat — behaviour appropriate to dealing with newly hatched infants, not with those nearly fledged. He brought six insects that afternoon and five the next morning. The mother worked tirelessly, but for the most part merely showed her insects to her children, then hopped off leading them slowly and surely away from the home hemlock and into the branches of other hemlocks.

The other nest, discovered July 26, was also cared for by the female alone. The two chicks left when eight days old and were quickly tolled off into the woods by their mother.

This lack of interest by the fathers of these birds seems to be exceptional. In three instances reported in the literature the males were as devoted to the young as were their mates, while this was true in a nest we had found at Grey Rocks in 1928. Moreover, over the years, we had recorded no less than nine examples of male Black-throated Green Warblers feeding young out of the nest.

I wrote a long and detailed paper on the history of these two nests, concluding with a table comparing brooding and feeding young at 16 warbler nests as described in nine papers by four authors (1932). My friend, Henry Mousley of Canada, had published accounts of the home life of seven species (1924, 1926, 1928). These were the last of my studies on warblers — seven nests of five species of this choice family. Many of our visits to Grey Rocks in subsequent years were late in the season, while in 1938 and 1940 I concentrated on searching for Song Sparrow nests.

It was a report on this study of the Black-throated Green Warblers that I gave at the A.O.U. meeting in October*. This took place in a large hotel in Detroit, Michigan, under the chairmanship of an enterprising woman, Mrs. Etta T. Wilson, active in bird watching and in conversation. Blaine and I drove there in our car — his first chance (because of teaching duties) to attend a gathering of the Union.

The American Ornithologists' Union was an old, proud and exclusive society founded 48 years previously. In 1931 there was a heirarchy of 50 Fellows, 100 Members, and perhaps 1,500 Associates. Fellows and Members were proposed and elected by their peers. All business was transacted by them, but Associates participated in the scientific and social activities. Dr. Witmer Stone, editor of the *Auk* for 25 years wrote: "The 'Fellows' of the A.O.U. represent the fifty leading ornithologists of America; standards may always be so characterized" (*Auk*, 1915:138). Such an ideal, however, did not always work out in practice.

At this time there were four women Members — Mable Osgood

*The 49th Stated Meeting of the American Ornithologists' Union, Detroit, Michigan, October 19-22, 1931.

Wright, Althea H. Sherman, Elsie M. Naumberger of the American Museum, a specialist on Brazilian birds, and May T. Cooke of the United States Biological Survey. Two years previously Florence Merriam Bailey had been elected to the class of Fellows, the first woman to be so honoured. (The Associates finally grew so weary of the lowly estate that in 1955 their designation was changed to that of Members while the former Members, now numbering 200, became Elective Members.)

We were delighted to visit with Miss Sherman and the Joseph Grinnells at the meeting. Dr. Grinnell was the President of A.O.U. at that time while Dr. Palmer was still Secretary and McAtee still Treasurer. I was happy to be elected to Membership, proposed by Miss Sherman, Dr. Oberholser, and Dr. Palmer.

In 1919 William Brewster had died. "To him more than to any-one else was due the founding of the Nuttall Ornithological Club from which sprang the A.O.U." (1919) wrote Dr. Stone. As evidence of the esteem and love felt for this noble man a fund of $7,250 was raised by some 260 friends of his to establish the Brewster Memorial Fund, the income of which was to be used every two years for a medal and honorarium to the "author of what, in the judgment of the Council of the Union, is the most important work relating to the birds of the Western Hemisphere, during the period in question." Later the award was given annually, while the pertinent period extended over six years.

This year the Brewster Medal was awarded to Florence Merriam Bailey for her splendid volume on the *Birds of New Mexico* (1928).

On the third day of the meeting we all went to the University of Michigan at Ann Arbor to visit its Museum. Since our family planned to attend the International Physiological Congress in Rome in 1932, I asked Dr. Frank Chapman, Representative for European birds on *Bird-Lore's* Advisory Board, what book to obtain for the trip. He referred me to Dr. Ernst Mayr, a young German ornithologist working in the American Museum of Natural History in New York City. Thus started a warm and enduring friendship that became exceedingly important to me.

Ernst was delighted to find an American "interested in more than faunistic records and pretty pictures" (*in lit*). (To judge from the papers at the meeting, the chief interests of the speakers appeared to be in matters of explorations by ornithologists, distri-bution and migration of birds, and conservation of endangered species.) Ernst started me reading the German journal *Journal für Ornithologie* in the University Library that very day; he told me of the most important European ornithologists interested in life history work and gave me their addresses.

I wrote to these men and received in return friendly letters and many reprints, the most important of which for my future work was Oskar Heinroth's classic paper on the relationships between bird weight, egg weight, set weight, and length of incubation (1922).

Mr. Charles L. Whittle, retired geologist, was the able and dedicated editor of *Bird-Banding: A Journal of Ornithological Investigation*, published for the Northeastern, Eastern, and Inland Bird-Banding Associations. He lent me several years of three German journals: *Ornithologische Monatsberichte, Der Vogelzug,* and *Beiträge zur Fortpflanzungsbiologie der Vögel.* These I diligently read and from them took many notes. I was greatly impressed with the solid foundation of life history studies on birds in Germany.

Back at Interpont, winter came but the weather remained mild. On January 6 and 13 in 1932 swamp tree frogs gave their songs — *greek greek* — while two days later a misguided bat fluttered by. The resident Song Sparrows, old and young, settled down to proclaiming territory in the balmy weather of late January and of February. Interpont rang with music.

On February 15, however, I began to notice that silence had descended in many spots.

"Does every one have a mate?" I wondered. "Yesterday was Saint Valentine's Day."

Investigation showed no less than 16 mated pairs, proving the presence of an unprecedented number of resident females. One notable event was the remating of 60M and 60F, the first instance of this situation in the known history of Interpont. Most unexpected of all was the mating between a brother and sister, offspring of two residents, banded in the same nest and wintering in the same weedy ditch some two-fifths of a mile from their birthplace. I named them Siegmund and Sieglinde. In May all three eggs of their first nest hatched and one little bird was fledged: I never found Siegfried again. Siegmund disappeared that first summer but Sieglinde lived in the same locality until the spring of 1934.

February's exceptional mildness brought home most of the male summer resident Song Sparrows and the first of the migratory females. But how did the weather treat these little birds it had lured north so early? The coldest temperatures of the whole winter descended in March — bitter wind and snow, the thermometer hovering between 8° and 12° F. above zero. On March 6, instead of the glorious chorus we had come to expect, the only song at dawn came from a brave Mourning Dove. Territory was suspended; birds flocked to the feeding places from near and far, and everything reverted to a winter basis. Trapping was rewarding; ten Song Sparrows were taken on the 6th and the same number on the 7th, as well as numbers of Tree Sparrows, Juncos, and Cardinals.

On the 11th the thermometer rose to 17° F. above zero, the wind rested and all the unmated Song Sparrows were singing once more.

Before the end of March Interpont was full to overflowing with Song Sparrows, a total of 69 males on the forty acres. This was its peak of population during our stay in Columbus. There was still a fine representation of the 27 males with which the population study had started in 1930 — six residents and six summer residents. Six of the eight males (one a summer resident) banded as nestlings in 1930 still flourished. All 69 breeding males were banded, and the same was true of 67 of the females.

Cold weather in April delayed the start of nesting and an early drought brought starvation to some of the nestlings. Sixty nests were located and 76 fledgelings banded before we left for the East on June 14, five of us bound for Europe.

XV

To Europe in 1932

Leaving eight-year old Janet at Grey Rocks with my mother and my sister Katharine, the rest of us sailed for Europe, reaching France on June 26. Our aims were three-fold: to attend the International Physiological Congress in Rome in late August, to give our three older daughters a comprehensive trip from the sight-seeing and educational points of view, and incidentally to become acquainted with some European birds and ornithologists. I was handicapped in bird identification by the inadequacy of my bird guide in France, but later did much better with a small three volume set of German books.

We all understood and talked French to some extent. Constance and Marjorie were our chief historians, while Barbara sketched what took her fancy. Mont St. Michel was the most perfect, the most fascinating place I had ever visited. The sheer beauty of the medieval architecture of this ancient fortified abbey, the tiny ferns of many kinds on the walls, the bright colouring of stonecrop and red valerian, and the ever circling swarms of swifts[1], swallows, and House Martins[2] – all these made an unforgettable picture. In the garden we heard our first nightingale – an ecstatic, warbling, bubbling, joyous strain. How could this have ever been called a lament?

As soon as we reached Paris, I wrote to M. Jacques Berlioz, Assistant Director of the Laboratory of Ornithology of the Museum of Natural History, sending him the letter of introduction given

---

[1] *Apus apus.* [2] *Delichon urbica.*

me by Ernst Mayr. The next day a letter in English came from him expressing his regret that he was on the eve of departure for Canada.

Much in need of help in the identification of the birds I had been seeing, I started out for the Musée d'Histoire Naturelle, M. Berlioz' kind note in my handbag.

This museum, oldest in the world, has a long and glorious history, having been founded by the Comte de Buffon in the reign of Louis XIV; it is an extraordinary place, but according to our standards seemed a bit old-fashioned. All the birds and other animals were arranged in rows, and I saw but two tiny attempts at habitat groups.

Since all I could find were "Birds of the World," I searched for a guard, but the one on duty was fast asleep, and my footsteps in his vicinity failed to bring any reaction. So I looked further and came upon three guards engaged in conversation; in response to my inquiry as to *les oiseaux de la France*, one of them detached himself and led me to a small room. Here all the large birds – raptors, geese, etc. – were arranged around the wall on the low shelves, while near the ceiling were all the small birds, the only access to them being a gallery to which I could see no stairway.

As my chief purpose in coming to the museum had been to study these small birds, I asked the guard how I was to see *"les petits oiseaux."*

"Mais, regardez bien, regardez bien."

I told him I couldn't possibly *regardez* from my position and inquired how one mounted.

"Mais non! C'est réservé pour les professeurs!"

As if the professors would have the slightest interest in looking at these small specimens! It was the most absurd arrangement possible.

I handed my letter from M. Berlioz to the guard; he was much impressed and tried to read it. He caught one word.

"Ah, vous êtes du Canada!" he exclaimed.

He mumbled away as he pretended to read it, saying *"Avec mes meilleur sentiments"* when he came to "Yours very sincerely." He conducted me downstairs to *L'Administration,* a group of three guards by the front door. He told his tale and was greeted with *Non, non!* from the others. He showed the letter, which all examined with interest, but which not one could read.

"C'est en anglais," they remarked.

My guard insisted it must be a *permission* for me to enter the sacred gallery, but the others were equally sure it was not. My guard turned about and started upstairs, and I followed him. Fortunately, a mass of small boys, some 60 in number, were engaging the attention of the other guards, so we were able to get to the small room unobserved.

Here with great show of secrecy my guard produced an immense key and unlocked a door; we cautiously crept up the stairway and after a second unlocking were on the gallery!

"Dix minutes," said he.

"Quinze," said I.

I must be in a special place, and he would return. Then with more *chuts, chuts* he departed.

I began to look at *les petites oiseaux* with great interest. Suddenly I heard a commotion in the room beneath me. Another guard had discovered the enormity and was reproving my guard at the top of his voice. I remained completely absorbed in *les oiseaux* and never glanced around, but I could not fail to hear the angry recriminations and to catch out of the corner of my eye a few of the gestures. The clamour went on for some minutes below me, then the scene of battle was transferred to the main hall, where for some time I could still hear loud, excited vociferations.

I was fortified by the knowledge that my desire to see the little birds was innocent, reasonable, and laudable, and that if M. Berlioz had not been on the ocean, he would have personally conducted me into the forbidden precincts. I had an interesting time, discovering the French names of many of the birds, as well as the identity of several I had seen out-of-doors. After *vingt minutes* my guard reappeared and let me descend. His enthusiasm over a sizable *pourboire* was so great that he offered to show me all the Birds of the World.

From Paris, Dr. Hans Scharnke, a student of the distinguished Prof. Stresemann of Berlin, conducted us on a trip to St. Germain-en-Laye. After all my lone efforts to learn the birds, it was satisfying to have an ornithologist tell us the name of every singer, to corroborate or correct my own identifications, and to name each new bird. We heard the delightful songs of the Redbreast[1], the Blackcap[2], and the Wren[3] — the same species as our Winter Wren but with a much inferior song. The chief singer was the Chaffinch[4] with his unforgettable chant; we found this handsome bird everywhere throughout our trip in parks and on the mountainsides in the Tyrol. Sadly enough, our kind guide was to lose his life in the Second World War.

---

[1] European Robin, *Erithacus rubecula.* [2] Black-capped Warbler, *Sylvia atricapella.* [3] Northern Wren, *Troglodytes troglodytes.* [4] *Fringilla coelebs.*

On July 18, leaving my family to take the Rhine trip and explore southwestern Germany, I took the train to Berlin. Here political posters were violent in the extreme: the Communists and National Socialists called each other liars, murderers, and so on, while still another party attacked them both. Alas for the world, it was the Nazis that were to come into power.

At the *Zoologisches Museum* I met with the warmest of welcomes from the famous ornithologist, Erwin Stresemann, and from Ernst Mayr, who was visiting his former professor. All of Dr. Stresemann's great array of books and journals were placed freely at my disposal. For ten days I worked eagerly in this library.

Everyone was most friendly and helpful. Students of Dr. Stresemann — George Steinbacher and Werner Rüppell — took me on two expeditions to see birds. Some of the most notable were the handsome Red-backed Shrike[1], the brilliant Golden Oriole[2], and a pair of Hobbies[3], where the screaming female met her mate in the air and snatched prey from his claws. Most thrilling of all my bird experiences that summer was the sight of five Great Bustards[4]. The immense birds, all males, with their long white necks and brown speckled backs, walked slowly across a mown meadow, dwarfing a Buzzard (*Buteo buteo*) that perched near. As we approached, they flew, giving a most striking display of the white patches in their great wings. W. H. Hudson had called this species the "finest of British birds . . . wantonly extirpated (in Great Britain) during the first half of the present (19th) century" (1897 a).

At this time, Germany was not allowed to maintain an army — a cause for rejoicing with some of the young men, a bitter disappointment to others. Ornithology benefited, for students did not have their time frittered away in military exercises.

Dr. Oskar Heinroth, Director of the Berlin Aquarium, showed me this great and fascinating institution one morning and the Zoo on another morning. It was a keen disappointment to me that Frau Magdalena Heinroth was in Rumania and that this season for the first time in 30 years no young birds were being raised. The Heinroths had done the most extraordinarily interesting and important researches, having brought up from the egg, or soon afterwards, hundreds of different species, making careful studies on the growth, development, and behaviour of the young birds. Everywhere in European ornithological literature one finds the

[1]*Lanius collurio.* [2]*Oriolus oriolus.* [3]Northern Hobby, *Falco subbuteo.* [4]*Otis tarda.*

Heinroths quoted as the authorities on life-history matters. It was a shock to learn after my return home that Magdalena Heinroth had died in August — a great loss to her friends and to ornithology.

The chief benefits of my visit to Berlin lay in discussions with Dr. Stresemann. At Columbus I had missed the stimulus of talking over my Song Sparrow problems with other naturalists for these were organized into the strictly masculine Wheaton Club, of which Blaine was a member but from which I was excluded. Dr. Stresemann listened with attention to my descriptions of my study, and he gave me valuable suggestions. For instance, when I spoke of 4M as an "old" bird at five or six years of age, he said small passerines are not "aged" after that span of years; in captivity they may live for 17 years or even longer.

When I told him of the difficulty of getting long papers published in America because of the non-selectivity of the editor of the *Auk*, Dr. Stresemann told me that he returned two-thirds of the papers sent him as editor of the *Journal für Ornithologie*, the oldest still continuing ornithological journal in the world, having been founded 80 years previously. "I do not want to die of indigestion," he said. He added that he was usually able to suggest publication for rejected papers elsewhere.

To my amazement Dr. Stresemann invited me to send him a paper, 100 pages long if I wished. He would have it translated into German and published in his journal. It would be funny, thought I, to have by far the fullest account of my Song Sparrows appear in German, while only partial papers would have come out in America. At that time I knew of no journal in America where anything like an adequate presentation could be given. The *Auk*, for instance, published nothing longer than 20 pages in one contribution.

I felt that the long hours of trudging up and down Interpont in cold and heat, rain and snow, day after day, month after month, at last were meeting with a reward. At a dinner at the Stresemanns' home we all drank to the health of the Song Sparrows. I was a proud person since I had visited Berlin.

It was a joy in Munich to meet my family after their happy trip to Brussels and up the Rhine. After a week in the Tyrol, we again separated; the daughters travelled to Venice while Blaine and I went to Luzern. Here we took the funicular to the peak of Mt. Pilatus, an hour's ride from a level of 1200 feet to nearly 7,000, through beech woods, through spruces and finally above tree-line. We were delighted to find a large number of the Alpine Choughs[1]

---

[1] Yellow-billed Chough, *Pyrrhocorax graculus*.

sailing and diving and circling as gracefully as gulls following a ship. With their strange screams, which suited the wildness of the crags, and the marvel of their flight, they gave the finishing touch to the wonderful scene. They came within a few feet of people in hopes of crumbs, their red feet and legs and yellow bills contrasting strongly with their glossy black plumage. On the trip down the mountain an Englishman, despite my statements to the contrary, condescendingly explained to me that these birds did *not* belong to the crow family as I had told him, but were "a kind of buzzard, a bird of prey, like a vulture."

The following day we visited Herr and Frau Josef Bussmann at Sempich to see the terragraph — an electromagnetic instrument for recording the activities of birds and mammals. The Bussmanns spoke no English, but Blaine and I marshalled our best German, and we got along famously. Herr Bussmann was a zealous bander and had made many studies of hole-nesting birds, recording parental visits by means of the terragraph. I told him that one of my problems on Interpont was the shooting of my Song Sparrows by boys.

"This is not done in Switzerland," said he. "If boys shoot House Sparrows or any other birds, their parents are severely punished." Every man had a gun but shooting is mainly performed at targets.

There were a thousand participants at the Fourteenth International Physiological Congress in Rome* and wonderfully well did the authorities look after us. Blaine gave a speech on the changes in the specific gravity and chemical elements in the blood after emotional excitement (1932); we were greeted by Mussolini; blessed by the Pope; given a banquet; and taken on excursions to Tivoli, Hadrian's Villa, and Ostia at the mouth of the Tiber. At each of these places we were served with elegant refreshments.

Although since we had reached Italy it had seemed almost magical to me how my Italian, dormant for a quarter of a century, had come back to me, nevertheless I had fondly hoped that the zealous bander, Prince Francesco Chigi, would talk English. Instead we conversed in Italian. Between his Quail[1] banding station on the seashore and his home at Castel Fusano at Ostia, there stretched a beautiful woods of live oaks, maritime pines, and much undergrowth. The bird life was rich under strict protection, and a large

---

*The XIVth International Physiological Congress, Rome, Italy, August 29-September 3, 1932.

[1]*Coturnix coturnix.*

number of hawks nested — Black Kite[1], Buzzard, European
Sparrow-Hawk[2], and Honey-Buzzard[3]. It was an inspiring sight to
see two Short-toed Eagles[4] and the graceful Red Kite[5].

Prince Chigi showed me his trammel nets on the sand dunes for
capturing migratory quail and smaller nets in the *boschetto* where
thrushes and other migrating passerines were lured by the calling
of caged birds and the whistling of his bird-catchers. I took notes
as best I could, but after I had jotted down that his helpers had
discovered 1,000 nests that spring, I was dismayed. After some
reflection on how to phrase it, I asked him whether he would not
write an article on his banding activities, and I would translate it
for *Bird-Banding*.

Sure enough, his paper said nothing about 1,000 nests. With the
help of a dictionary I translated his "Methods of Capturing Birds
at the Ornithological Station of Castel Fusano" and it was
published (see Chigi. 1933).

In London we called on Mr. H. F. Witherby, editor of *British
Birds*. Ringing of birds (which we call banding) was not financed
by the government as it is in our country; it was managed by his
journal; every cooperator subscribed to it and paid for the rings he
used. Most of the ringing has been of nestlings and young precocial
birds but, of late, trapping of adult birds had been coming more
into vogue. During 1931, 7041 birds had been trapped and 22,513
nestlings and precocial chicks had been marked. It was interesting
to learn that Starlings were increasing in numbers and spreading
into new localities in England. In Spain, the people caught them
by the thousands and ate them.

Our last day in England — September 17 — was satisfactory in
every way, for we visited both Winchester and Salisbury, delighting
in the quaint old towns, in the magnificent cathedral and a beautiful vesper service. As we were sitting out in front of Salisbury
Cathedral, I suddenly noticed that what I had taken for a carved
ornament on a spire moved its head! At once I trained my glasses
on it and found it to be an immature Cormorant[6]. As we were
exclaiming over it, a sweet old lady sitting on the same bench told
us it had been there for 36 hours and had aroused great interest in
the inhabitants of Salisbury. She and the verger had decided it
must have been a falcon or one of "those birds from Belgium that
live on roofs" (I suppose a stork!). "It must have come here to rest,

---

[1]*Milvus migrans.* [2]*Accipter nisus.* [3]*Pernis apivorus.* [4]*Circaefus gallicus.*
[5]*Milvus milvus.* [6]*Phalacrocorax carbo.*

just as we all do. It's the human in it."

As we watched the graceful Jackdaws[1] flying about the Cathedral I told our friend that the Austrian investigator, — Konrad Lorenz, — had discovered that these birds mate for life. She was greatly delighted. "They're not like these writers nowadays with their horrid theories!"

On shipboard the second day out on our return voyage, a female Merlin joined us. Two days later she was eating a fellow refugee. And that was the last that we saw of her. Very few birds were noted later. I worked undisturbed on translating Herr Bussmann's article and on a report for Mr. Whittle on "Some Ornithological Experiences in Europe (1933)." On landing in New York we rejoiced to be reunited with our youngest daughter and on the 27th of September we were home again on Interpont.

---

[2] *Corvus monedula.*

XVI

'Zur Naturgeschichte des Singammers'

The next morning we were happy indeed to hear a song from 4M. Although he was at least in his seventh year, I noted on October 1, "4M still sings the most of any of my Song Sparrows." Little could he realize that shortly he was to become famous as the most important of the "Song Buntings" through the publication of "Zur Naturgeschichte des Singammers" in the *Journal für Ornithologie* (1933-34).

A shock awaited me when I went out to view Interpont. "Tremendous destruction by the city of trees and underbrush all along the river bank," I wrote in my journal. "The most beautiful spot on all Interpont has been demolished. 'Janet's Mountain' leveled. The weeds cut down; a desert made. I'm thankful I was 4,000 miles away this summer."

In November the Wilson Club met in Columbus at the University and the State Museum*. In contrast to the formal atmosphere of the A.O.U. the W.O.C. was a very friendly, democratic association.

The meeting was well organized by the Secretary, Lawrence Hicks of the Botany Department of the University. He gave a paper on a "Statistical Survey of Ohio Winter Bird Life"; Edward S. Thomas of the Ohio State Museum spoke on "Returns from Starlings Banded at Columbus," while I talked on the migratory status of my Song Sparrows and on my European experiences with birds and ornithologists. Programmes of bird meetings in those days were much less sophisticated and technical than they are now.

*The 19th Stated Meeting of the Wilson Ornithological Club, Columbus, Ohio, November 25, 26, 1932.

Sixty-four of us joined in the field trip to Buckeye Lake under the leadership of Milton Trautman, who later published an exhaustive study of the birds around this lake (1940). The total list of species for the day came to 59.

My chief project of the fall and winter was the preparation of the report for Dr. Stresemann. I learned much from his quarto volume (889 pages long) on *Aves* (1927-34). In a review of this book in *Bird-Banding*, I wrote: "Dr. Stresemann is both a scholar and a naturalist; he is a great systemist; he has an astonishing grasp of the literature, and he knows birds in life. Moreover, he has a keenly discriminating grasp of the significant in research."

On January 29, 1933, I wrote in my journal:

I am now spending *all* my available energies on Song Sparrows – an hour or so outdoors with them in the morning; the rest of the day on writing, except for what has to go for sleeping, eating, getting breakfast and lunch and a little more house work. (Our daughters prepare dinner and wash all the dishes.) I write all morning after coming in, rest perhaps an hour after lunch and then write again all afternoon. In the evening I am now going through all the great Song Sparrow note books, having reached No. XII with ten more to go. I'm finding many important items . . . Sometimes I grow weary of this everlasting grind. Sometimes I feel very happy over it, but at other times I feel discouraged.

On February 26 I began typing the great thing. On March 18 it started on its way to Germany – 150 pages long with 28 tables, 2 charts, and 15 maps. Working up this interim report proved of much value to me, for during the next three seasons I was aware of new problems and able to work more intelligently than if Dr. Stresemann had never asked me to prepare this paper for him.

It was warmly welcomed by Dr. Stresemann who found that "we had correctly understood each other and that you had organized the *magnum opus* just as I could have wished it. What wealth of important observations, findings and interpretations! Once again a work from which German ornithologists will draw counsel and inspiration for many years to come. My heartiest congratulations" (my translation).

Dr. Herman Desselberger had kindly undertaken the task of translating the manuscript into German. He wrote me: "The translation of your paper is not very difficult, but rather wearisome." He had my sympathy.

In the meantime, in the spring of 1933 Interpont had been taken over for gardens for the unemployed. The plan was to make a clean sweep of everything that grew there except for some of the trees. By determined efforts I was able to persuade the authorities to leave much of the cover along the dikes and in a few other spots that could not be cultivated. Many of the Song Sparrows were driven away completely, while others had to shift their territories into the few places which had not been denuded. In late March the workmen departed and the birds and I were left in peace.

On March 30 I had a busy morning trapping five birds in the field. The first female, 121F, entered the trap for seeds. I left her in the small gathering cage inside the big trap and shortly captured her next door neighbour, 134F. With the second female as bait I soon caught her neighbour, 23F, who had arrived the day before. With this last individual in the trap I took two males, one a bob-tailed, unbanded male, the other, 169M, banded in the nest on May 14, 1932, 200 yards to the south of his birthplace. It was so unusual to catch Song Sparrows with a decoy of the opposite sex that I concluded that 23F must have been too new for all of her neighbours to have become personally acquainted with her. I noted:

Today Song Sparrow work has been thrilling. Sometimes it is quite the opposite. It is fascinating to know these little birds, to realize how they do things, how they order their lives, how they influence one another. I get joy, grief, deep satisfaction and keen adventure from Interpont.

Spring was late in 1933. On April 23 I wrote:

The Song Sparrow work hasn't been going a bit well. I haven't found one single nest yet and my birds keep disappearing and new ones continually appearing that need to be caught but that refuse to be caught.

On May 5 I was indeed discouraged after fruitless efforts at nest finding, both by watching the birds and by "whick-whacking" over likely looking spots with branch or sapling. I wrote:

The Song Sparrow work is going disastrously. Only 5 nests so far. I'm at my wits' end! I haven't found one nest by seeing the bird build. They won't call their mates off. It seems as if they'd 'caught on to me' and are determined to deceive me.

My luck changed and in the next eight days I located nine nests. Six of these came to their ends in two floods; a small one occurred on May 11 but three days later the second flood covered Interpont entirely except for the dikes. Every inch of the territories of 14 of my pairs was under water. The Song Sparrows perched on weeds above the waste of waters or retired to the trees on the dikes. One bird kept flying out and hovering over a spot in the flooded field as if her nest were just below here. I was glad that all the nests had contained eggs, not young.

The floods receded. I looked eagerly to see whether the Song

Sparrows would place their new nests higher than before, having "learned from sad experience," as we often read that birds do. On the contrary, in those localities where nests might have been built above the flood line, they happened to be put even lower than before!

The authorities seemed to have forgotten their plan to cultivate Interpont. The weeds towered above my head and my birds were busy with second attempts at nesting.

And now the third calamity befell. On the 6th of June men arrived with a tractor prepared to plow Interpont three days later. And most of the Song Sparrow nests had babies two to three days old! One pair had lost their first nest in the first flood; their present brood of four was nearly ready to leave, so early on June 9 I slipped the chicks into a stocking and released them in a nearby grove of cottonwoods to the great indignation of their parents. Two survived and returned to Interpont, the brother nesting there for one year, his sister for two.

Four other nests were in the path of the plow. Happily I knew of four nests in the ditches, so I distributed nine endangered refugees into what I hoped would be safe havens. The plowing, however, attracted a host of grackles and these visitors, not content with grubs turned up, searched for additional prey. All four nests were robbed, although I believed that some of the young left in safety.

One little Song Sparrow I rescued a second time. It was a great grandchild of Teazel, a female who nested on Interpont for at least four years. I put this important individual into the House Wren's nest on our grounds. Here, in company with three small wrens and another refugee, a yellowthroat, this "great grandchild" fledged at the age of 11 days and was cared for out of the nest for at least a day by its hospitable foster parents. We left for the West the next day and never again found Teazel's descendant, although it carried fine new coloured bands, supplied by the Biological Survey, at Mr. Whittle's suggestion to the Bureau.

On our five-week trip the six of us visited Oklahoma, New Mexico, and Arizona, going as far as the Grand Canyon. We camped in woods, on prairies and deserts; it was at these times that we made most of our observations on birds. My choicest experience was in a woods in Illinois where on June 21 at 3:30 a.m. C.S.T. I started to record the twilight song of a Wood Pewee for my friend Wallace Craig. It was he who had opened my ears to the melodiousness of the song of the Mourning Dove and to the rare beauty of the pre-dawn song of the Wood Pewee (1943). This is composed of three phrases: the two of the daylight song combined with one heard almost always in twilight. The first seems to me to express aspiration or striving, the second peace, while the third is an exquisitely beautiful phrase that to me signified calm and holy joy. Only in the very early morning is this secret of life revealed, and only to those who truly love nature, who will arise betimes to study her ways.

It was on this trip that I mastered Dutch, after a fashion. Dr. H. N. Kluijver's fine volume on the biology and ecology of the Starling (1933) reached me at Norman. Alas, it was in Dutch with a three-page summary in English. It was my plain duty to read and review it. With the help of a little Dutch grammar and dictionary in the University Library I puzzled out the essentials in the text and was able to write a two page review of the book for *Bird-Banding* (1933). After that I could read and review factual studies on birds in this language, but theoretical discussions remain beyond me.

On graduation, *cum laude*, our daughter Marjorie had received a Graduate Resident Fellowship in history at Columbia University. It was to visit her as well as to attend the Jubilee Meeting of the A.O.U.* at the American Museum that in early November I travelled by bus to New York City. It proved a delightful trip — the happy visits with Marjorie in Johnson Hall, the friendships with the members at the meetings, as well as inspiration from some of the papers. My talk was on "Problems in the Study of Song Sparrow Eggs."

For this Fiftieth Anniversary of the A.O.U. a memorial volume was published, entitled *"Fifty Year's Progress of American Ornithology: 1883-1933."* It contains articles by 14 ornithologists on "educational work in the fields of migration, bird banding, life histories, territorialism, economic ornithology and paleontology." I had been asked by the Secretary, Dr. Palmer to write the paper on "The Theory of Territorialism and its Development (1933)."

Marjorie and I went to the Bronx Zoo on one of the excursions; here we shared a complimentary luncheon with fellow ornithologists and were greatly impressed by seeing many Birds of Paradise. The trip to New York was also notable to me in making the acquaintance of five young men all of whom became true friends — Joe Hickey, Bill Vogt, Roger Tory Peterson, Bob Allen, and Warren

---

*The 51st Stated Meeting of the American Ornithologists' Union, American Museum of Natural History, New York City, November 13-16, 1933.

Eaton.

On the way home I spent a night at Glenolden, Pennsylvania, with John and Mabel Gillespie — a delightful couple — enthusiastic bird banders and bird watchers. Mabel had made an important contribution to bird banding terminology by clarifying the terms "repeat," "return," and "recovery" (1930).

Until my meeting Ernst Mayr at A.O.U. in 1931, I had been almost completely ignorant of what bird students were doing in other lands. I thought, because their species of birds were largely different from ours, that there was little to learn from foreign bird-watchers. This mistaken viewpoint, I believe, was rather generally held by American birdwatchers, although professional ornithologists, of course, knew better. Gradually, from reading foreign journals and, in 1932, meeting so many foreign birds and ornithologists, I resolved to try my hand at educating Americans, as to what was being done in other countries in life history studies, and for foreigners as to what was being done in this country in the behavioural field.

I told the Gillespies about these ambitions.

"Nobody will read them," said they.

So I resolved that my reviews should be presented in as disarming and inviting a manner as possible.

Witmer Stone, eminent ornithologist and botanist, past-president of the A.O.U., edited the *Auk* from 1912 to 1936. He was a kindly gentleman, too courteous to criticize adequately contributions sent him or to judge the many publications he mentioned in his journal. This resulted in two situations unfavourable for American ornithology: difficulty in getting good papers published and the virtual absence of any real criticism of what did appear.

Mr. Whittle, editor of *Bird-Banding*, always eager to improve the scientific value of bird banding and of ornithology in general, welcomed my plans with enthusiasm. From its start in 1930, *Bird-Banding* had had a small review section written largely by Herbert Friedmann of Cowbird fame (1929), and John B. May, author of *Hawks of North America* (1935); they had mentioned briefly the contents of a number of foreign journals but without giving definite titles and references to the articles.

In January 1934 the first of my Review Sections appeared; 18 items were covered. By April and July there were 50 items each and this number was representative through 1942. In the early days I headed my reviews as follows:

The articles have been selected and arranged under subjects of importance to students of the living bird and also for the purpose of suggesting problems or aspects of problems to those banders who wish to make the most of their unique opportunities.

Titles and references in foreign languages were relegated to footnotes. In April 1938 I decided my readers would no longer be repelled by foreign words; I dropped the introductory paragraph and placed titles and references at the beginning of each review.

My aim was to pack as much pertinent, definite information as possible into each citation; to praise good work and honestly to reprove poor work.

Instead of presenting my reviews in alphabetical order according to authors. I arranged them under subjects, such as Banding and Migration, Censuses, Longevity, Weight, Life History, Ecology, Behaviour, Books, etc. This innovation met with some disapproval at first, but as the years went by, I was glad to note that more and more journals, abroad and at home, used this idea.

The benefits to me of conducting the Review Section were many. A great amount of literature, both domestic and foreign, came free, and I *had* to read it. "The only solution to achieving all this work," I noted, "is greatly increased efficiency in reading, grasping the essentials, and expressing them!" As a rule I wrote my review immediately upon reading the article, using a 4 x 6 inch card, which I afterwards filed in my burgeoning card catalogue. Undoubtedly the Reviews were a serious responsibility.

This fall 4M sang but little. I recorded singing from him only five days from September 30 to October 5.

On November 27, 1933, the first part of "Zur Naturgeschichte des Singammers" appeared in the *Journal für Ornithologie* splendidly translated by Dr. Desselberger. A proud sight. The same day a letter came from Dr. Stresemann, saying that "the more important second part is wonderful and I really know no other similarly oriented study that is anywhere near so full of substance and which should advance science so far forward" (translation mine).

Then, Dr. Stresemann, as President of the Eighth International Ornithological Congress which was to meet in Oxford, England, in July 1934, invited me to give a paper on my Song Sparrow researches. This was an exciting prospect.

The second part of the *Naturgeschichte* came out in January 1934. The kind *Deutsche Ornithologische Gesellschaft* made me a gift of 40 copies of my study. "A reward," I noted, "for the mighty labours of the past five years. It is really thrilling to me to read it — to get the continuity and fullness and something that approaches adequacy, instead of the brief articles I've published in English."

A welcome letter came from Ernst Mayr: "I consider your Song Sparrow work the finest piece of life-history work, ever done." And for the entire study he offered publication in the Linnaean Society of New York. "Even if it runs to three volumes." This promised to be a most welcome solution for the publication of my great study.

The Linnaean Society of New York, founded in 1878, two years after the Nuttall Club, is the second oldest natural history society in this country that is still flourishing. Established by several prominent ornithologists, among them C. Hart Merriam and A. K. Fisher, it numbered among its corresponding members John Burroughs and Theodore Roosevelt. In the 1930s it had a large and active membership of men and women and this remains true at the present time.

Another honour that spring consisted in the naming of a sub-species of Bewick's Wren for me by George Sutton. *Thryomanes bewickii niceae*, inhabitant of the far western Panhandle of Oklahoma was named "In honour of Mrs. Margaret Morse Nice, author of *The Birds of Oklahoma*." I was very pleased to have a race of such a choice little bird christened after me. And it was disappointing when this new race was rejected by the A.O.U. Committee on Nomenclature.

As to my Song Sparrows on Interpont in 1934, there were many discouragements. Twenty-eight of the 29 nesting males were banded and 18 of the 25 females. Cowbird parasitism was heavy. Only 13 nests were found, from six of which 14 Song Sparrow fledgelings were raised when I left for Europe by the 22nd of May.

XVII

The Ornithological Congress at Oxford*

Fortunately for me, my sister Katharine had decided to join me on the trip to Germany, Scandinavia, and England. On May 26, 1934, we embarked on the *S.S. Bremen*; travelling third class on this Norddeutscher Lloyd ship proved a pleasant experience.

In Germany we found that *Heil Hitler* had taken the place of *Guten Tag* and *Aufwiedersehen*. University students had to spend their Sundays in military exercises rather than in studying birds. In Berlin we saw the outsides of a *Museum gegen das Marxismus* and a Museum of War in which the "Big Bertha" of World War I was the chief attraction.

A memorable experience for me was an all-day hike in the Unterspreewald, 50 miles northeast of Berlin, with Herr Gottfried Schiermann who had published a notable study of censuses of these woods and meadows. We saw 55 species of birds; the most exciting of these to me were 11 individuals of five species of hawks, as well as the colony of White Storks nesting in ancient oaks, two, three and four nests in one tree.

I was glad to meet Dr. Hermann Desselberger, translator of my Song Sparrow manuscript for the *Journal für Ornithologie*. It was very pleasant to take tea with Herr Ludwig Schuster, his wife and their three small daughters, all dressed alike, and with their hair in braids. Herr Schuster was a tireless worker; busy all day in the Ministry of Agriculture, his evenings were devoted to his very interesting journal *Beiträge zur Fortpflanzungsbiologie der Vögel*

*The VIIIth International Ornithological Congress, Oxford, England, July 2-6, 1934.

(Contributions to the Breeding Biology of Birds) which appeared six times a year. Besides publishing original articles, he reviewed the pertinent literature from Germany and abroad. Sundays and vacations were spent in the field. Enough work for three men!

Our two-and-a-half weeks in southern Sweden and Norway were full of happiness. Both countries have fascinating outdoor museums to which ancient carved, wooden churches, and picturesque peasant houses have been moved. In Stockholm the Stadthuset is a noble building of modern design. The scenery on the railroad from Stockholm to Norway is magnificent.

Norway in June was a country of unsurpassed scenery with a wealth of wild flowers and interesting birds. To us one of the most striking of the latter was the Fieldfare (*Turdus pilaris*), a large, grey-headed, spotted-breasted thrush, a species that during the last 50 years had spread from the forests into parks and villages. The Norwegian ornithologist, H. Lövenskiold, told me that these birds are a nuisance because of their hearty appetite for fruit. The only notes we heard from them was a peculiar loud, grating, snarling *shak-shak*.

In contrast to two other abundant nesters that were strictly territorial — the Chaffinch and Willow Warbler[1] — the Fieldfare nests in groups. In an apple orchard near Hardinger Fjord we found five nests within 40 to 50 feet of one another; some held handsome eggs, blue with brown speckles, while others had babies covered with fawn-coloured down. And what an ear-splitting up-roar greeted our kindly interest! The reception of an intruding Hooded Crow[2] at one colony and a Magpie[3] at another made clear the advantages of gregarious nesting to this positive character, the Fieldfare.

On reaching Oxford on July 1 we were quickly aware of the thoughtfulness of the Local Executive Committee, for we found ourselves assigned to the same boarding house as Konrad and Margarethe Lorenz. I had read Dr. Lorenz's paper on the "Ethology of Social Corvids" in the *Journal für Ornithologie*, and he had read mine on the *Singammer* in the same journal, so we greeted each other with delight.

Three hundred and eleven ornithologists from 25 countries had gathered together for the purpose of telling their discoveries, sharing their experiences, becoming friends, and protecting the birds.

Mornings were devoted to papers which were given in English,

---

[1]*Phylloscopus trochilus.* [2] Now called Eurasian Crow and considered conspecific with the Carrion Crow, *Corvus corone.* [3] Black-billed Magpie, *Pica pica.*

German, French, and Italian. Section I was concerned with Taxonomy, Zoo-Geography, Life-History and Behaviour; Section II with Anatomy and Physiology; Section III with Migration and Ecology; and Section IV with Aviculture and Protection. I was listed as one of four Vice-Chairmen of this last section, but was never called upon to officiate.

Banding was much to the fore in Section III, both in the matter of homing experiments and of migration. A notable report was given by my friend, Werner Rüppell, on Starlings, 353 of which had been caught at their nesting boxes from all over Germany and released at Berlin, 106 having been subsequently captured at or near their homes. Long papers illustrated with many maps on migration as shown by recoveries of ringed birds were shown by Dr. E. Lönnberg for Sweden, Dr. Ernst Schüz for Rossitten, Dr. Rudolf Drost for Heligoland, and Mr. H. F. Witherby and Miss E. P. Leach for England.

Censuses of water birds, game populations and of Common Herons[1] were discussed by three Englishmen – A. D. Middleton, Julian Huxley, and E. M. Nicholson. The last gentleman told us of the comprehensive census of herons in England in 1928 and of sample censuses in subsequent years. He suggested that such counts might be a good project for international study, but the consensus of opinion appeared to be that any publicity given to the numbers of herons might lead to increased persecution by fishermen.

Few papers dealt with life history or behaviour studies. There were Jean Delacour's on "First Rearing of Pittas[2] in Captivity (1938)." L. Studinka's report on the breeding habits of Montagu's Harrier[3] in Hungary (1938). Dr. Schüz's on the biology and ecology of the White Stork (1936), Julian Huxley's on "Threat and Warning Coloration in Birds (1938)," mine on "Territory and Mating in the Song Sparrow (1938)" and Dr. Lorenz's important discussion on "Comparative Sociology of Colony Breeding Birds (1938)".

One afternoon there were moving pictures. Notable were Edgar Chance's "The Cuckoo's Secret" which showed the bird laying in a Meadow Pipit's[4] nest and another film on the ejection of a Reed Warbler[5] chick by a nestling Cuckoo[6] and later the little foster parents alighting on the head of the great changeling to feed it. There were fine pictures of the Golden Eagle in Scotland by Captain Humphrey Gilbert, and a marvellous one of the Gannets[7]

---

[1]*Ardea cinera.* [2]Hooded Pitta, *Pitta cucullata.* [3]*Circus pygarus.* [4]*Anthus pratensis.* [5]European Reed-Warbler, *Acrocephalus scirpaceus.* [6]Common Cuckoo, *Cuculus canorus.* [7] Northern Gannet, *Morus bassanus.*

at Grassholm exhibitited by Professor Huxley. Finally the home life of the Osprey was shown us by Horst Siewert with superb lantern slides.

On another afternoon we went to Foxwarren Park in Surrey. On the way we saw much pretty country, but the driver of our charabanc drove like the wind through narrow curving lanes and several times we almost had collisions. Mr. Alfred Ezra had many rare birds in his aviaries and his waterfowl collections of which the beautiful Pink-headed Duck (*Rhodonessa caryophyllacea*) of India was probably the rarest. It was an entertaining sight to watch the wallabies and blackbuck antelopes rushing over the hill-sides, and a disconcerting experience to meet a Sarus Crane[1] ready to attack us in defense of its nearby nest.

The Congress was distinguished by the number and brilliance of its social occasions. The first reception was given in the Town Hall by the Mayor of Oxford, Miss L. S. Tawny, a gracious, grey-haired lady in scarlet robes with a gold chain around her neck. After a bountiful tea, Her Worship showed some of us the ancient charters of the city of Oxford and the gorgeous gold and silver plate belonging to the city.

That same evening the Vice-Chancellor of the University, Dr. F. Lys, Provost of Worcester College, received us at the Ashmolean Museum, where, besides the art treasures, there was a special exhibit of contemporary British ornithological art with some notable pictures. For this occasion we were requested to wear academical and evening dress and many were gorgeous in the brilliant gowns pertaining to their colleges.

One of the members of the Congress was His Majesty, Ferdinand, Ex-King of Bulgaria, travelling incognito as "Graf Murany." I asked Dr. Stresemann at the reception to show me the King. He said he had not come but there was a Princess just behind me. She was Her Serene Highness, Princess Victoria, Countess of Solms, niece of "Graf Murany." She did not look very regal to me.

On Wednesday evening the President and Council of the Royal Society for the Protection of Birds invited us to a reception in Exeter College. Here, thanks to Miss Phyllis Barclay-Smith, distinguished worker for international bird protection, ornithologists danced to tunes played by the band of His Majesty's Coldstream Guards – a festive "proceeding never before recorded in the eight centuries of Oxfordian history," according to Dr. Stresemann.

---

[1] *Grus antigone.*

The dinner given by the British members of the Congress to the overseas guests was a very splendid affair. In the Great Hall of Christ Church — one of the most beautiful halls in England with Queen Elizabeth the First and King Henry the Eighth looking down at us, we sat on benches at seven long tables, the officers and chief dignitaries in robes and with decorations being seated at the top table. Here in the centre the President sat with the Ex-King at his right and the Princess at his left.

After dinner the Toastmaster, a special official, gained our attention by announcing in a stentorious voice, "My lords, ladies, and gentlemen, pray silence for your President, Prof. Dr. E. Stresemann," and so on for each of the speakers. After proposing the health of the King of England, Dr. Stresemann gave an excellent speech on the achievements of Oxford University in ornithology; Mr. Witherby spoke entertainingly on "Our Over-seas Guests;" while Sir Peter Chalmers Mitchell made a fine plea for bird protection.

The great event of the dinner for me was meeting Eliot Howard, author of *Territory in Bird Life* (1920), the book that opened the eyes of the ornithological world to this subject of fundamental importance. He talked to me about how each bird must be born with a consciousness of the size of territory he needs. I asked him whether he had read Bernard Altum's *Der Vogel und sein Leben* (1868), but apparently he had never heard of this book. He was eager to get hold of it and wanted to borrow my copy, but when I asked him whether he read German easily, he confessed he did not read it at all. He hoped it would be translated, but I feared there was little chance for this. So I said that I would translate the part about territory and send it to him, for which offer he was very grateful. Actually, the following year Ernst Mayr did publish a translation of Altum's statements on territory (1935). I introduced Mr. Howard to A. Landsborough Thomson, and they talked together until Mr. Howard hurried away. He was much of a recluse, practically unknown personally to British ornithologists except for Julian Huxley who was a close friend.

The Long Excursion proved a fitting climax to the Congress. One hundred and forty-five of us travelled all day in buses to the quaint little town of Tenby on the coast of Pembrokeshire in Wales.

For the trip to the bird islands we were guests of the British Admiralty who had put two destroyers at our disposal — the H.M.S. Windsor and H.M.S. Wolfhound. On the former a retired navel officer, Capt. H. L. Cochrane, conducted a number of us including Dr. Alden Miller of the University of California and several Germans, over the ship, explaining the guns, the three sets of steering gear, and other features. We climbed down ladders to visit the sailors' quarters and the engine room where the temperature was 120° F., but that was nothing to what it would be when the boat was really going! Capt. Cochrane was so cheerful in his explanation of the various death-dealing devices that it was gruesome to me. Here were we — the epitome of international friendship and cooperation, guests on a ship, that if politics should change a little, would do everything it could to blow us to bits.

On the first of the bird islands — Skokholm — the owner, R. M. Lockley, author of fine books on puffins, shearwaters (1942) and Islands in general, had birds and their nests carefully labelled for us; Puffins[1], Storm Petrels[2], Manx Shearwaters[3], Oystercatchers[4], Greater[5] and Lesser Black-backed Gulls[6], Razorbills[7], and others. At the next island — Skomer — there were incredible numbers of the absurd little Puffins; the ground was honey-combed with Shearwater nests in rabbit burrows, while the greatest sight of all was an immense cliff crowded with thousands of Guillemots[8] on their nests with here and there a snow-white Kittiwake[9].

By an old stone wall Captain Gilbert, author of *Secrets of the Eagle and Other Rare Birds* (1925) had inadvertently broken into a Manx Shearwater's nest and the owner was biting his leg. He took out the egg which proved to be addled. "We'll give it to one of the foreigners," said he, but one of the Englishmen asked for it. Captain Gilbert was sorry that he had disturbed the bird but comforted himself that he had saved the pair from their useless task. We went on, but three of the group stayed and hunted on the wall. "That's all they came for — just to get eggs," he exclaimed. Later Dr. Carmichael Low, author of *The Literature of the Charadriformes*, i.e. shorebirds (1924), told me of the reprehensible activities of some of the oölogists. His only solace was that eventually the miscreants would die.

And then we sailed to Grassholm, and when we drew near it seemed as if the island were covered with new-fallen snow. It was a marvellous sight — acres and acres of the great white gannets on their nests! We circled the island twice and were lucky enough to see some great grey seals.

---

[1] Common Puffin, *Fratercula arctica*. [2] British Storm-Petrel, *Hydrobates pelagicus*. [3] *Puffinus puffinus*. [4] Common Oystercatcher, *Haematopus ostralegus*. [5] Great Black-backed Gull, *Larus marinus*. [6] *Larus fuscus*. [7] *Alca torda*. [8] Common Murre, *Uria aalge*. [9] Black-legged Kittiwake, *Rissa tridactyla*.

The return trip in the evening was beautiful with the graceful gulls following the ships. And then came the Manx Shearwaters in a great stream hurrying home to Skomer. Before reaching the island, however, they settled on the water, waiting for the darkness to fall which would protect them from the Great Black-backed Gulls on the return to their nests.

When we reached Pembroke Dock Dr. Stresemann made a speech of thanks to the British Admiralty, Commander Wilson, and the officers and men for this great treat; he said they must have had a special understanding with Neptune and St. Peter for the calm and perfect weather that had prevailed. (Some of us had to inquire about this allusion, and we found out that in Germany St. Peter makes the weather.) The Commander answered saying it had been a most amusing event for them; they were all amazed to learn that the official name of the Manx Shearwater was *Puffinus puffinus puffinus*!

On the bus from the dock to Tenby I was seated by genial M. Charles Dupond, editor of the Belgian ornithological journal, *Le Gerfaut*. He could speak and understand very little English and less German; my French was poor and choked by German, but we both could read and write English, so we communicated in writing. This was mostly about exchanging his journal with *Bird-Banding*. I thought I'd try a little spoken English so I said, "Have you ringed many birds this year?" He thought a moment and then had an inspiration: "Oh, thousands and thousands," at which statement I was surprised. He continued. "How grand those *Sula bassana* were!" So he must have thought I had asked him about the gannets.

The return trip to Oxford was a very friendly experience. People moved about in our bus and visited with one another. The Rev. F. C. R. Jourdain, Secretary of the Congress, was scandalized by the informality of some of the men in taking off their coats in response to the heat; he insisted that all coats be put on before tea at Stanway House as guests of the Earl and Countess of Wemyss. After this pleasant break Konrad Lorenz shared my seat. He described dramatically the behaviour of his hand-raised Jackdaws that looked upon him as their mate: they insisted upon feeding him and if he didn't open his mouth, they jammed the tidbits into his ear!

No one at the Congress wore his name and there was little interest in introducing people, so I feel sure some of the members had lonely times. Dr. Stresemann said to me: "Because of your paper in the *JFO* you are well known in Europe. The other

Americans have published good work in American journals but Europeans do not know of them." So thanks to Ernst Mayr, Erwin Stresemann, and the Song Sparrows, my experience at the Congress had been most gratifying. Of all the new friends I had found, Konrad Lorenz was the most important. I felt that with his statement that a display releases or inhibits action in another animal of the same species, he had given us a fundamental key to animal behaviour.

The Eighth International Ornithological Congress was a very great occasion for those fortunate enough to participate. Many elements made up the picture: Oxford with a cloudless sky and all the glory of the ancient colleges; the unselfish labours of the officers and members of committees; the generous hospitality of our many kind hosts; the conversations with ornithologists from many lands; the charm of the President, who, with his delightful humour and gift for friendship always says the happy gracious thing; and finally the never-to-be-forgotten day with the sea-birds. Dr. Stresemann wrote me afterwards, "Der Congress war zu schön um wahr zu sein."

XVIII

4M Sings 2,305 Songs in One Day

After the Congress, Katharine and I attended the Drama Festival in Malvern where we saw many plays, as well as George Bernard Shaw in person. On our return to London we both worked in libraries, Katharine at the famous British Museum, for she was a writer of distinguished poetry and prose (1951). I laboured at the Natural History Museum.

One warm morning I grew weary of reading and copying notes and decided to take a trip to try to find a Reed Bunting[1], prototype of territory-holders in two of Eliot Howard's books – *Territory in Bird Life* (1920) and *Introduction to the Study of Bird Behavior* (1929). I took a bus to Tring, famed for Lord Rothschild's Museum with its great collection of bird skins. Out we trundled past Featherbed Lane, Raven's Lane, and Roast Cow Hamlet, as well as eating places called Spotted Cow, Hit or Miss, and Hog in Pound.

At my destination I found it hard to discover a bit of shade not pre-empted by thistles and nettles, but at length I succeeded. As I was eating my picnic lunch, I suddenly heard a loud song from a bush near by. Here at last was an *Emberiza schoeniclus*, unafraid, singing and preening himself. He was a handsome fellow, larger than a Song Sparrow, looking somewhat like a Harris' Sparrow with his black hood and throat (1944 a).

His song has been described as a tinkling *tweek, tweek, tweek, tittick* with variants. In some ways it would be an easier bird to study than the Song Sparrow, because the female lacks the black

---

[1]Common Reed-Bunting.

on the head, and first winter plumages are somewhat different from those of adults. Nevertheless, I was thankful that my special territory holder was *Melospiza melodia* with his great variety of pleasant, original, and often beautiful songs.

On July 28 we boarded our old friend the *S.S. Bremen* and five days later were met in New York by Blaine and Janet, and whisked up to Pelham. Here we rejoiced in a reunion both with the family and with the well-loved birds of Grey Rocks.

My young nephew, Will's son Alfred, fired by reading a book *The Friendly Stars* (1935) by Martha Evans Martin, had been studying the evening stars with enthusiasm. I was aware, of course, that there were bright and beautiful stars and I knew a fair number of constellations, but never before had I known a star by name except Polaris. Study of the individual first-magnitude stars came as a revelation to me.

I wrote on September 1:

Last night I made acquaintance for the first time with two ancient, splendid stars — Arcturus and Vega. It is like enjoying the individual singers of the spring chorus instead of hearing it as a general blur of song. It is like the first year I knew Uno and the delight afterwards when I distinguished his six songs.

Ten days later I noted:

Last night was marvelously clear and I was able to identify practically every constellation visible — Pegasus, Andromeda and Aries, Aquarius, Pisces and Capricornus. Also the great stars — Fomalhaut and Antares. I want to make the map of the heavens a permanent possession.

We returned to Columbus on September 20. Ten days later 4M started to sing. This was a blessing and comfort in face of the unspeakable desolation we had found on Interpont. The surly overseer of the gardens for the unemployed told us that "The Government has taken up the land and has been cleaning up the trash." By this he meant most of the shrubs, many of the trees, and the weed patches. All cover had been burnt. Our own place was an oasis and a refuge.

A partial compensation for the loss of the wealth and variety of wildlife came through a mighty roost established by Starlings and Grackles in shade trees in town a half mile to the east of us. The birds were not welcomed here but all efforts to dislodge them proved fruitless. They stayed until the leaves fell in mid-October.

I was rising early each morning to study the awakening song of 4M and to check in relation to light values with a photometer borrowed from the University. A discovery awaited me: here on the first of October were the winter evening constellations in all their glory — Orion and Auriga, Tauris and Canis Major, with their great stars, Betelgeuse and Rigel, Capella, Aldebaran, and brightest of all, Sirius. To think that I had lived 50 years and never before had known Sirius!

On the clear morning of October 9, the earliest singers were roosters, and I could not help thinking how fortunate we are that the chant of this barnyard fowl is so musical. The crow of the Ring-neck Pheasant[1] is a pitiful excuse in comparison. Black-crowned Night Herons *quawked*, and Killdeer uttered their lamentable cries. A young Song Sparrow gave his pretty warbling while all the first magnitude stars still shone, but 4M waited until all were gone but Capella and Sirius. Then at 25 minutes before official sunrise he started with A. The sweet high hymn of the White-throated Sparrow, the rollicking song of the Carolina Wren and the bubbling explosion of the House Wren, as well as an occasional *cheer cheer cheer* from the Cardinal — all these were heard before a clamour in the distance turned into a roar. The blackbirds were preparing to leave. The roar continued and just as Sirius faded, out burst the first flock of Starlings.

My notes each minute from 6:26 to 6:36 (the time of official sunrise) read as follows:

First flocks — Starlings and a few Grackles. More Starlings. More Starlings. More Starlings, a few Grackles. More Starlings, many Grackles. No one coming. Flocks of Starlings; still the roar from the roost. *Immense* flocks, all Grackles. A few flocks. *Tremendous* flocks of Grackles, a few Starlings.

Six minutes later, I wrote:

Now they come, the last great exodus — Starlings and Grackles flying northwest. Still going, all Grackles, or nearly all, flying north and northwest. Small flocks, no, *multitudes* of Grackles and a few Starlings. A few Grackles have alighted in trees in our neighbours' grounds to the east and south. Silence from the roost.

In 21 minutes the roost had been emptied.

The morning flights were exciting, but they were outdone by the spectacle in the evenings. In the morning, the birds left the roost in many directions but all seemed to return over Interpont. About a half hour before sunset the show began. Great flocks of one or both species flew rapidly overhead to the meeting place. Sometimes a group dropped down into the neighbours' trees; at

---

[1]*Phasianus colchicus.*

first it was only Grackles perching there and keeping up a constant chorus, but soon a company of Starlings dove down to join them, and I had hopes that a small roost might be established in our vicinity. But no, a sudden silence, as multitudes whirled off for their goal. As sunset neared, the cohorts increased. They came in clouds and armies that blackened the sky and when we thought that all the blackbirds in Ohio must have passed over our heads, suddenly a new host appeared. At sunset the pageant ceased. All had assembled.

Shortly after our return to Columbus, I was proud and happy to learn that I had been elected a Corresponding Member of the Deutsche Ornithologische Gesellschaft.

A.O.U. met in Chicago this fall*, partly to enable us to visit the Century of Progress. This Fair proved disappointing to our family because it did not emphasize the best in our civilization but was largely a glorification of features that many of us deplore — the indifference to beauty in form, colour, and sound, the artificiality, the purposelessness — or, as Tagore had said — "the stupendous unmeaning" of so much of modern activity. I contrasted it most unfavourably with the dignity and beauty of the Columbian Exposition in Chicago which I had visited as a nine-year-old child forty-one years earlier.

At the meeting Albert R. Brand of Cornell University reported on his new method for intensive study of bird song by photographing songs on motion picture film (1935). George Saunders, whom we had helped in bird study when he was a high school boy in Oklahoma, talked on the natural history of Meadowlarks. I spoke on "The Inheritance of Song in Song Sparrows," which really should have been entitled "the non-inheritance." William I. Lyon of Waukegan, Illinois, gave a paper on "Results from Banding 65,000 Birds." Mr. Lyon was a tireless bander, but, despite all Mr. Whittle's endeavours, never reported his findings adequately in print.

In December Blaine and I drove to the Wilson Club meeting in Pittsburgh, Pennsylvania*, taking with us our good friend Ed Thomas, Curator of Zoology at the Ohio State Museum, chief sponsor of the Wheaton Club, photographer and writer of a distinguished nature column for the *Columbus Dispatch*. Highlights of

---

*The 52nd Stated Meeting of the American Ornithologists' Union, Chicago, Illinois, October 22-25, 1934.

---

*The 20th Stated Meeting of the Wilson Ornithological Club, Carnegie Museum, Pittsburgh, Pennsylvania, December 28, 29, 1934.

the meeting were an exhibit on Wilsoniana by Bayard Christy, a fine conservationist and a humanitarian; a description of the discovery of the Harris' Sparrow eggs by George Sutton near Churchill, Manitoba (1932, Semple and Sutton); talks by the Secretary, Lawrence Hicks, on research on 52,000 Starlings and distribution of breeding birds in Ohio; and a plea for "Our Vanishing Raptors" by Warren Eaton. I talked on the Congress and on "Six Years' Records on the Singing of One Song Sparrow." It was a treat to meet Mrs. Rosalie Edge and to hear her describe her achievement in purchasing Hawk Mountain in Pennsylvania as a sanctuary for persecuted migrating hawks. Dr. C. Kingsley Noble of the American Museum was a new friend; he told me of his card catalogue of 10,000 references on bird behaviour. Dr. Josselyn Van Tyne was elected President of the society, while I was made Second Vice-President.

The winter was largely devoted to working on the "Population Study" volume for the Linnaean Society of New York. On January 29, 1935, I wrote:

I have all my references, i.e. things to look up in the libraries. There must be over 50! Selous certainly simplified life by reading nothing published on birds!

Preparation of reviews four times a year was personally helpful in giving me information and suggestions. Some were simple to do, others took much time and thought. One of the most significant was that of Konrad Lorenz's great article on "Der Kumpan in der Umwelt des Vogels" (1934). These reviews were published in *Bird-Banding* in July and October 1936, and excited considerable interest. Dr. Lorenz wrote me:

I was very much impressed with the way in which you have handled my paper. I know very well it was not the easiest thing reviewing it, all the better because I had to do it myself last week, in a psychological colloquium. You would have been surprised how very much the same points I picked out in my review, as you did in yours! That is what I liked so much in your reviews: you have picked out just those items that I myself should think most important.

I had asked several Americans to send reprints to Dr. Lorenz and in consequence, warm friendships arose. Wallace Craig wrote me that he had sent a whole set of his reprints to Altenberg and had received a seven-page letter in reply. I wrote Lorenz a five-page letter. I told him that his *Betrachtungen über das Erkennen der arteigenen Triebhandlungen der Vogel* (1932) is, to me, the most interesting paper I ever read on bird behaviour. His work reminds me of that of "my revered master, Professor Charles Whitman." Dr. Lorenz, in turn, informed me that he considered Dr. Craig "one of the most intelligent men existing" and he spoke of the "most fruitful discussion" they were having across the ocean.

Another friendship sprang up between Dr. Lorenz and Dr. Francis Herrick of Cleveland, Ohio, pioneer bird behaviour student, who had made notable contributions on the home life of many species — various passerines, Black-billed Cuckoo (1935) and Bald Eagle (1924). He wrote me that he considered Dr. Lorenz "about the ablest ornithologist alive." It was due to Dr. Herrick's initiative that Dr. Lorenz prepared a summary in English of his views on the *Kumpan* which was published by Dr. Witmer Stone in the *Auk* in 1937.

The brilliant and neglected English naturalist Edmund Selous had died in 1934. I wrote an article about him for *Bird-Banding* (1935), concluding thus: "he shows us the glory and wonder of nature with breath-taking passages that quicken our pulses, fire our imaginations, and fill our hearts with love for the wildlings. May his high and noble words help the wild creatures that were so dear to his heart."

Since the population of the Song Sparrows had dwindled so drastically, I resolved in 1935 to devote myself largely to 4M. From January on I spent many mornings recording his awakening song — the seventh season I had studied this wonderful bird. On January 7, 8, and 11, I heard four of the nine songs of his repertoire. Silence then till February 9. By March 2 the Song Sparrows had reached the spring level in their singing, the first songs starting about 34 minutes before sunrise on clear mornings.

Two days later I caught an exciting bird — 4M's daughter, hatched May 14, 1934. She was a small, permanent resident settled on a territory some 60 feet south of her birthplace. In late April she built on a lattice and astonished me by laying *large* eggs, despite her known youth and small size. Her mother was of medium size and had laid medium-sized eggs. These had been greenish in ground colour, closely speckled with tiny red-brown spots; those of her daughter had large, handsome, irregular splotches. Alas, 4M's daughter soon disappeared, probably a victim of the neighbour's cat.

I was not at all pleased when on March 7 4M's awakening song had come to an abrupt end. A mate had arrived — an unbanded bird. She proved to be a cold, old-maidish creature, tyrannizing over her fine husband like a veritable Xantippe. I tried to capture and displace her, but she ignored the trap. On April 9 I discovered 4M's pleasant mate of 1934 in a "miserable territory next the river with an unbanded mate." How I wished she could have rejoined 4M, instead of this good-for-nothing, trap-shy individual. Six days later I did catch Xantippe. She struggled the most and bit the hardest of any Song Sparrow I ever captured. Unfortunately it was now too late to carry out my plot for fear it might have left 4M without any mate at all.

On April 20, wonder of wonders, Xantippe started to build! This was in the neighbours' raspberry patch to the north where 4M's second mate in 1935 had nested. The next morning I watched for *three and a half hours*. She picked up six loads, dropped four and carried *two* to her nest. I heartily echoed the discouragement of Selous: "How barren is this watching! How little does it lead to!"

Nine days later she started to line her nest, taking two loads in an hour, a great achievement for her. On May 3 she finally started to lay. The eggs, however, were punctured by House Wrens and 4M's poor excuse of a wife disappeared never to be seen again.

From earliest dawn the deserted 4M was now singing gloriously every day. Here was my opportunity to record the total amount of song given in a day by a Song Sparrow. Vega, Arcturus, and Jupiter shone down on me as I came out into the garden at 4:42 a.m. C.S.T. on May 11. Wood Thrushes and robins were already singing. Two minutes later (36 minutes before official sunrise) 4M began and until 5:50 a.m. sang steadily five times a minute before stopping for 35 seconds for a bite of breakfast. Until noon he sang almost continuously, giving from 200 to 278 songs an hour. The next three hours he averaged 150 songs an hour but after that he sang but little. The total for the day was 2,305 songs – this from a bird eight or more years old!

4M's nearest neighbours were the 221s, nesting in 5M's former territory; their nestlings hatched on May 13th and two left the nest on the 22nd. On the 28th I noticed that 4M had become silent. Was it the rain, or fatigue, or could he possibly have become engaged to 221M's mate? On the 30th I braved the eager mosquitoes and found 221M feeding a chick in his own land. His mate – Dandelion – however, was busy in our garden, feeding two chicks and making love to 4M who followed her hither and yon, occasionally bestowing a morsel on his step-children.

This situation presented a problem to us. If all went well, 4M and Dandelion would have a newly hatched family about June 20, just when we were due to leave for the East. For our daughter

Marjorie had become engaged to Carl Boyer, a fellow student at Columbus University, and instructor in mathematics at Brooklyn College. They planned to be married at Grey Rocks the end of June. Suggestions from me for a postponement were summarily rejected.

Dandelion had built her new nest in the north rose bush, the same place which two of 4M's former mates had used. She laid her eggs from June 2 to 6 and started to incubate. I resolved to exchange her set of fresh eggs with a set ready to hatch. I installed a canvas blind by the nest for I planned to make a careful study of the nest life of the pair. Ed Thomas had promised to take photographs, both moving and still, of 4M caring for babies.

The first egg hatched late in the afternoon of June 9. I slipped into the blind while 4M was not looking and cautiously peeped through the slit. There sat Dandelion, the picture of content. The extraordinary precocity of her brood apparently troubled her not at all. She yawned, then pecked at something and ate it, and soon slipped off. Nine minutes later she returned and gently fed a small insect to the baby, mincing the food into tiny fragments.

She preened herself, rose and looked beneath her, shook her feathers, and settled down once more. Presently she caught a mosquito and ate it — a helpful deed. At 5:27 she stood up and ate egg-shell. The second baby had hatched.

After supper I returned and until dark watched Dandelion's tender care of her foster babies. 4M evidently was unaware of the astonishing happenings in his household; he sang a good deal and twice guarded the nest during his mate's absences. She fed the infants seven times in the three hours I was in the blind.

The next morning I was out early, eager to continue the charming story of mother care and to see 4M's devotion to the babies. Alas, the nest was overturned and empty! What vicissitudes attended the Song Sparrows and my study of them! This was a major calamity for it would be too late now to make a second exchange with the next set.

The birds were not discouraged. The next day Dandelion was building in a tangle of bedstraw with 4M proudly watching her. On the 15th she laid her first egg. Fate was again against them, for Blaine, not knowing of the nest, cleared out the weeds and laid the nest bare. The next day the only new egg was a Cowbird's. We hoped that 4M and Dandelion would have better luck with a third attempt!

XIX

'The Population Study of the Song Sparrow.'

On June 19, 1935, we left in our car for Grey Rocks. Ten days later we witnessed a beautiful wedding between Marjorie and Carl in the same place where Blaine and I had been married 26 years earlier. Constance, Barbara and Janet were the bridesmaids and their gracious grandmother was full of pride and joy.

This summer I made no effort to find a warbler's nest. I rejoiced in the beauty of the Hermit Thrush's singing, and I thought of the debt we owe to birds for the wild magic of their songs with their unchangeable quality in this world which we have nearly ruined.

The absorbing task for me was working up the *Population Study of the Song Sparrow* for the Linnaean Society (1937). On July 13 I noted:

For nine days I've been working steadily on this project and it has been mostly a chore — a duty that *had* to be done. I merely plodded on and on in the heat. At last today, I grew enthused. Finally my creative daemon seized me and I had happy, triumphant feelings.

On August 24 I wrote:

Although I've worked so intensively on the Population Study all summer long, I haven't been able (except rarely) to have been really captured by the spirit of the thing, to have been engrossed by it, to make discoveries about it at odd moments. I think it's partly due to the fact that this is the second or third working over of the material for myself, which makes me feel it's old and well known and goes without saying. It's difficult for me to grow enthused over former discoveries. I always want to make new ones! In the meantime I leave my readers behind, because it needs repeated dinning in of new facts to impress the majority. Hence I often do not make enough of my discoveries, don't discuss them from enough angles, don't see their full significance.

The last of August, Blaine and I drove to New York City where I had helpful conferences with two friends. Ernst Mayr gave me some excellent, concrete suggestions on the Population Study. Bill Vogt, editor of *Bird-Lore*, explained his ideas on the popular book he had been encouraging me to write. He proposed my sending him several chapters on the lives of Uno and 4M for him to publish in his magazine, illustrated by Roger Tory Peterson. He felt almost positive he could get such a book published.

On our return to Columbus September 12, we found Interpont a fine tangle. Apparently there had been no destruction during the summer. Janet, her shephard dog, Rex, and I went around to the ancient sycamore by the Olentangy River and saw exactly one Song Sparrow, an unbanded juvenile without a tail.

A week later "4M sang A. He is alive, alive, alive. So life is good. And Interpont is a riot of colour."

I heard him sing a small amount on September 20 and 29 and from October 11 to 20. Again on the 30th, also on November 25 and 26, the last song I ever heard from him. 4M, who had surmounted difficulties and dangers for so many years, must at last have fallen a victim to some enemy.

In a letter earlier that year Dr. Stresemann has sent his regards to "world-famous 4M. May he reach a Biblical age!" And this he did in comparison with most small birds in the wild. Of my banded breeding Song Sparrows 76 males were recorded for two years, 24 for three years, eight for four years, one for five years, one for six years, and 4M for eight years. Juvenile Song Sparrows can be known as such by their warbling during their first autumn and winter; I never recorded the singing from this species during our first year on Interpont. So 4M must have been at least in his second year when he arrived on Interpont in September 1927; this would make him nine and a half years old (or possibly older) at the time of his death. Banded song birds of various species have been known to survive ten years and longer.

During the early years 4M was an overbearing individual, picking quarrels with his neighbours and dominating them, but by 1932 he had become much less quarrelsome. He was the most zealous singer of any of my Song Sparrows; he started in late January or in February according to the weather and sang well into July. The last of September he started once more and sang splendidly on pleasant days in October, the picture of abounding energy and joy in living. During the last two falls of his life he sang but little, but on May 11, 1935, he had sung a prodigious amount, as told in Chapter XVIII.

4M had had at least 11 mates while we knew him. Seven times he had been left a widower. Of the 17 nests started while we were on Interpont, only five succeeded, fledging 13 chicks. A son survived from a brood in 1931; he nested away from Interpont, two-thirds of a mile north of his birthplace. Here I banded two of 4M's grandchildren but never found either again. A daughter, hatched in 1934, started to nest some 60 feet south of her birthplace but lost her life shortly afterwards.

Since 1930 was the only year in which we spent all summer on Interpont and thus were able to carry on continuous observation, it is probable that in the other years 4M and his mates might have raised one or two families late in the season.

That he was intelligent was shown by his ignoring of a mounted Song Sparrow placed in his territory, in contrast to the displays and furious attacks dealt this intruder by 4M's male neighbours to the west and south when confronted by the dummy. Although not shy toward me, he must have been cautious in regard to boys with guns and especially alert in escaping other dangers. Bill Vogt once wrote me: "I am sure 4M bids fair to become the most famous bird in the world. He was, after all, one of the most important birds that ever lived."

For eight years I had devoted myself to Song Sparrows. During the seasons of alternating expectation and frustration, of triumph and failure, there had been one unfailing comfort – the dauntless cheer of this treasured bird and the wonder of his long life.

This college year, Janet was our only daughter at home, for Constance was in a Teachers' College in Iowa, Marjorie in New York City and Barbara was a junior at Massachusetts State College in Amherst. To lighten my correspondence I started a series of "Interpont Chronicles" and thus typed a half dozen or more copies at one session. These chronicles gave vivid pictures of our life in Columbus.

Lawrence Hicks drove Mr. James C. Hambleton and me to the A.O.U. meeting in Toronto, Canada.* Mr. Hambleton was a genial gentleman, just retired from the post of supervisor of Nature Study in Columbus schools. Lawrence proved a most interesting guide, pointing out the geology, ecology and biology of all sorts of things as we sped along.

---

*The 53rd Stated Meeting of the American Ornithologists' Union, Royal Ontario Museum, Toronto, Canada, October 21-24, 1935.

The President of A.O.U. was kindly Arthur C. Bent, while the posts of Secretary and Treasurer were still held by Messrs. Palmer and McAtee. It was a crowded program of 67 papers that required three double sessions. Marguerite Heydweiler (later Mrs. Fred Baumgartner) gave a fine talk on "Sex and Age Studies of Wintering Tree Sparrows." Two papers were on Cowbirds. Dr. Harry Hann of Ann Arbor told of watching females of this species laying at dawn in Ovenbird nests, from which they usually removed a host egg the day before or after depositing their own. These were new and exciting discoveries. In my paper on "The Cowbird in Ohio" (1936 a), based on Lawrence Hicks's and my experiences, I told the audience that, as a matter of patriotism, we should boost our parasite that has had so little fame in comparison to the European Cuckoo.

Dr. T.S. Roberts's moving pictures "Adventures in Kodachrome" were disappointing for, although the yellows and buffs came out in natural colours, this was far from true with the greens. It was thrilling to see and hear Arthur Allen's sound pictures of the booming of the Lesser Prairie Chicken. Especially noteworthy were the sound pictures of Paul Kellogg of Cornell University of the Ivory-billed Woodpecker at its last stand as known at that time in this country in the primeval forests of Louisiana.

After the meeting we drove to Drehersville, Pennsylvania. For some 50 years this had been the scene of merciless slaughter of migrating hawks, but in 1934 the mountain was purchased by that wonderful woman, Rosalie Edge, who made it into a sanctuary for hawks and other wildlife. On October 27 we spent seven hours on top of the mountain. The weather was too mild and there was too little wind for a spectacular flight, but 99 hawks seemed quite a number to us. Some came very near, while others flew exceedingly high. We saw seven species of hawks, a great flock of Turkey Vultures, and 40 Canada Geese. There were 160 human visitors that day; at times they have much larger crowds. Hawk Mountain is proving of great educational value both in this country and abroad. It has been fortunate in its dedicated and efficient guardians, Maurice and Irma Broun.

After Christmas, Lawrence Hicks drove Blaine and me to the Wilson Club meeting at St. Louis*. On the trip we had great discussions on Song Sparrow problems. It was a treat to meet the fine ornithologist, Lillie Ernst. I found it fun being Second

*The 21st Stated Meeting of the Wilson Ornithological Club, St. Louis, Missouri, December 29-31, 1935.

Vice-President.

On January 21, 1936, after seven months of labour, I sent off two copies of "The Population Study of the Song Sparrow" for criticism. One went to New York City for Ernst Mayr and Bill Vogt, the other to Ames, Iowa, for Paul Errington. (Paul and Carolyn had visited us for several days in the fall, and I had benefited from Paul's suggestions.)

A great event for Columbus naturalists was the five-day visit to us in February of Erwin Stresemann. He talked on "Homing in Birds," first to the Audubon Society, later to the Biology Club of the University. On a bitterly cold morning I showed him over Interpont. "Many ornithologists will envy me the opportunity to see this place," said he. Alas, there was no 4M to grace the study area. Dr. Stresemann liked to watch the feeding shelf and to handle the birds I caught, several of which were new to him. On Sunday, three carloads of us drove out to Buckeye Lake where we saw some gorgeous Red-headed Woodpeckers (a great delight to our guest), some "famous poison ivy," (native only to North America), and at Newark, impressive Mound-builder Earthworks made by prehistoric Indians.

The winter of 1936 was record-breaking in the persistence of low temperatures, snow and ice. It was not until the last week of February that spring came for a three-day visit, bringing with it the first migrants as well as a great flood over the river bottoms.

After this winter of winters it was strange to have little birds hurrying back to us at the first hint of a let-up in the cold, at the first excuse of a few mild days. First came the robins, then Killdeer, Red-Winged Blackbirds, a flicker, and finally a Fox Sparrow — my only record for February. Interpont was littered and jammed with great ice cakes after the flood. It was curious to see bright-breasted robins running about in the open places between the massive chunks of ice. It looked like the Arctic, not central Ohio.

In late March we drove to New York City to take my mother to the homes of her youngest and eldest sons. The weather was stormy; the car slipped and would have backed down a steep hillside but for a strong fence that held it. Rescued from this predicament, we continued on our way. The mountains of Pennsylvania had never looked lovelier — a fairyland of soft snow with a brilliant sunset to add to the glory. But soon we were stuck in a snow drift with a blizzard howling around us and no anti-freeze in the car! Blaine put on the chains, and we thankfully started again while the wind whirled blinding snow in a thick mist around us.

It was a happy experience visiting Marjorie and Carl in their attractive flat. Barbara joined us at Marjorie's and told us the glad news of her engagement to Stanley Thompson, a senior at Amherst College.

I had helpful conferences with Ernst Mayr on the Population Study and also with Bill Vogt on the same subject, as well as on the first of my contributions to *Bird-Lore*, "The Way of a Song Sparrow" (1936).

Tributes came to my work with the Reviews. In June 1935 I was made an Associate Editor of *Bird-Banding*. That same month came a letter from Dr. James Schenk of Budapest, saying I had been elected a Corresponding Member of the Royal Hungarian Institute of Ornithology — "in appreciation of your merits in Bird-studies." In the German Ornithological Society I was promoted from Corresponding to Honourary Membership.

In the February 1936 issue of *Bird-Lore*, Bill Vogt devoted the whole editorial page to my Reviews. He wrote:

We are fortunate in having in the United States a guide to literature concerning the living bird . . . and *Bird-Banding* is rendering real service in devoting its pages to these reviews.

To devote 29 per cent of an issue may, without knowledge of them, seem disproportionate; but to one who is familiar with them, and comes more and more to depend on them for an account of what is being done by students of bird life, there often recurs the wish that they might be even more extended.

Mrs. Nice comments, compares conclusions and criticizes. More than this, she distills from each paper its essence, in a few words she conveys results, and an idea of methods to the reader . . . We do not with to leave the impression that these pages in *Bird-Banding* are a compound of scientific dullness and egregious profundity. They are not; they skim the very cream from a growing knowledge of how birds live, and while they are all but indispensable to the "serious" worker, they are as alive as a morning full of May migrants.

One joint undertaking with the central Ohio naturalists consisted in our broadcasts over the State University's radio station WOSU. In the spring of 1933 I had been asked to give a number of broadcasts on birds, and this gave me the idea of planning a series of nature talks by a group of naturalists. Six three-month sets were given from the fall of 1933 through March 1936. I organized the project, got speakers and prepared the announcements which were put out by the University. Twenty-six people gave 78 broadcasts. Wheaton Club members were my chief standbys — Lawrence Hicks, Ed Thomas, J. C. Hambleton, Blaine, and others. It was a fine set of talks with a wide variety of topics, yet the response was not great.

For each program I listed the talks and the speakers, gave a brief note on each speaker, recommended bird books and devoted a page to propaganda. The authors quoted were Euripides, Thoreau, Herbert Sass, Edmund Selous, Edward Forbush, and W. L. McAtee. I will quote here the selection from the last author's bulletin on "Preface to Fish-eating Birds" (1935), as it is excellent, yet seems to have been generally overlooked:

With a feeling of fellowship, and a desire to understand, it is a revelation what enjoyment there is in every contact with a bird, a beast, a tree or a flower. With every such experience, conviction deepens that after all we are fellow creatures, each in its own way engaged in the pursuit of happiness. It does not take many realizations of this vital truth to make a nature lover — one whose attitude toward wild things, on every possible occasion, will be that of appreciating and protecting because he may, instead of dominating and oppressing because he can.

I had not intended to do much with Song Sparrows this spring but it was hard to ignore them. Nine of 18 nesting males were banded, four of 12 females. Twelve nests contained 52 Song Sparrow eggs, of which 17 hatched and fledged safely (32.7 per cent). They also contained 12 Cowbird eggs from which five young were fledged (41 per cent).

I will quote from Chronicles XVI and XVII some details concerning these Cowbirds:

May 18, 1936. There are great Cowbird excitements on Interpont nowadays. Three hatched Saturday and four Sunday. One hatched six days later than its brother and lived only one day. Two in another nest hatched the same day.

But the one that had the greatest adventures was the egg laid in 253M's nest. A possum or some other enemy had dragged out the nest but failed to eat the eggs, which I found hidden under the nest material. As an experiment I put the Cowbird egg into a Robin's nest in which I knew incubation had just started. Robins often do not tolerate Cowbird eggs, but this Robin did so very nicely. I feared, of course, that the egg might have been addled from its rough treatment, but what was my astonishment yesterday to discover that two Robins and my experimental Cowbird were hatched!

I don't blame Cowbirds for seldom laying in Robins' nests. Although these birds are the same age, the poor little waif is entirely dwarfed by his giant companions. But he is holding up courageously. This morning Robin No. 3 was just hatching as I reached the nest and he looked three times as big as the egg out of which he had just emerged. This evening my tiny orphan was still asking for food. I do hope he survives but I fear that would be a miracle. Most things are relative in this world; usually it is the Cowbird that is the monster.

May 22. My brave little Cowbird was found squashed on the third morning. How those Robin "foster-parents" do hate me! They come rushing to the scene when they see me approaching and shriek and scream their loudest!

In April I had plunged into the final revision of the Population Study. On May 15 I noted:

I'm gloriously, gloriously happy. I'm perfectly fascinated by the "Population Study" and am making discoveries every day. The "Start of Laying" is my greatest delight. I'm whipping it into something to be proud of.

On June 25 I sent the finished manuscript to Ernst Mayr. I noted in my journal:

It has taken *one solid year of work writing it up*, not counting the half year I spent preparing the first version for *JFO*. Have done almost no field work for a year, no trips (except two to New York and two to bird meetings), very little other writing except four sets of Reviews and translating Dr. Schüz's article on the White Stork for *Bird-Banding*. Well, it's an achievement.

This was our last year in Columbus, for in late August we moved to Chicago. We left Columbus with many regrets, for we hated to leave the wildlife and the friendly naturalists. We had enjoyed the Audubon Society with its monthly lectures, given for the most part by members of the Wheaton Club, and its monthly field trips led by the same gentlemen. I had finally been admitted to the monthly meetings of this club as an "unofficial honorary member." How I would have benefited from this opportunity for discussion of my problems earlier in the study of Song Sparrows! Blaine had just been elected to the presidency of the club. I was vice-president of the Columbus Audubon Society and slated to be its next president but neither of these presidencies came to pass. Our delightful German friend and neighbour, Mrs. Gerhard Lamers, said, "Columbus will be empty for me." And Ed Thomas lamented, "It is nothing short of a tragedy for Columbus."

It was sad to leave Interpont, but we had no control over most of it, for our land comprised only about one of its sixty acres. We regretted leaving our loved Fossil Canyon, just north of Columbus, where in early spring there was a glory of hepaticas and snow trilliums. And south of Columbus nature was exciting in the Hocking County spectacular State Parks as well as in Athens County on the Nice family farm.

I owe a great deal to Interpont and the opportunity at our doorstep to study such a notable species as the Song Sparrow. Indeed, with its rich variety of individual songs it seems to me the most admirable bird imaginable for an intensive study, for each male is a unique personality. And when he dies these songs are lost forever. This is the sorrowful aspect of a study such as mine.

XX

A
Warm Welcome
to Chicago

Blaine was now head of the Physiological and Pharmaceutical Departments in the Chicago Medical School on the west side of the city at 710 Wolcott Avenue. Although he had to drive seven miles each day to reach the Medical School, he was happy in his teaching, for he had never given nor helped give better courses than here. As in his other teaching positions he was loved by his students because of his warm sympathy for them.

I had written to our friend of Oklahoma days, Marjorie Allee, gifted author of books for girls, asking her advice as to where best to settle in Chicago. She recommended the vicinity of the University saying that the house of our friends the Percival Coffins was on the market, for Mr. Coffin had recently died and Mrs. Coffin had left the city. The house at 5708 Kenwood Avenue was old-fashioned with four very large rooms on the first floor, two large and three small ones on the second floor and a spacious attic. The small back yard boasted a large and handsome bur oak and a smaller ailanthus. We lived here for eight years.

Janet liked her school which was just around the corner from our house and Constance enjoyed Gregg Secretarial School.

As for me, for the first time I had an adequate study, usable both summer and winter. We bought from Mrs. Coffin's niece four large glass-enclosed book cases for my books and journals, and rescued from the basement a sizable filing case which Mr. Coffin had used in his business. This had four tiers of drawers: the top with four small drawers for 3" x 5" cards, the next with three larger drawers for 4" x 6" cards, and below four still larger drawers in two tiers. Here I established at the top an elaborate filing system for references to reprints, while in the next tiers I housed my annotated references on the behaviour and ecology of the bird: as individual, as mate and parent, and as member of society. In the bottom tiers I arranged my life history cards by species, families, and orders. Reprints were lodged in numbered boxes in a book case on the sun porch. The pieces of furniture from the Coffins proved life-savers for me in caring for my ever-growing ornithological library.

Constance, Barbara, and Janet all helped with the formidable task of filling in the multitudinous cards. As I read for the reviews, I customarily made a card for each article or book, composed the review from this, then filed it in the most appropriate spot. It was an ambitious scheme and a helpful one until at length it broke down, for lack of a full-time ornithologically trained secretary to take care of it.

We were given the warmest of welcomes by the bird people. W. Clyde Allee, author of *The Social Life of Animals* (1938), invited us to the weekly meetings of the Zoo Club at the University of Chicago and to the Ecological Seminar which met each Monday evening either at the Allees' or at Alfred Emerson's, specialist on termites. These meetings were stimulating, and I was invited to speak at both.

R. M. Strong, founder of the Chicago Ornithological Society in 1912, and at this time again its president, invited us to its meetings. The C.O.S. had started as an exclusive body of expert bird students. Dr. Strong was its first president and Mrs. Coffin the first secretary; later she became president, as did our friend, Mrs. W.H. Richardson. During the presidency of Rudyerd Boulton of the Field Museum, the requirements for membership were liberalized and by 1936 everyone interested in birds was welcomed. I was promptly elected to a vice-presidency in this eager group. Our family enjoyed the monthly meetings and monthly field trips.

As for the Illinois Audubon Society, I soon found myself a Director. This Society, founded in 1897, was one of the earliest State Audubon societies in the country. Orpheus Schantz, who later helped establish the Great Smoky Mountains National Park, was president from 1914 to 1930; from then until 1941 C. W. F. Eifrig held the chair, after which Dr. Strong headed the society for another decade. Monthly meetings of the directors were devoted to discussions on conservation problems. Starting in 1916 the society has published a quarterly *Audubon Bulletin*. Of late years they have presented each year without charge to the public a half dozen of the National Audubon illustrated lectures.

Native birds were scarce around our home, but were abundant in migration at nearby Jackson Park. On the lake front in winter we found many ducks of which the charming little Oldsquaws[1] were our favourites.

Chicago is fortunate in its splendid Forest Preserves that surround it on three sides. They were established from 1904-1915 by the Cook County Forest Preserve District after the plans of Jens Jensen, far-seeing landscape architect for the Chicago West Park Commission. Mr. Jensen had a deep respect and love for our native landscape; he believed firmly in the brotherhood of all living things. The aim of the Forest Preserves is the preservation of their 55,720 acres of native landscape in their natural condition.

At the start people were invited to gather wild flowers and to camp. At that time access from Chicago to these areas was either by taking a train, a very long buggy ride, or, in a few cases, an electric interurban. In 1920 Jens Jensen considered the recently created Forest Preserves to be so remote that they could never be of importance to the citizens of Chicago. "But by 1927 the horse and buggy had disappeared, [and] the automobile had taken the country by storm" (1939). Camping had to be forbidden and automobiles restricted to the main roads.

Our favourite Forest Preserves were the Orland Wildlife Refuge and Long John Slough, both attractive to ducks, geese, and hawks. There were other choice places. The Morton Arboretum is a magnificent tract of 11,000 acres with a wealth of native and exotic trees and shrubs that make it an excellent haunt for birds, particularly of owls and northern finches. The Indiana Dunes, 50 miles to the southeast, presented a great deal of interest and charm for the naturalist.

In short, in those happy days before the curse of pesticides had come upon the world, there was a rich and varied bird life in the Chicago region.

In late October I travelled by train to Columbus where I visited with Barbara, now a senior at Ohio State University. Lawrence Hicks drove me to the A.O.U. at Pittsburgh*, a delightful meeting. My talk on "Do young birds return to the place of their birth?"

---

[1]*Clangula hyemalis.*

---

*The 54th Stated Meeting of the American Ornithologists' Union, Pittsburgh, Pennsylvania, October 19-22, 1936.

roused considerable discussion. In America, many banders believed they did not, while in Europe the evidence confirms the opposite view. With my Song Sparrows I had found that 26 males and 14 females out of 317 fledged nestlings returned as breeders — 4.5 to 20 per cent each year of those banded, averaging 12.6 per cent. Of these only five — 1.6 per cent of the total banded — were caught in our garden; the others had had to be captured on their nesting territories. The Song Sparrow is particularly faithful to the vicinity of its birthplace and especially to its nesting place. Some other species seldom return to the place of their birth; for instance, of 1,000 catbirds, banded as nestlings by Walter P. Nickell of Bloomfield Hills, Michigan, only one returned to nest in its natal locality (1965).

After Thanksgiving the Wilson Club* and Inland Bird-Banding Association met at the Chicago Academy of Sciences for two days of 30 papers, while the third was spent at the notable Brookfield Zoo. Dr. Van Tyne, President of the first society, presided on Friday; William I. Lyon, President of the second society presided on Saturday. Dr. Sewall Pettingill of Carlton College, Northfield, Minnesota, became the new Secretary of the Wilson Club, and I was promoted to first Vice-Presidency.

One ever-recurring occupation was the preparation of reviews for *Bird-Banding*. Mr. Whittle was always appreciative, writing: "a fine consignment," "a wealth of important material," "a mammoth piece of work." He was alert for possible papers for his journal, writing to many banders, urging them to work up their results for his journal. He once wrote me:

Regarding "conciseness," I surmise that you have very little idea of the labor put in to reduce and rearrange most notes and some articles and still maintain friendly relations with contributors. S . . . has been a problem. His July paper was reduced from 11 pp. to two! And just now it's M . . . who is likely to throw up the sponge. What do you think of a man who will prepare a major M.S. without having a *title* in mind?

Professor Frederick Saunders, President of the Northeastern Bird-Banding Association, asked Thomas T. McCabe, Research Associate in Botany at the University of California at Berkeley, to write some articles for *Bird-Banding*. Mr. McCabe declined, but suggested that: "Mrs. Nice might care occasionally to assign something [to him] for somewhat extended review." Thus started our

*The 22nd Stated Meeting of the Wilson Ornithological Club, Chicago, Illinois, November 27-29, 1936.

cooperative efforts. From April 1936 through April 1940 *Bird-Banding* published, in 15 issues, 111 of his reviews as well as 719 of mine.

Mr. McCabe was ornithologist, mammalogist, and botanist — a brilliant man, original and rather erratic. Time and again he wrote entertaining reviews but often failed to give the gist of the contribution. I tried to impress him with the technique I used in *Bird-Banding*, once writing him: "My basic idea in the reviews is to abstract papers, giving the meat of each article, some definite facts that will be of distinct value to the student, even though he may not be able to read the original." He would try to do better but without consistent success.

He had great ambitions for our reviews. On August 14, 1936, he wrote me:

There is an immediate need for a complete set of abstracts and reviews of ornithological matters in the country. We have a chance, by supplying it, to force *B-B* into a recognition it might take a generation of luck and good generalship to achieve otherwise. But to occupy this position we require, within our field, systematic, encyclopaedic completeness. Mere happen-chance, hit-or-miss à la *Auk*, will do us no good. I would like to see the day when we might get some help and make the department absolutely complete in all bird fields. It is in some such future achievement, not in writing occasional bright reviews, that my interest lies.

Needless to say, Mr. Whittle and I were appalled at this astonishing goal, and we regularly returned to him those of his reviews which did not fall within our field of "subjects of importance to students of the living bird."

Mr. McCabe agreed to review some 14 foreign journals, so our coverage was broadened. As he was well acquainted with German, I asked him to review Dr. Friedrich Goethe's paper of 120 pages on the biology of the Herring Gull. He answered on a postcard: "I'll take on the Herring Gull horror, expecting thereby not only to cancel my sins of the present and past incarnations, but to acquire merit enough to last several more! I detest the wretched language." He wrote an admirable review nearly two pages long, which was published in July 1937.

Eventually he grew tired of writing reviews, for his last contributions appeared in April 1940. I was hoping to meet him eight years later when I visited California. To my great disappointment I found that he had died of a heart attack some four months earlier. Although he had often been a trial to me, he had also been a help in my heavy, self-imposed task.

Some of my reviews were not welcomed by the authors criticized. The most indignant was the Norwegian, Thorlief Schjelderup-Ebbe, pioneer in the study of peck-order as shown in the barnyard fowl. For this work he had received a Ph.D. in Germany and later was getting another Ph.D. in Oslo for a study of germination of ancient seeds. He wrote me that he was "vice-leader" of the Norwegian Antivivisection League.

In April 1936 I had reviewed his "Social Behaviour of Birds," as follows:

The author has done pioneer work on the matter of despotism and peck-order in the domestic fowl and it is a fine thing to have a summary of his studies in English. Very many of his observations are illuminating, not only in regard to the biology of chickens, but of mankind as well. He makes the mistake, however, of applying his findings too widely, as Allee has shown, and as, indeed will be evident to any careful student of the behaviour of wild birds.

This sentence was largely in reference to his dictum that peck-order was a universal phenomenon in birds in nature; that every bird in a flock knew its exact position of rank.

A wrathful letter arrived from Dr. Schjelderup-Ebbe:

The latter part of the recension . . . was — I am sorry, that I must say it — very unjust and has disappointed me . . . I demand you to do a correction in 'Bird-Banding' of what you have written there on the named point — and to send me that please. [Signed with a big red seal beside his name.]

In my answer I told him that his letter was a surprise both to me and to Dr. Allee who was sending him reprints that showed that the researches of himself and his students "were at variance with your statements." I quoted from Lorenz's *Der Kumpan* (1935), in which he discusses bird species where "contrary to Schjelderup-Ebbe's view, there is no rank-order." I concluded with a fine sentiment:

The role of a critic is not merely to give praise, but to point out errors and weaknesses. In this way scientists can help each other in their common search for truth.

Schjelderup-Ebbe never answered me directly but he wrote to Dr. Allee, saying that some of the statements in his own articles should "be taken with a grain of salt" and that my sentences on the role of the critic would be true of a "just (*gerechtete*) critic."

Dr. Allee told me that this Norwegian scientist had written him that observations by him (Allee) and his students must have been in error, because they differed from his own!

On the strength of my work with the reviews in *Bird-Banding*, Dr. Allee procured for me the privilege of a card to the libraries of the University of Chicago. This proved a real help.

From March 12 to 25 there was a rewarding trip to New York City. The highlights were: Barbara's and Stan's wedding in a simple ceremony in Marjorie's and Carl's apartment; visits with Marjorie and Katharine; my speech on the Song Sparrows to the Linnaean Society; dinner with the Vogts, tea at the May's; lunch with Bill Vogt, Ernst Mayr, Joe Hickey and Bob Allen; an opera — Aïda; two plays — Richard II and High Tor; and a visit to the Metropolitan Art Museum. Another thing — I finished the page proof of the "Population Study" while in New York.

I had dedicated this book to "My Friend Ernst Mayr" to whom I was deeply indebted for his labours on its behalf, both in finding a place for its publication and in his creative criticism. I wrote him:

I am happy to have the opportunity of showing something of my appreciation for a true scientist and a true friend.

He answered:

It certainly makes me very happy that you dedicated your wonderful Song Sparrow paper to me . . . I accept this honor in the spirit in which it was bestowed upon me and I shall try to live up to it. To have this paper dedicated to me makes me more proud than any honorary fellowship could do!

That spring (1937) the *Population Study of the Song Sparrow* was published. It made quite an impression. Mr. Whittle wrote me, "Your monumental Song Sparrow paper has come and has been read with pleasure and wonder too at the wealth of data you have so painstakingly gathered; it's really an ornithological epic."

Of the many published reviews I will quote from two.

Mr. E. M. Nicholson wrote in *British Birds* (1939):

This modestly presented paper includes at least as much original and significant observations of the essential facts of bird behaviour as almost any dozen ordinary bird books . . . a fundamental and original study of how birds live, worked out in the field in the terms of one species, but checked and illuminated by frequent references to work on the same problems with many species in many countries.

Jean Delacour, in *L'Oiseau* (1937), said,

In its form, this book is a model of clarity; in its substance, it is perhaps the most important contribution yet published to our knowledge of the life of a species.

In the spring of 1937 Constance and I drove out to Oklahoma where for five weeks we searched for birds and flowers and where we met with a royal welcome from our many friends. At the 12th Annual Spring Meeting of the Oklahoma Academy of Science at Robbers' Cave Camp in Latimer County in eastern Oklahoma I talked on "Oklahoma Birds" and led a field trip early in the morning. It was good to see again our warm friend Edith Force, leader of the bird watchers in Tulsa. Although, in contrast to my trip to Tahlequah in 1923, the warbler migration proved disappointing, yet we had happy and exciting experiences: the sight and sounds of displaying Lesser Prairie Chickens on a cloudy afternoon in northwestern Oklahoma; the glory of the prairie flowers in southeastern Oklahoma and best of all — the discovery in McCurtain County in southeastern Oklahoma of two new breeding birds for the state — the American Egret and the Anhinga[1]. These were nesting in the Buzzard Roost Cypress Brake. Professor Paul B. Sears, then head of the Botany Department at the University of Oklahoma, as well as our old friend Dr. Charles Gould of the National Park Service, and Hugh Davis, Director of the Tulsa Zoo, all took an active interest in trying to preserve this unique heronry with its fine birds and great cypress trees. Nonetheless the following summer it fell to the lumberman's axe.

One of my chief projects during our first year in Chicago was working on my book *The Watcher at the Nest*. This was designed to reach a wide public and, we hoped, to bring in a little financial reward. For all my labours on birds during the last 18 years or so had meant considerable outgo of money but very little income.

It was Bill Vogt who had encouraged me to write a book on the subject of "4M, His Life and Loves"; he proposed to publish several chapters in *Bird-Lore*, of which he was editor.

So I composed three chapters: "The Way of a Song Sparrow," "The Nest in the Rose Hedge," and "Uno and Una Return." Bill gave me constructive criticism; Roger Tory Peterson supplied engaging illustrations and these appeared in 1936. They were much admired. Aldo Leopold, distinguished conservationist and writer, wrote me, "It is not often that one who has done anything scientific succeeds in giving it literary expression." Paul Errington

---

[1] *Anhinga anhinga.*

complimented me "on the freedom and grace" of the articles. "Your subject matter could easily have been made dry, but you have made it living fabric, indeed. I think that the effectiveness of your writing lies chiefly in its simplicity."

I settled down and wrote and wrote and wrote. My principle critics were Constance and Katharine. At times I was very happy over my work but much of the way proved an uphill battle. After I had described the adventures of a great many Song Sparrows, Katharine wrote me that I was telling too much, that my readers would become confused. She suggested that I confine the narrative to Uno, 4M, their mates and descendants, then turn to other species for the rest of the book.

This I did, devoting ten chapters to the Song Sparrows, and eight to other birds, with the final chapter a burning plea for conservation. Constance, however, told me this last chapter would not do; it was too drastic, it would antagonize people. She suggested instead an enthusiastic account of our recent trip to Oklahoma, incidentally including propaganda for saving choice samples of prairies and swamps. "You write it," I answered. And this she did. Between us we made a satisfactory final chapter. But I had had enough of "popular" writing and vowed I would never attempt another such book. The middle of October 1937 we consigned the manuscript to the kind care of Bill Vogt.

The A.O.U. meeting that fall in Charleston, South Carolina*, was notable. In mid-November Lawrence and Thyra Hicks drove Constance and me to this historic city.

As soon as we entered the Fort Sumter Hotel, James L. Peters of the Museum of Comparative Zoology in Cambridge, Massachusetts, said to me, "Mrs. Nice, I congratulate you. We did the deed at last." So I knew I had reached the proud pinnacle of Fellowship in the A.O.U., the second woman to be elected. It was fun receiving the congratulations of Fellows and Members and later of many others. Lawrence said someone told him that the *Population Study* had done the trick.

I was delighted that Ernst Mayr was the other new Fellow and sorry he had not come to the meeting. Two of my friends were elected to Membership – Dr. Olin Sewall Pettingill and Dr. Miles Pirnie (Director of the Kellogg Bird Sanctuary in Michigan). To the horror of many old-timers, but to the satisfaction of younger folk, we elected Lawrence Hicks as Secretary, thus retiring

---

*The 55th Stated Meeting of the American Ornithologists' Union, Charleston, South Carolina, November 15-19, 1937.

Dr. Palmer after 20 years in this office. He was an ardent conservationist, a tireless worker and a scholar, but he had, we felt, become too much in love with having his own way. As to Mr. McAtee, he resigned as Treasurer the following year after 18 years of energetic and faithful service.

There were many good papers and fine motion pictures. I talked on "The Biological Significance of Bird Weights," a paper later published in *Bird-Banding* (1937). I was glad to meet Amelia Laskey of Nashville, Tennessee, an ardent bird bander and author of life history studies on many species, especially Bluebirds (1939, 1940), Cowbirds (1950), and Blue Jays.

After the banquet we enjoyed a wonderful treat, for the Society for the Preservation of Spirituals sang for us. These were Charlestonians who had been brought up on plantations and had a great love for spirituals and sang them the way the Negroes do with clapping, patting, and shouting which means bodily movements, such as swaying or getting up and performing something like Indian dance steps. It was a unique experience seeing these aristocratic southerners, the women in hoop skirts, the men in corresponding costumes of Pre-Civil War days, singing and shouting. It was hard for the audience not to join in, and when they asked us to do so at the end, we responded joyfully.

Charleston is one of the most beautiful and picturesque cities we had ever seen in this country. It is rich in old colonial houses with wrought-iron gates, with flowers and palmettos. One evening the A.O.U. members were taken to visit five notable houses, built between 1723 and 1762 — a great privilege. The panelling and carving of the woodwork were very fine.

We rejoiced in Mockingbirds, Red-cockaded Woodpeckers, and Brown-headed Nuthatches. The all-day trip to Bull's Island was a memorable experience with cypresses, live oaks, sweet gums, and Spanish moss, with green tree frogs and chameleons, handsome sea shells and many, many birds.

We drove back from Charleston through the Great Smoky Mountains — a strange and beautiful scene with snow on the road and loading the pines and hemlocks, with a bitter wind and temperature 5 degrees above zero. We were glad when we reached Gatlinsburg, where we found our friend from Columbus, Arthur Stupka, a former Wheaton Club member, now Park Naturalist. We had passed from summer to winter in a day.

Such a nice letter came from Joseph Grinnell. "I am delighted at the outcome of the elections. Congratulations to *you* on election to *Fellow*-ship! Scholarly accomplishment in ornithology *scores*. There should, of course, be no other criterion."

The Wilson Club meeting in Indianapolis, Indiana*, December 1937, was also noteworthy for our family. Blaine drove us all there — my mother, Constance, Janet and myself. In Lafayette, Indianna, we stopped to call on my 91-year-old step-grandmother with whom I had gone to Europe 34 years earlier. Mother had been my guest at A.O.U. in Washington in 1920 and 1927 and in Philadelphia in 1929; this was her first experience of the Wilson Club and she greatly enjoyed it, especially the fine movies by Cleveland Grant and Sewall Pettingill. I spoke on "Konrad Lorenz and Bird Behavior." Mother was very proud when it was announced that I had been elected to the Presidency, as were all the rest of our family. It was a position of trust and serious responsibility.

---

*The 23rd Stated Meeting of the Wilson Ornithological Club, Indianapolis, Indiana, December 27, 28, 1937.

XXI

The Ornithological Congress in France*

Back in July 1937, Ernst Mayr had written me that Niko Tinbergen, famed colleague of Lorenz in ethology, had "spent a couple of months" in Altenberg, Austria, with Dr. Lorenz. "Now why," I thought I, "couldn't I do that next summer? Get some sort of a grant, go to the Congress in France, and afterwards to the Lorenzes?"

On September 29 I wrote triumphantly in my Plans V:

The great event today that has stirred me deeply and thrilled me amazingly was the letter from Dr. Lorenz: "We should be very happy indeed, if you would come to Altenberg for a few months as Tinbergen did.

Now, I see why I toil unremittingly on my birds. This is a reward and a wonderful opportunity.

Dr. Albert R. Brand of Cornell suggested that I work up a party of American ornithologists and thus earn my passage on the *S.S. Newport News*, due to leave Baltimore on April 28, 1938. So, I busily invited bird people to join our party for the Congress. Although most people declined, we did get a group of eleven, which ensured us a jolly, friendly trip to Europe.

The ship was a small, comfortable, one-class boat that carried its 66 passengers across the Atlantic in ten days. Our party consisted of Mr. and Mrs. Brand and their daughter Alice; Lawrence and Thyra Hicks; Arthur A. Allen of Cornell University; Hugh Birkhead of Pelham Manor, New York; James H. Flemming of Toronto,

*The IXth International Ornithological Congress, Rouen, France, May 9-13, 1938.

Ontario, former President of the A.O.U.; George Sutton of Cornell; Mr. W. E. C. Todd of the Carnegie Museum in Pittsburgh, Pennsylvania; and myself. It proved a thoroughly congenial group. On May 8 we landed at Le Havre and travelled to the fascinating old city of Rouen.

We were just in time for the opening of the Ninth Ornithological Congress by the President, Professor Allesandro Chigi of Bologna, Italy. Some 260 members from 32 countries were gathered there, England leading with 60 representatives, while Germany and North America tied for second place with 24 each.

Jackdaws shouted from the clocktower of the railroad station in Rouen and Black Redstarts[1] gave their plain little songs from the house tops. This species was extending its range northwards, finding cottages in villages and apartment houses in cities acceptable for nesting as substitutes for the mountain cliffs that were its original habitat. In the little park on the Rue Jeanne d'Arc where six years previously I had met my first Chaffinch, a Chaffinch was again singing. A Mute Swan[2], guarded by her mate, was sitting on a nest full of eggs, and a sign warned us: *Le coup d'ailes des cygnes est brutal.* In the Jardin des Plantes a pair of Moorhens[2] (the same species as our Common Gallinule) were nest building in a pool about 50 feet in diameter; Madame sat on a wee island in the centre while Monsieur paddled busily about, picking up great waterlily leaves and bringing them to her.

The papers were divided into four sections: Taxonomy and Zoo-Geography, Anatomy and Physiology, Biology and Applied Ornithology. A number dealt with experimental studies of migration: Count Kazimerz Wodzicki of Warsaw had worked with White Storks on their sense of orientation (1939), while two papers reported on homing experiments – Dr. Werner Rüppell with Hooded Crows (1944), Goshawks[4] (1940), and Black-headed Gulls[5] (1939); and Dr. Rudolf Drost of Heligoland with the European Sparrow Hawk (*Accipiter nisus*, 1939). My paper on "What Determines the Time of the Song Sparrow's Awakening Song" (1939), proved to be a somewhat specialized topic.

Two mornings were spent at the Cinema Normandie. Here we saw Dr. Allen's sound film of disappearing North American birds, Marquis Yamashina's movies of Japanese birds, the most unusual of which were those of Cormorants trained to catch fish for their

---

[1]*Phoenicurus ochruros.* [2]*Cygnus olor.* [3]*Gallinula chloropus.* [4]*Accipiter gentilis.* [5]*Larus ridibundus.*

masters; Capt. C. W. R. Knight's films of the Crowned Eagle[1] and Secretary Bird[2] ; Dr. Lorenz's illuminating exposition of the behaviour of the Graylag Goose[3] ; and Horst Siewart's pictures "Through the Year with the Moose" and the extraordinary "Courtship of the Great Bustard."

The program was so full that it was difficult to get sufficient time to visit the sights of the wonderful old city — the splendid Palais de Justice, the Cathedral, beautiful St. Ouen. One morning we went to the Natural History Museum, founded in 1828, and saw, besides mounted birds from over the world, a local collection and various habitat scenes, mostly of French birds. There was a reception at the Town Hall; a garden party celebrating the centenary of the Jardin des Plantes; and a grand banquet at the Circus (Salle des Fêtes du Cirque) decorated with immense banners showing insignia of Rouen and other cities of Normandy; for this occasion we had been told to wear evening dress and medals. On all these festive occasions we heard many long speeches, all in French.

One afternoon we travelled out in buses to Clères, the Zoological Park of M. Jean Delacour, the efficient and charming Secretary of the Congress. The Château was a stately structure, some of it dating from the first half of the 13th century. M. Delacour (1935) tells us in an article on "The Ornithological Collections of Clères" that "Jeanne d'Arc when taken to Rouen, stopped there a night, and two kings, Charles IX and Henri IV were also guests of the Château."

On the spacious grounds antelopes and wallabys dashed about while capibaris — large South American rodents, were more dignified in their movements. Two gibbons leaped around in the trees on an island in the duck pond, wonderfully skillful in jumping from place to place. The number of birds was bewildering: many kinds of cranes, egrets, Scarlet Ibises[4], Roseate Spoonbills[5], and flamingos from Europe and America wandered over the meadows and waded in the stream. A great variety of geese, ducks, and swans were swimming on the pond and in the brook. Many of these nested each year, while Wood[6] and Mandarin Ducks[7] bred in full liberty. Several Rheas[8] were on the hillside, one of them incubating on a nest. Near the Château were large aviaries in which many rare

---

[1]Crowned Hawk-Eagle, *Stephanpaetus coronatus.* [2]*Sagittarius serpentarius.* [3]*Anser anser.* [4]*Eudocinius ruber.* [5]*Ajaia ajaja.* [6]American Wood Duck, *Aix sponsa.* [7] *Aix galericulata.* [8] Common Rhea, *Rhea americana.*

birds were kept, while tropical birds — Cocks-of-the-Rock[1], Birds of Paradise[2], and hummingbirds — were housed in greenhouses. It was an extraordinary array of beasts and birds that met our eyes recalling, as M. Delacour wrote, "the Garden of Eden."

After a sumptuous tea in the Château we sat on the lawn and were delighted by immense blue and red macaws that flew from tree to tree. Most of M. Delacour's birds had been brought back by himself from his trips to distant corners of the world. A number of young birds were raised each year. "Many species," he writes, "of which the habits, the courtship, the eggs and young were unknown, have been studied here for the first time." His article is illustrated by a coloured plate of the magnificent Imperial Pheasant (*Hierophasis imperialis*)[3], the male of which is dark blue with red cheeks and legs, the female brown. This bird:

was discovered in the Province of Quantri in Annam (Indochina) in 1923. A single pair was captured and brought to Clères, where they bred in 1925. No other wild specimen has been found since then, but there exists in European and American Museums and collections of live birds a good number of individuals that came from the original pair, the male of which still lives (in 1938), is in excellent condition and breeds each year, although at least sixteen years of age.

Disasters were to come. On February 15, 1939, a fire completely destroyed the interior of the Château, consuming all of the great library, and its owner's notes and personal treasures. In May 1939 it was bombed, in June it was machine-gunned from the air and taken over by German troops. All the mammals and birds were disposed of. Since then, however, it has been restored to almost the same standard at which the Congress enjoyed it in 1938.

On the long excursion into the valley of the Seine we found Jackdaws on the ruined arches of the ancient Abbey of Jumièges and harts-tongue ferns and European Robins at the Abbey of Saint-Wandrille. After a delicious lunch at Caudebec-en-Caux we drove through fine forests of beech and hornbeam and Scotch pine, finally stopping at a heath. Here in a bush of gorse one of my life's ambitions was realized. Ever since reading of the Dartford Warbler[4] in one of W. H. Hudson's books, I had longed to see this little red-breasted bird (1897 b). In a bush of gorse was a nest with babies, and not far away were the troubled parents, their bills stuffed with

---

[1]Guianan Cock-of-the-Rock, *Rupicola rupicola.* [2]*Paradisaeidae.* [3](Now called *Lephura imperialis.)* [4]*Sylvia undata.*

insects. In an adjoining field a pair of the curious Stone-Curlews[1] stealthily left their eggs. We saw our first Wheatear[2] and heard our first Skylark for the trip. We visited a Wood Lark's[3] nest with four eggs that looked like those of a Song Sparrow. And a pert little Crested Tit[4] brought food to its four chicks in a broken stump.

On Saturday the Congress moved to Paris, and in the afternoon we went to the Menagerie du Jardin des Plantes, which had had a good collection for those times, of native and exotic birds as early as 1804. The most important of the birds were three Kangaroo Island Emus (*Dromiceus novaehollandiae diemenianus*) brought from an island south of Australia; they lived until 1822 and 14 years later the race had become extinct. We looked at the Museum of Natural History, finding in contrast to my visit in 1932, the small birds all on the lower shelves instead of the highest.

The next morning we were taken to the Parc Zoologique du Bois de Vincennes, one of the finest modern zoos I had seen. The animals were enclosed by moats and many had great heaps of pinkish artificial rock to climb over. Instead of conventional buildings we walked into caves. There were severe warnings against exciting the animals and against feeding certain ones, especially against offering them stones! On the other hand, it was possible to buy bread and fish for other animals. Over the pool of the walruses and sea-lions the sign read: *Chers visiteurs, excusez-nous, nous ne mangeons pas de pain.* (Dear visitors, pardon us, but we don't eat bread.)

There were no small birds at this zoo, but a great flying cage for herons, storks, and gulls, and large pools for ducks and waders. One of the prettiest sights was a dance of a pair of Demoiselle Cranes[5]; they waved their wings and bowed and skipped lightly about in a way that was utterly charming.

That night we travelled in *wagon-lits* to Arles where we saw old churches, the well-preserved theatre where classic plays are still given, and the Roman arena in which bull fights take place. Monday afternoon we started out again in buses, stopping at Nîmes to see the fine arena and to visit the Natural History Museum where we were shown mounted specimens of birds of the Camargue. Then on and on across the monotonous plain to the remarkable walled city of Aigues-Morte from which Louis IX sailed in 1270

---

[1]*Burhinus oedicnemus.* [2]*Oenanthe oenanthe.* [3]*Lullula arborea.* [4]*Parus cristatus.* [5]*Anthropoides virgo.*

on the crusade from which he was never to return.

On our way back to Arles we saw birds — a great heronry in low pines of Night Herons and Little Egrets (*Egretta garzetta*) — hundreds and hundreds of them. Blue egg shells were scattered hither and yon, while as many as six nests might be in one tree. Dr. Hans Noll from Switzerland climbed a tree and found eggs, small young and large young in different nests. We were shown an occasional Squacco Heron (*Ardiola ralloides*), about the size of the egret but buffy rather than white. Hoopoes[1] with amazing crests frequented the vineyards and nightingales sang along the border of the woods.

The drought of a year's standing was broken at last; at 6:30 on Tuesday morning we started off in a pouring rain for our chief day in the Camargue. Fortunately, it cleared after a few hours and later became so bright that some of us were sunburned.

New birds to me were the European Avocets[2], about a dozen of which were running along the shore at Romieu; they are less brightly coloured than our American species. Cetti's Warbler[3] sang loudly from the reeds but refused to let itself be seen. A charming sight was the nest of a pair of Penduline Tits[4] on which both birds were working; it hung from a tree, shaped something like a Baltimore Oriole's nest. Later we were shown a finished structure with its funnel-like entrance near the top; Mr. Jourdain remarked that it resembles a swarm of bees.

The chief glory of the Camargue lies in the Flamingos[5] that visit it from Egypt. It was one of the most wonderful sights of my life — 2,000 of the extraordinary birds standing together in the shallow water. They are pale pink instead of the bright pink of our American birds but when they fly they are gorgeous beyond words, because the colours on the undersides of their wings are black and deep rose. At rest they are rather inconspicuous but when hundreds rise together it is a marvellous spectacle.

After an ample lunch we started on a long walk to visit Black-Winged Stilts[6]. A herd of black cattle lowed and bellowed as if they would have liked to get at the impudent ornithologists who were taking pictures of them, but *gardiens* on white ponies stood between. The chief singers were Skylarks, Whitethroats, (*Sylvia communis*)[7] and always the cheerful Nightingales. Flocks of Ruffs[8]

---

[1]*Upupa epops.* [2]Pied Avocet, *Recurvirostra avosetta.* [3]*Cettia cetti.* [4]Eurasian Penduline Tit, *Remiz pendulinus.* [5]Common Flamingo, *Phoenicopterus ruber.* [6]Common Stilt, *Himantopus himantopus.* [7] Greater Whitethroat. [8]*Philomachus pugnax.*

wheeled about over the shallow ponds. The Stilts were handsome creatures with white bodies, black wings, and red legs stretched backwards in flight. They called *pee-wee* as they flew about, disturbed by their admirers. The walking was more than wet and streams had to be jumped, the ladies assisted by the gentlemen. Dr. Allen waded about with water half way to his knees, and a French ornithologist exclaimed, "Ce monsieur n'a pas de bottes!" We were shown a nest of the Stilt just above water; it held four astonishingly large eggs.

Tea and cakes were served at the headquarters of the Sanctuary. Here we saw a gaily coloured Goldfinch[1] building a nest, and were shown a nest of the Spectacled Warbler[2] with five eggs. One of the loveliest nests I have ever seen was that of a fan-tailed warbler (*Cisticola juncidis*), woven out of spider webs between blades of grass. It held five tiny babies, but was so fragile that the *gardien* warned us emphatically, "Ne la touchez pas!"

My last day in Provence was also memorable. Five of us Americans and Dr. Erwin Stresemann hired a taxi and visited a desert and a mountain. La Crau is part of a glacial moraine of the Rhone and the most stony place I have ever seen. Large flocks of brown sheep, accompanied by a few black goats, a shepherd and a dog, cropped the sparse vegetation so closely that we wondered how any birds could raise families. Nevertheless La Crau is the home of innumerable larks — our old friend the Skylark, the small Short-toed Lark[3] with its unpretentious song, and the Calandra Lark[4], the largest lark in Europe. "You would have to go to Thibet to see a larger one," Dr. Stresemann told us.

The strangest inhabitant of La Crau was the rare Pin-tailed Sandgrouse (*Pterocles alchata*) with short legs and long tail. Unfortunately the birds were shy and gave us only fleeting glimpses.

Les Baux is a picturesque mountain group rising abruptly from the plain; in the Middle Ages it was strongly fortified but now its palaces are mostly ruins, destroyed by Richelieu. Many of the rocks have been quarried into rooms, while in one spot a large number of pigeon holes is thought to have served as a crypt.

For a picnic lunch we climbed to some rocks in the midst of prickly gorse; from this vantage point we saw and heard Melodius[5]

---

[1]European Goldfinch, *Carduelis carduelis.* [2]*Sylvia conspicillata.* [3]Lesser Short-toed Lark, *Calandrella rufescens.* [4]European Calandra Lark, *Melanocorypha calandra.* [5]*Hippolais polyglotta.*

and Subalpine Warblers[1], Blue Rock-Thrushes[2], Serins[3], Nightingales, Hobbies, and many Common Swifts. A Short-toed and a Bonelli's Eagle[4] soared overhead. Dr. Allen found the nest of a handsome Cirl Bunting[5], and finally, we had the pleasure of sighting two rarities — Alpine Swift[6] and Crag Martin[7].

Reluctantly we left this fascinating place, stopping at marshes to hear the grasshopper-like song of Savi's Warbler[8], and by a farm house to admire the curious Hoopoes and to look at the wool-lined nest of a Woodchat Shrike[9]. There were hills here that made me think of mesas in the Oklahoma Panhandle, but an old monastery furnished different local colour.

Dr. Alexander Wetmore, Secretary of the Smithsonian Institution, was chosen as the new President and North America as the next meeting place. Little could we foresee what the world situation would be in 1942.

---

[1]*Sylvia cantillans.* [2]*Monticola solitarius.* [3]*Serinus serinus.* [4]*Hieraaetus fasciatus.* [5]*Emberiza cirlus.* [6]*Apus melba.* [7]*Ptyonoprogne rupestris.* [8]*Locustella luscinioides.* [9]*Lanius senator.*

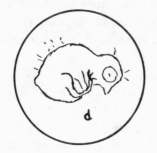

XXII

The
Month with
the Lorenzes

MAY-JUNE 1938

Konrad Lorenz, son of the distinguished orthopedic surgeon, Adolf Lorenz, was born in Altenberg, Austria, in 1904, and brought up, as he wrote to Wallace Craig, "in country surroundings and on a social footing with very many animals and few scientists."

He received an M.D. from the University of Vienna and for some years taught anatomy there, but his heart was with his birds in Altenberg. He acknowledged in a letter to Dr. Craig his immense debt to Oskar Heinroth (1871-1945), President of the *Deutsche Ornithologische Gesellschaft*, and author, with his first wife, of *Die Vögel Mitteleuropas* (1924-1933) in four volumes:

It was a remarkable experience for me to read this book, as even I myself had a queer feeling that I'd written it myself and couldn't remember when I'd done it! In every sentence that Heinroth has written in all his life, there isn't a word that has not been important to me and he never left anything out, that I would have thought relevant. The consequence of this incredible congruence of viewpoint between Heinroth and me is that I really am in the unique position to "command another man's experience."

From Arles I had travelled by train to Vienna where I arrived on May 24. The next day Konrad met me and, together with a pair of Wood Ducks, for which he had traded a pair of Egyptian Geese[1], we drove out to his father's home in the village of Altenberg.

Here, in a wonderful great house that seemed a cross between a castle and a palace, lived the Lorenz family, consisting of genial Professor Adolf and his gracious wife, of Konrad and his wife, the

[1] *Alopochen aegyptiacus.*

PROF. DR. KONRAD LORENZ

charming and efficient Dr. Margarete, a physician who left each morning for work in a Vienna hospital, and their two delightful children, Thomas, nine, and Agnes, seven. There were also Resi, Konrad's old nurse who helped care for the birds, and a staff of three women — a cook and two maids.

Overlooking the Danube Valley, Lorenz Hall rose from terraces with ivy-covered walls, crowned with carved stone railings from ancient bridges. The garden was adorned with statues and the house with a profusion of paintings and art treasures, while a great clock on the roof of the guest room struck the quarter hours for the benefit of the village. On the top of Lorenz Hall lived the famous colony of Jackdaws.

The porch that led off the kitchen and the guest room was largely devoted to young birds. Here was a brooder that served as nursery for baby ducks and geese, Muscovies and pheasants, and even for an orphaned Jackdaw that, sitting in an old blackbird nest, was inconsiderately tramped upon by its companions. Two young Magpies shrieked and begged and flapped their wings and made expeditions into the kitchen. Since the food for all the young birds was mixed on this porch, it attracted hordes of House Sparrows. I asked Konrad whether he ever did anything to lessen their numbers. "No, I never kill birds," said he. "To a certain extent I am a friend of successful species. This goes so far that I even like weeds."

Over the spacious grounds roamed a bewildering array of birds, many in full liberty. Since Konrad was studying the courtship of river ducks, he had many species of these, both native and foreign, as well as numbers of hybrids. The Graylag Geese were Konrad's favourites; these were now moulting so I missed the fine sight of their flights. Sometimes they would be frightened at night and fly away, getting lost in the mist; but later most of them gradually found their way home.

Four yearling geese were his children and used to fly after him in the Danube meadows; at this time they would approach and lie down near him when he sat by the pond. In the fall he expected them to follow him more closely, for then the yearling geese rejoin their parents. In February when he had been away on a lecture tour, these geese had become very restless, flying about and calling. (Young geese do not migrate independently of their parents; if these are pinioned the young stay with them.)

This year Agnes was mother to five goslings and several times a day she took them out of their pen. It was a pretty sight — the little girl in gay peasant costume with flaxen braids down her back, closely followed by the solemn grey goslings.

A decorative note was added to the terraces and garden walls by a gorgeous Peacock[1], that went about by himself, while his mate and three yearling sons kept each other company. All four males displayed, although the young birds lacked the splendid upper tail coverts. There was no jealousy nor fighting among them. A male Peacock does not display to any special object; he merely stands with his tail outspread, advertising, "Here is a male Peacock." At such a time, if a fowl of any description — peahen, bantam, or even pigeon — starts to pick up food in front of him, he becomes excited, grows more and more agitated and gradually lowers his tail over his head in a sort of tent over the pecking bird.

One morning Konrad and I went together to seine the ponds for mosquito larvae and other tidbits for the ducklings. The flowers in the Danube meadows were bewilderingly lovely; many were friends

---

[1] *Pavo cristatus.*

of my childhood – buttercups, daisies, and red clover, while others were strangers – the purple meadow salvia, a white catnip, and here and there a lavender harebell. There is something very appealing in such a mingling of the familiar with the new. The one caddis fly larva we discovered was somewhat different from any I had met in America; it had made itself a long slim tube of bits of green leaves. There were two species of newts or tritons in the pools, both with crests on their backs. *Rana esculenta* sang determinedly with a bladder puffing out each side of his mouth; this edible frog is about the size of our leopard frog, not large like our bull frog.

Most exciting to me was the discovery of the author of the most insistent sound on the meadows – a low, musical *mmm mmm mmn* that made me think of the sound of telegraph wires in the wind that I had heard as a child – Thoreau's "telegraph harp." All this came from a *Feuerkrote* or *Unke, Bombinator igneus*, a creature that looked like a fat black toad. Konrad fished one out of the water and it lay stiffly on its back with its legs held up, and bright orange spots showing on its belly. It belongs to the bell-toads, the *Discoglossidae*, and is a relative of the midwife toad. Around some water plants we found a ribbon of its eggs. It gives off a disagreeable secretion from its skin that makes it safe from snakes, turtles and birds. "If you go out to catch food for your birds," said Konrad, "you will soon find that many of the things that are abundant and easy to catch are not good to eat." *Bombinator* sings all summer long.

To carry out the project that I had planned, I needed a nest with young birds. I had come to Austria to learn first how to raise little birds so they would be healthy individuals; second, what to watch for in their development, and, finally, how to distinguish between innate and learned behaviour. Birds were everywhere but nests, that was a different matter. Some that we found were just started, while in others the nestlings were too old for adoption.

On June 1st I noticed European Redstarts carrying food into a crevice near the top of the chimney of a small, unused house on the grounds. Konrad climbed to the roof while I watched with breathless interest; the nest might be inaccessible, or the infants too young or too old. Fortune favoured us at last; "Six babies just the right age!" Three of these were transferred to a handkerchief, and the package, held in the finder's teeth, journeyed to the ground.

With much excitement I looked at the wee Redstarts aged about five days, for they matched well pictures of birds of this species at that age in the Heinroths' volumes. Long down sprouted from their heads, while scattered over their bodies was the promise of feathers. They could not be said to resemble their pretty mother with her soft buff colouring and red-brown tail; and still less their handsome father with his red breast, black throat, and white forehead. (European Redstarts, *Phoenicurus phoenicurus*, belong to the thrush family and are about the size of our Eastern Bluebirds.) It was a triumph at last to have our family.

Konrad contrived a snug nest of flannel in a paper box; the babies opened wide their golden mouths, swallowed bunches of fresh ant pupae (purchased in Vienna by Konrad) and were content. I put them on my bedside stand and at 3:30 the next morning a pleasant twittering awoke me. That day I fed them 26 times. I gave them a late supper, drew the curtains of the windows, and covered the little birds with flannelette; thanks to these measures, they let me sleep until 4 a.m. I fell asleep again, but not for long; as I dozed, I tried to persuade myself that it was merely a Barn Swallow calling outside, instead of three foster babies on my stand. I soon learned to lie motionless, for the least sound on my part meant an explosion of piteous pleas from my starving infants.

In my walks after tea up the hill into the beech woods or down in the meadows by the Danube, I was always on the look out for a second family. Nothing came my way, but on June 8 on my return from a morning walk, I found a present awaiting me from Hermann Kacher, a young bird student and friend of the Lorenz family. A branch of Norway spruce hung on the wall; in it was a dirty little nest holding three extraordinary looking babies. "Serins!" I said in dismay. Konrad had told me that these birds, *Serinus canarius serinus*, close relatives of the wild canary of the Canary Islands, were hard to raise by hand, since their parents fed them by regurgitation. The best way to bring up young Serins was to give the eggs to a Canary and let her do the work.

We fixed up a mixture of cooked millet seed, chopped nettle leaves, egg yolk, milk and bread, but the problem was to get it down them. The ridiculous little things stood up straight, stretching as high as possible, frantically waving their wee wings and screeching with wide open ruby-coloured mouths. They had a weazened look and I called them the "Three Ungraces." It was difficult to get their little crops filled and they kept up a constant peeping. We tried medicine droppers and by using spruce twigs pushed nourishment down their throats. I found them quite a trial. According to pictures in the Heinroths' book, they appeared to have been about 11 days old when found by Hermann.

At 14 days of age the Redstarts all climbed out of the nest. I gathered them up and installed them in a roomy cage; here they lived contentedly, cuddling together side by side like little birds on a Christmas card. I called them Gelb, Rot, and Blau, according to the colour of their bands.

That evening as we were in the upper garden gathering green food for the baby ducks and geese, Konrad uncovered in the grass a little Redstart about two days younger than ours. Since no parents seemed to be about, we adopted him. He proved to be tame enough, but he just wouldn't open his bill to be fed! He often hopped up beside the bird I was feeding, but the loud food-call, energetic wing fluttering and open gapes of his companions brought no response from him. We had to feed him forcibly the first morning.

At last in the afternoon when the others started to fly about, he opened his mouth and I was able to stuff something down him. Twice I excited him by rapidly moving the forceps in front of him. Gelb jumped on his back; open came his bill and in went some ant eggs. I hit him on the back, and got in one more mouthful, but no more. Head tappings did not prove to be the open sesame.

The next morning started auspiciously; Wildling, the orphan Redstart, begged from sheer hunger at breakfast. After that he begged whenever a comrade alighted nearby; by noon he was begging as well as any of his foster brothers. A week later he was the tamest of them all.

At the age of 16 days Rot first picked up ant pupae for himself. All three Redstarts now flew skillfully about the room, their landing technique perfected. It was often a problem to capture them to get them back into their cage; they had no notion of coming to call and their favourite perches on the curtain rods or the top of the chandelier brought them above my reach even with the furniture serving as step-ladders. In desperation I presented the end of my closed umbrella to Blau; she begged to it! The next minute, however, she stepped on it and rode in state back to the cage. But her brothers were terrified of the queer contraption.

The day that the Redstarts left the nest, I moved the Serins, estimated then to be 16 days old, into another cage, well furnished with spruce branches; the little birds climbed about unsteadily, stretched and preened themselves, and seemed well pleased with their new home. Two days later one of them flew to the window. The others contented themselves with flapping their wings very rapidly, occasionally letting go of the branch and rising a bit in the air. They looked for all the world like the moving pictures of Dr. Francis Herrick's young Bald Eagles.

Two of the Serins were named Bluet and Snowdrop in accordance with the colour of their bands. Their brother was a noisy creature; no matter how well-filled was his crop, he still continued his tiresome *yip yip yip yip*. To the amusement of Thomas and Agnes I called him "Cry-baby." All three moved about with tiny steps and sometimes would travel the length of my arm in a sort of Susy-Q dance. Grey and yellow, they were still a bit fluffy, but were far from the Redstarts' picture of baby innocence.

To quote from my diary:

8 a.m. My breakfast of tea and rolls is brought in. Rot comes to visit me, alighting on the edge of the tray. I offer him a crumb; he begs, but seems disconcerted by my fingers instead of the forceps from which for the last two weeks he has received all his meals. Bluet, seeing something is up, alights on my left hand. She is pleased to nibble the crumb, then turns her attention to the clasp of my watch ribbon and finally to my sweater. Snowdrop alights on my head. Rot, in the meantime, has caught his first ant.

When the Redstarts were 18 days old, I heard something new — a soft warbling song. It came from Gelb, who sat on the perch with closed bill and vibrating throat, Wildling and Blau pressed tightly against him. The next day Rot also sang, and two days later Wildling. It seemed an extraordinarily early age to start singing.

So far the two families had been good friends and Wildling had even tried to cuddle against the Serins on top of the cage, pushing these small creatures farther and farther along and finally off the edge, all with the best of intentions. But on June 16, Rot drove Bluet off the rim of the Redstarts' cage and chased her about the room! Soon afterwards, I was shocked to see Blau seize Cry-baby by a feather of his head and pull at it.

The next day I wrote:

7:30. The Redstarts are a delight; they stand so straight and alert, and wag their red-brown tails so busily after alighting. Two were cuddled together on the curtain rod when Anna brought breakfast.

"*Das muss ein Liebespaar sein!*" she exclaimed.

8:20. Bluet flies to my hand, then back to the top of the Redstarts' cage. Rot opens his bill at her and she retreats. The next minute Cry-baby lands on top of Rot, knocking him to the bottom of the cage!

I hear a loud, disagreeable, new note; it comes from Cry-baby, who is saying *ga-ga-ga-ga-ga* at Rot, completely bluffing the latter. It was an absurd sight — the pigmy Cry-baby repulsing the Redstart that looked three times as large — from the Redstarts' own cage. It was a brand new note and brand new behaviour.

Later in the day I discovered that Bluet was also using the threat note; there was a set-to between her and Rot on the window sill with passes back and forth until he left. Later Cry-baby, Gelb and Blau were on the floor of the Redstarts' cage; Cry-baby opened his bill and scolded; the others pecked at him. He drove them up on to the perches!

When Cry-baby was about three and a half weeks old, he again surprised me by a new note; standing on his left leg he sang, giving a rather loud twitter, much like the song of the adult male Serin. The next day he was again singing, but this time *with his head under his wing*! It was the most ludicrous sight — *twichy weech weech* coming from a shaking, feathery ball with a tail attached! It almost appeared as if some grotesque little monster were singing, the sound issuing from the rising and falling breast feathers.

As a child I had been intrigued by a picture in our beginner's German book of a hedgehog and by its curious name, *Der Igel*, pronounced like our word "eagle." Although this was my fourth visit to Europe, I had never come upon an *Igel*. My friends said it scratched noisily in dead leaves, but whenever I investigated such sounds, up flew a Song Thrush[1] that had been probing about for snails. One day my room became a real menagerie, visited by all the household from Professor Adolf Lorenz down: I had been given a new bird and Hermann had brought me my hedgehog. It was an absurd little beast, capable of making itself into a complete ball, but its prickles were mild affairs in comparison to our porcupines. It retired for the day behind the cushions of my sofa; in the evening we released it in the garden.

The new bird was a European Cuckoo, a handsome black and white-mottled creature about three weeks old, found in a Black Redstart's nest. When Konrad tried to feed it, it spread its wings and tail, shook its body and opened its mouth to bite. For the most part it sat with its bill obstinately closed. My baby birds were out on the porch at this time; soon I brought them in and opened their cages. At once the cuckoo's mouth came open. Whenever a little bird flew near, the great red cavern gaped. Gelb and Rot stared as if astonished. I improved the occasion by stuffing food down its throat. When the mouth had snapped shut, I could sometimes get it open by bringing a Serin nearby, or by taps on the head, the place from which small fosterers customarily feed the large parasite. It never fluttered its wings; its begging note was a faint *yip*; the irresistible attraction to fosterers resides in the great red mouth. Wildling landed nearby; at once the yawning cavity turned toward

---

[1] *Turdus ericetorum.*

him and was held there in solemn expectation, but Wildling failed to understand.

The next day the cuckoo remained in a cage on the porch and by afternoon I had it trained to take food from the forceps. The following day I brought it back near my little birds and immediately the lower mandible dropped down in the former automatic fashion. We released it in the garden, Konrad assuring me that it would be fed by strangers.

It was time for me to leave. Konrad took the little birds into his room and later wrote me news of them. Of the Redstarts, Wildling became wild again, but Gelb, Rot, and Blau stayed tame and peaceable, always sleeping side by side. In September they flew away. Of the Serins, Bluet was the only one kept by Konrad. She sang a little as long as she was alone, but not after the wild-caught male was put in her cage, although she remained rather dominant over her shy husband.

It had been a rich and happy experience for me with the kind Lorenz family and their household and the trusting little birds. In Altenberg I had learned what I had hoped for. I started on a round-about route for home, ready to raise and study baby Song Sparrows.

XXIII

Birds of an
Hungarian Lake
JUNE, 1938

At the Congress in Rouen I had met Dr. James Schenk and Dr. Andrew Keve of the Royal Hungarian Ornithological Institute; they had cordially invited me to come to Hungary to see their birds. After my month's stay at Altenberg I travelled to Budapest for a visit with Marie Engel-Lamers, daughter of our good neighbour in Columbus, Mrs. Gerhard Lamers. Marie was a delightful hostess and took me hither and yon in the city, where by myself, entirely ignorant as I was of the language, I would have felt quite lost.

At the Hungarian Ornithological Institute, I was intrigued to find a pair of Barn Swallows nesting on a chandelier in one of the rooms, flying in and out of the open window as they cared for their brood. The Institute was one of the pioneers in marking birds. H. C. C. Mortensen in Denmark started this activity in 1899; J. Thienemann, Vogelwarte (Bird Observatory) of Rossitten, Germany, followed in 1903, and James Schenk took it up in 1908 when he became Director of the Hungarian Ornithological Institute. His special interests lay in migration, in return of adult birds to their nesting areas and of young birds to their birth places.

The ornithologists at the Institute had arranged a two-day stay for me at Lake Velence, an hour's distance from Budapest. On June 23 Dr. Schenk and I took the train to Dinnyés, a village by the lake. Here we were met by our tall guide, Juri Müller, and accompanied him to his flat-bottomed boat. We took our places on the seat in the centre, while Juri stood aft to pole. But first we each had a drink of white wine. "So Juri will pole more diligently," said Dr. Schenk. And then we started on our journey through the great reed beds.

Some open spaces were bright with a little yellow pea-like flower dotting the surface, and others were coloured orange by a handsome stonewort, *Chara*, growing under water. Occasionally we came upon a purple nightshade among the reeds. Immense snails (*Paludina vivipara*), two to three inches long, appeared to be the most abundant inhabitants of the lake. Brilliant damsel flies, the males shimmering blue, the females pale green, darted over the water, as did occasional gorgeous red dragonflies. Happily enough, we did not meet a single mosquito.

Our punt followed narrow, straight channels through the mass of reeds, channels made by fishermen for the capture of carp; the exits were covered under water with nets. At frequent intervals the fishermen had broken over the reeds some three feet above water to make supports for drying their nets. Under this shelter, many small birds nested. We had heard the Great Reed-Warbler[1] as we started and soon afterwards the grasshopperlike trill of Savi's Warbler, as well as the songs of the Reed Bunting and Little (European) Reed-Warbler. The most constant singer was the Moustached Warbler (*Luscionala melanopogon*) that gave an energetic, varied performance with occasional phrases resembling those of a nightingale. None of these songs was high in the musical order, but all were likable and all seemed fitting to the spirit of the reed beds. Kind Dr. Schenk did not tire of mentioning the name of each singer — again and again — a great help to me in my inexperience.

We soon began to find nests, mostly empty. There was one each of Great and Little Reed Warblers, and many of *L. melanopogon*, some old, one with four eggs, one brand new, all wet and green; and finally one with four babies. Dr. Schenk banded these with large rings which he lapped over, saying that he had many more returns from the larger bands than the small ones, since the latter were so hard to read. The inscription on one ring read "Budapest Ornith 121262."

The most abundant nests were those of the lovely Bearded Tit[2], a whitish and buff-coloured, long-tailed bird with a pleasant metallic note. The nests were deep with ample foundations of leaves of reeds, and lined with feathers and plumes of reeds. All that we found this morning contained only two or three eggs or were empty.

We came upon torn-out reeds, the work of muskrats. This

---

[1] *Acrocephalus arundinaceus.* [2] *Panurus biarmicus.*

American animal had escaped some twenty years earlier from a game farm in Bohemia and had since spread over much of Europe. It burrows into dikes and ditches and is said to cause wrecks of automobiles and trains. Even its fur has deteriorated so as to be of little value! "A very harmful beast," said Dr. Schenk.

Juri backed the punt into the reeds and showed us a nest with seven big brown eggs, while the parent Little Crake[1] scolded *jip-jip* in the reeds. Some 20 Black Terns made a tremendous commotion as we cruised about their nesting colony, seeing nests with one or two great dark eggs. Again Juri stopped the boat; he handed us the most ridiculous baby Little Bittern[2]. A gawky, buff coloured creature with great eyes and immense yellow feet, it sat on its haunches and pointed its bill to the sky.

By now, it had grown hot on the lake so we were glad to return to land and walk to the village. To my delight I found that Dinnyés had two White Stork nests, one of them new this year. The three solemn black and white chicks on the roof of the mill appeared to be about half grown. Flocks of white ducks and geese were standing by the shallow pond. Little girls called, "I kiss your hand," and Dr. Schenk answered, "God give you a good day."

The Müllers' house, like all the others, was low, white, thick-walled, and covered with a thatched roof. The north door led into the kitchen, from which one entered the family bedroom; the south door led into a supplementary kitchen and from there into the guest room in which I was to stay. The middle door opened directly into the bedroom of five cows, two calves, and a bull. Dr. Schenk and I had dinner on a little table in my room and made plans for the rest of my stay. Since he had to return to Budapest early in the afternoon and Dr. Koloman Warga, assistant at the Institute, would not arrive until 9:00 the next morning, it was necessary to give instructions to my hosts. He and I communicated in English and German, whereupon would ensue animated conversations in Hungarian between him and Mrs. Müller, followed by a translation for my benefit.

"No, thank you, I do not care for beer. White wine and mineral water would be better."

"No, indeed I do not wish rum in my tea!"

"Pure tea would suit me very well."

Late that afternoon Juri and I started out to search for a Blue-throat (*Erithacus svecicus*). We were silent partners, our conversation limited to a few exclamations on his part when he wished to show

---

[1]*Porzana parva.* [2]*Ixobrychus minutus.*

me birds, and a few requests on mine that he would write the name of some new bird in my note book for later translation by Dr. Warga. A bird flew up from some weeds; Juri searched about and motioned for me to come. "Reed-Bunting," he said, pointing to the nest with three large young. I wished his one English bird name had been of something of which I did not already know the identity.

We walked over the village goose pasture, and then across a dry, treeless plain, seeing flowers familiar in America, thistles and yarrow, and St. John'swort. Flocks of young Starlings and gorgeous Lapwings flew past. At last we came to a boat and pushed off into another reedy lake. Herons rose with loud *quarks*, and Mallard mothers splashed away feigning injury. The main body of open water showed a wonderful array of bird life — Common[1] and White-eyed Pochard (Ferruginous Duck)[2], Coots[3], and Crested[4] and Red-necked Grebes[5] on the water, Black Terns and Barn Swallows skimming over the surface, and Lapwings and Snipe[6] on the shore. We landed on the far side of the lake, borrowing another boat to cross a drainage ditch to a field of sedge. Redshanks[7] screamed in protest at our approach; Little Reed Warblers sang in the air and a handsome Yellow Wagtail[8] called *tsip* from a weed.

"Kickbagg," said Juri, pointing, and there was a bird I had long hoped to see, the beautiful little Bluethroat. With his scintillating blue throat bordered with red, and his brown tail spread, he sang with all his might, at times in his exuberance flying straight up in the air. It was a varied, pretty, happy melody, making me think of a Mockingbird's on a small scale, that is, his own song, not the imitations. All in all, I quite lost my heart to the Bluethroat.

In the distance I noted what I took to be flocks of sheep, which, strangely enough, had not yet been shorn at this late date. Examinations with the binoculars showed, however, that they were, in fact, large grey hogs, attended by swineherds and their dogs. Off to the left was a herd of cows watched by a cowherd on horseback. But, to me, the chief point of interest in the landscape lay in a long stretch of white — some 80 Spoonbills[9] resting on the plain. These great white birds with their extraordinary bills were a fascinating sight.

Despite much searching Juri discovered no nest of the Bluethroat, but a flock of Graylag Geese in flight was a delight. We started to

---

[1]*Aythya ferina.* [2]*Aythya nyroca.* [3]*Fulica atra.* [4]*Podiceps cristatus.* [5]*Podiceps grisegena.* [6]*Gallinago gallinago.* [7] *Tringa totanus.* [8]*Motacilla flava.*
[9]Eurasian Spoonbill, *Platalea leucorodia.*

push home through the reeds, scaring a muskrat from our path. A Crested Grebe preened its remarkable self, then joined its striped-neck half-grown child; the adult flew at our approach, the young bird dove into the water.

The trip home was a memorable experience in the cool evening with the long shadows over the water — the chorus of *melano-pogons*, the strange sad call of the Lapwings, and the throng of Mallards flying against the gold and rose of the sunset sky. As we walked home over the plain, on every side we heard the exuberant songs of the tireless Skylarks.

The next morning my smiling hostess came in, inquiring in pantomime as to how I had slept. Every one was so friendly and talked so earnestly in Hungarian that I felt most ignorant and rude to think that I could not even say "Good day" or "Thank you." I answered them in German, feeling that since it was a foreign language to me, it ought to be less foreign to them than English. This was true of Juri's sister, who understood and spoke a little German. They brought me tea and rolls and three eggs for a break-fast, and appeared to be inquiring what I would like for picnic lunch. They produced an Anglo-Magyar phrase book and I started to hunt for something helpful. "Your father is sitting in his two rooms" did not seem very much to the point, and even less usable was "Are you sure you love me very much? Which is the way to the marriage bureau?" So I said the German word for egg and let it go at that.

Loud squeals came from an outbuilding; upon investigation I found that Hungarian pigs did look woolly; they had long noses, large ears and long coarse hair, while one of them had the fanciest curls all over her back. By the goose pond an old man with a whip was watching two sows and their offspring. Reeds were extensively used by the peasants both for thatching roofs and making walls for outbuildings. Flocks of geese, mostly white but some with splotches of grey, marched to the pond, talking the same language and using the same greeting ceremonies as the Graylags of wild stock I had known at the Lorenz home. The birds around the village were House and Tree Sparrows[1], Barn Swallows and Pied Wagtails[2], while a little outside were Crested Larks and Corn Buntings[3].

I was glad to welcome Dr. Warga, who had done splendid work in banding, both of water birds at the large lake of Kish-Balaton

---

[1]Eurasian Tree Sparrow, *Passer montanus.* [2]White or Pied Wagtail, *Motacilla alba.* [3]*Emberiza calandra.*

and of box-nesting birds in the garden of the Ornithological Institute. Together we proceeded with Juri to the main lake and traversed some of the route of the previous morning. A cool wind was blowing and the birds were silent for the most part. Channels grew narrower and more choked and Juri had desperate struggles to push the punt along. Finally we came to the place where the wading was to begin. I pulled the trousers lent me by Juri over my slacks and changed my shoes for a pair of his; Dr. Warga made sure that his pencil, his notebook, his rings, and other paraphernalia were securely tied to his clothes – and we were off. I cheerfully started to follow Juri, only to find myself sunk to the knees at the second step; Juri hauled me out and after that I noted that the trick was to step sidewise on the reeds and thus provide oneself with some support. The water was not cold and most of the wading was not over a foot deep, but occasionally both Dr. Warga and I slipped into holes. Juri, however, skillful as a heron, sped over the reeds without mishap.

Overhead, Gray and Purple Herons[1] flapped and an occasional Great White Heron[2], a race of the same species as our Great Egret, while majestic Spoonbills sailed around with outstretched necks. A Marsh Harrier[3] objected to our presence with a note that matched well the reedy, froglike songs of the small birds.

Juri called us and we hurried as best we could to his side; there on a great heap of dead reeds stood three gorgeous white birds with extraordinary paddle-shaped bills. This was my first sight of a Spoonbill nest. With a quick movement Juri seized their legs and Dr. Warga banded them. I was surprised to learn that the nest was not built on an old foundation but was made new each year. Other Spoonbill nests were found by Juri, as well as several of Gray Herons, which were also heaps some two-and-a-half feet in height. The young often started to leave at our arrival but Juri was skilled in retrieving them for our benefit. From his long experience at Kish-Balaton, Dr. Warga told us the approximate age of each bird he banded.

Happily the sky was overcast and the air cool; nevertheless I was not sorry when we splashed and tumbled our way back to the punt and pushed off to find a clean place to wash our hands and a good position from which to watch a *melanopogon* – so often heard and so seldom seen. Juri took his modest share from the lunch basket, handing the rest to me. Dr. Warga gave me cheese and lemonade and accepted some of the delicacies I pressed upon

[1]*Ardea purpurea.* [2]*Egretta alba.* [3]*Circus aerunginosus*

him, a bit of smoked ham and wine and cake. The rest of my lunch consisted of no less than *seven* semi-hard-boiled eggs! Our morning conversation had borne fruit. Not even Juri could do justice to such a clutch.

The punt started again on its laborious way and once more we plodded through the reeds. Now Juri showed us Purple Heron nests; these were about the same height above water as those of the Gray Herons but were simple nests placed more or less on top of the reeds instead of being solid mounds. The young birds were gaily-coloured, the skin green, the feathers reddish brown.

Two years previously the first pair of Great White Herons had nested at Lake Velence; their three young had been ringed by Dr. Warga. The next year there was only one bird. This year there were two pairs. Juri led us to one of the nests in which were two young of about 10 and 12 days, odd-looking creatures, their green skin covered with white down. Big Brother struck continually at us and both were vociferous with shrill squeaks and harsh cries. Dr. Warga took careful measurements of the height and size of the nest, and of many fine points in the anatomy of the young birds, only regretting that he had not brought his scales.

The nest of the other pair, he said, should be found within 30 meters of this one. We all started to search and by following shrill cries soon came upon the expected nest with two young of practically the same age as those of the first.

On the way home we found a Bearded Tit's nest with five of the prettiest, fluffiest babies, the general colour buffy with a dark line through the eye. These were banded and carefully tucked back in the nest with a piece of folded reed laid on top. This is a scheme of Dr. Warga's for dealing with young nearly ready to leave the nest; it prevents them from scattering prematurely, and when the parents return they remove the cover.

Mrs. Müller had a supper of delicious fried chicken waiting for us and her little granddaughter gave me a bouquet of madonna lilies and roses. Too soon we had to hurry to the station to catch the train for Budapest, regretfully leaving the wealth of bird life among the reeds of Lake Velence.

Twenty-three years later (in 1961) Guy Mountfort with five other British ornithologists spent two weeks studying and photographing the abundant bird life at Lake Velence and in the marshes of Dinnyés (1962). It is sad to learn that Juri had died in a concentration camp during World War II. His brother Stépan had become the "highly skilled and obliging game warden" of the Lake Velence

Bird Sanctuary. There were then 12 pairs of *Egretta alba*, "the rarest and most magnificent of Europe's herons. It escaped extermination at the hands of the plume-hunters at the turn of the century by a hair's-breadth." The party found the 17 occupied nests of the Spoonbill colony "so close together that the sitting birds could rob one another of sticks without rising from their eggs; but most of the time they either sat or stood immobile, like statues." Mountfort gives a charming description of the songs and displays of a colony of White-spotted Bluethroats.[1] It is a comfort to realize that so many notable birds are still flourishing in this sanctuary.

---

[1]Formerly known as *Cyanosylvia s. cyanecula*, the central and southern form of the Bluethroat, *Erithacus svecicus*.

XXIV

Musical
Prodigies

It was indeed a joy to be home again with my family and at beloved Grey Rocks. Good news had come from Bill Vogt: my book, which at Katharine's suggestion had been called *The Watcher at the Nest*, had been accepted by Macmillan for publication in 1939.

A quotation from my 1938 journal will give a picture of the abundance of birds at Grey Rocks in those bygone, pre-pesticide days:

Here all sounds are beautiful and significant — the wind in the aspen, the rushing of the brook after a rain, the melodious crickets in the evening, and always the birds. In mid-July the bird voices heard from the house are not many. The regular singers number but six. In the background, all day long, there flow the placid, unhurried strains of the Red-eyed Vireo, a song endeared to me from childhood memories and many happy associations over the years. It is such a dependable friend; it is there through the heat of noon and of August days; it is never obtrusive, always pleasant and restful.

The Chewink[1] is different. His loud, emphatic *Towhee* and *Drink-your-tea* might weary us if uttered too often, but as they are given they have a pleasing, invigorating effect. The Scarlet Tanager's Song is loud and emphatic, but much less distinctive.

After the Red-eye, the bird that sings the most is the charming little Magnolia Warbler. His two songs — *weechy weechy wee* and *wichy wichy weasy* — are much-of-a-piece; they do not rank high in the musical order, but they have a quaint charm and earnestness. They are precious to me through the memory of the first warbler nest I studied (1926 b). Early in the

---

[1]Rufous-sided Towhee, *Pipilo erythrophthalmus.*

morning and again in the evening we can rejoice in the heavenly strains of the Hermit Thrush. Later comes our old friend the Whip-poor-will[1]; his vigorous notes are more than welcome.

In cities we must cultivate indifference to most of the sounds — raucous, trivial and unpleasant — that afflict us. Here, on the contrary, the more sensitive we become in this respect, the more aware of our environment we grow, the greater happiness we gain. How greatly we need wilderness!"

The imperative endeavour was to find a Song Sparrow nest with eggs. Many hours were spent watching and waiting and whick-whacking up and down wherever we saw Song Sparrows. At length we came upon a nest with three eggs two and a half feet from the ground in a little hemlock. Every day we visited it. On July 24 we were delighted with the sight of two wee babies and on the next day three.

This family throve, and on July 30 I transferred them to a berry basket and carried them home to a waiting nest. They seemed to me very much like the little Redstarts at Altenberg at the same age; their eyes were open and feathers were unsheathing. We gave the chicks red, blue, and yellow celluloid bands, and called them accordingly Redbud and Blueboy for the seven-day babies and Yellow Puccoon for the six-day one.

Much of the time they slept, all in a black heap, except for the cream-coloured bill-swellings and brown-coloured bills; when the nest was jarred, up came two or three heads like jack-in-the-boxes. That first evening I examined them to be sure they were all right; all three burst into life, standing upright, their necks stretched to the utmost, the insides of their ruby mouths shining in the candle light.

Janet and I busily used our nets for catching fresh insects for our charges; we developed great respect for parent birds. The babies throve splendidly. When they arrived at Grey Rocks they could stretch up on their legs, stand on their feet, and make preening movements although there was next to nothing to be preened. The following day Blueboy scratched his head and stretched his little wing sidewise, while Redbud climbed up on the side of the nest. The weather was sultry — 92°F. in the shade, and the poor babies panted. I put Blueboy into a separate nest and at noon he cowered. In mid-afternoon Redbud also cowered. At bedtime I picked Blueboy up to return him to his nestmates; he cowered and shrieked, causing the others also to cower. So fear had come spontaneously

---

[1] *Caprimulgus vociferus.*

at seven days and had been induced in the six-day-old by the loud scream of its brother.

On August 1 the babies were increasingly active and noisy. At 11:50 Blueboy fluttered his right wing as he begged for an insect; at 12:30 Redbud did likewise, and the next day Puccoon did so for the first time. They opened their bills definitely to the forceps, following it as I moved it about.

The next morning I was awakened at 5:30 by the hunger call. The two older birds looked quite like juvenile Song Sparrows with striped breasts and mottled backs. They were more alert than before and less hungry. They began to beg from one another. Blueboy and Redbud shook themselves.

On August 3 came the great event. Blueboy woke me at 5:10 by the hunger call, yet I found the little birds difficult to feed. I will quote from my record:

At 5:50, Blueboy leaves the nest! He hops to the edge of the box, then to the dish; I feed him, and the others beg frantically from him. He hops to my arm, then to the nest, then to the floor. I gently pick him up and he screams frantically. With big hops he makes his way to the Morris chair at the east end of the room; jumps up onto a rung but slips down. He is calling *eep* all this time and the others answer him. Then he jumps a dozen times to the top of the floor board, always, of course, falling down.

Redbud is on the edge of the strawberry box that holds the nest, preening; Puccoon is begging around him, fluttering one wing, then both; she won't be persuaded that Redbud isn't her parent.

6:07. Redbud now stretches sidewise, then fans his wings, while Puccoon begs hopefully. *They refuse food from me.*

Redbud hops out, then back in, then onto the floor. Now on to the rung of a chair, calling *eep*.

6:10. Blueboy is still trying to get to his floor board top. *I* offer him a mealworm; he shows no interest. I pick him up — he screams bloody murder. Put him in the bamboo cage and he tries frantically to get out.

6:20. The same thing happens with Redbud. Then *Puccoon leaves the nest!*

So the great step of nest-leaving had been taken at the normal ages of nine and ten days.

From then on, they begged constantly from one another. My whistle meant nothing to them; the forceps were ignored. They seemed bound to be fed by another Song Sparrow, especially from one perched slightly higher than they. Redbud and Blueboy begged from the swing in the cage.

That night Blueboy slept on the swing, Redbud on a perch, and

Puccoon on the water dish — as far as possible from one another. The two older birds put their bills in their scapulae for the first time; Puccoon kept up the baby way, but the next night, when she became ten days old, she did as her brothers had done.

The babies were now as winning as could be, fluffy and round and bob-tailed, their buffy breasts striped with dark brown. They were tame and confiding, letting us pick them up at will, apparently enjoying being stroked and liking to ride in our hands and contentedly napping there.

Song Sparrows in the wild separate on leaving the nest and for a week live hidden in the weeds or shrubbery, seeing nothing of any other Song Sparrow but their parents. They no longer have to compete between themselves but they must attract the parent to them.

Before they left the nest they had made themselves as conspicuous as possible at meal times — erecting themselves to a great height, with their red-lined mouths wide open, giving an explosion of loud cries. After leaving the nest they crouched low and bowed, begging with a soft *tit-tit-tit*. It was a ridiculous sight when all three bowed to one another!

The week of "retirement" was marked by many advances. Two days after they had left the nest, each flew a little for the first time — about two feet in distance. At 13 days they discovered that their bills were to be used as tools in exploring and manipulating the outside world. Until then they had merely opened them wide for the reception of provender, and employed them for preening their pretty feathers. But now they suddenly began to show interest in insects, especially moving ones. Blueboy pecked at a grasshopper and Puccoon at a spider, while Redbud picked a thrip off the window screen. Late in the afternoon Blueboy was pecking at all sorts of small things, his own and Redbud's toes, Puccoon's cheek, and a spot on the table. He caught insects on the screen and ate them!

At 14 days they all ate bread and hard-boiled egg out of the dish. Redbud scratched in dead grass, then fell off the table onto the floor.

The most astonishing accomplishment was that of singing. I had thought the Redstarts wonderfully precocious to begin at 18 days, but Redbud warbled *at 13 days*! This is the youngest definite age of starting to sing that I have been able to find for a bird of any species. The next day Blueboy warbled for four minutes at a stretch. I was very pleased that Puccoon did not sing. Surely this silence corroborated my hopes of her sex. When she was 16 days old she was discovered by Janet perched on top of a candlestick looking at herself in the mirror. Such behaviour appeared to be charmingly feminine, but the next day I had a shock:

Horror of horrors. *Puccoon is singing*! This is as good as her brother's efforts, louder than the songs with which they started. My one comfort is that Konrad said female fledglings of some species may sing.

For some days I clung to the faint hope of Puccoon's femininity, continuing to record her as "sister" and "she," but it was no use. The nest in the hemlock had cradled three little brothers.

At 17 days of age, tails were half-grown and the little birds could fly from one end of the long room to the other. They now started "play-fleeing," rushing around on the floor, making short and sudden turns. A new note appeared, a loud and prolonged twitter, given when two birds met; apparently it denoted antagonism.

The appearance of the net was a signal for all to hurry to the window-sill. As I gradually opened the net, out would come a Noah's ark in miniature; the grasshoppers would walk to their doom, the crickets would run, while spiders were adept at escaping.

I felt a responsibility toward my small wards in regard to these insect collections; I did not want to offer them indigestible, evil-tasting, possibly poisonous, tidbits, so in general I stuck to grasshoppers, crickets, caterpillars, moths and spiders. Leaf-hoppers and lace-winged flies and stink-bugs I released out the window. The little birds eyed large black beetles with suspicion and moved out of the way.

Once they were alarmed at the sound of a truck that came up to the house. Twice they were frightened at the chatter of a red squirrel, two dashing to shelter, the other freezing. There is some resemblance between these sounds and the fear note of the adult Song Sparrow.

Still another major activity appeared:

Aug. 12. The first flight! Blueboy, 19 days old, alighted on the roof of the cage near Redbud; they went at each other with out-stretched wings and out-spread tails. They pecked each other. Redbud drove Blueboy off. They gave angry-sounding notes. I am greatly pained.

Four days later there was another quarrel. Puccoon was on top of a curtain; Redbud flew up there. They pecked back and forth, first going through funny bowing motions, but I heard no notes. They spread out their wings and tails; they opened their bills at each other and bumped bills.

The course of development of the Song Sparrows had matched well that of the Redstarts in Altenberg; the order in which behaviour patterns had appeared was similar in both species but in correspondence with a four-day-later fledging date, some activities came later in the Austrian than in the American birds.

On August 18 a great change came into the lives of the three little brothers. They were tucked into the automobile in their small bamboo cage and it was not until six days later that they again enjoyed the freedom of a room. We had caught a jar full of grasshoppers with which to start the journey; at each relative's where we stopped we caught more grasshoppers. Carl and Marjorie procured for us a fine array of mealworms from the barn on Carl's mother's farm in Pennsylvania.

When we stopped for meals I carried the chicks with us, for the car, locked in the sunshine, became a bake oven. I replenished the water supply and sometimes gave them a bit of fried egg. They aroused much curiosity; no one knew what they were; indeed, no one had ever *heard* of Song Sparrows. At one little eating place in West Virginia, where neither loafing nor swearing was allowed, the proprietress told us of her canaries: one male was jealous of the other and refused to sing; the female was a good singer, but an indifferent mother, deserting her young before they were ready to leave the nest, shifting the burden to her mistress. One tourist home was crowded with canaries. Neither of these fanciers could tell me definitely when fledgeling canaries start to sing.

Our little birds soon adapted themselves to this new life; as we hastened on our way they warbled and at times quarrelled. I fed them out of my hand and for the first time they developed the skill of shelling canary seed.

At different Nice cousins we experimented with cats and dogs; we brought these enemies within five feet of the cage but the birds paid no attention. It was in the matter of showing them what to fear that I chiefly failed as a parent; I could not imitate the *melospizan* fear note and warn them of the death-dealing prospensities of these creatures.

In southern Ohio the young birds made a great hit with our small nephews and nieces. We carried the cage around in the fields and captured grasshoppers, the children eagerly assisting when offered a cent for each ten insects. Flying crows and nighthawks were intently watched by our birds. A clap of thunder was unheeded by them. Here, since no Song Sparrows had nested near the house at Grey Rocks, for the first time since babyhood they heard a little singing from adults of their species, but we could see no response from the brothers. The scolding *tchunk*, however, of a wild Song Sparrow did bring a reaction; our little birds listened with raised crests, and answered with the call note *tssip*.

They no longer begged from one another, but did so with fluttering wings to the forceps or to my hand holding a grasshopper. A sizable insect often changed beaks a number of times before disappearing; one bird would take it out of his brother's bill and then the third might seize one end and a tug of war would ensue. All such actions were carried on with the greatest good humour. Quarrelling, when it appeared, broke out spontaneously.

At the home of our fourth relative I had a scare. I was trying to get a bathing dish into the cage as it stood on the lawn, when out slipped Puccoon! He alighted on a bush, I approached cautiously; he flew to another, where to my great relief I was able to pick up the gentle little fellow. Little did I realize how important an individual he was to become — the central figure of my three groups of hand-raised Song Sparrows.

Late that afternoon we reached Chicago. The little birds had been very patient with the long journey, but they certainly seemed glad to be able to leave the cage and stretch their wings once more.

XXV

Song Sparrows in My Study

For a while the three little brothers made charming pets. They often alighted on our arms or heads, sometimes tugging at our hair. Almost always we could pick them up whenever we pleased.

Much of their life centred around the west window where they could look out into the small garden. At times they spied dangerous objects in the sky — gulls, I suppose. They jumped up and captured objects on the screen. I released grasshoppers on the sill and these were eagerly pursued. But one large, active orthopteron gave a great leap that induced them to cry *tik-tik-tik* in fear and to hide for ten minutes.

Constance had purchased a large horned toad at a pet shop; one day it slowly stood up on its hind legs and gazed solemnly into the Song Sparrows' cage. The birds hopped back and forth seemingly puzzled at this strange visitor; then Blueboy gave its "hand" a peck. No reaction from Horned Toad. Another peck. "Ouch," said Constance in sympathy for her pet and indignation at my laughter. This time the hand was withdrawn, although Toady still stood there gazing in.

One surprising thing that the Song Sparrows did was nestmoulding. Redbud started this behaviour when 35 days old; he was cuddled in the insect net as it lay on the floor; suddenly he crouched down with wide-spread wings, working them as if moulding a nest! A few weeks later all three often busied themselves thus in the black cloth with which I covered the bamboo cage at night or in my sweater as it lay on the table. Nest-moulding was seen occasionally until the birds were three and a half months old. Konrad Lorenz suggested that this behaviour might be an example where "young males perform female instinctive actions."

In mid-September they started to moult and in three weeks had renewed all their body feathers. After this, quarrels became more frequent and a stright-line hierarchy was established with Blueboy at the top, Redbud second in rank, and Pucky at the bottom.

On October 6, when the Song Sparrows were ten weeks old, I took an all-day record of their activities. They fed 30 times, spending about five of the 11 hours in eating. Other occupations were nest-moulding and fighting. Blueboy and Redbud gave short songs in connection with disagreements. Blueboy warbled for some 80 minutes, Redbud for 15, and Pucky for one. Four days later I noted: "Great quarrels today. Blueboy always has to interfere in fights between his brothers."

On the 14th we found Redbud dead on the floor. We supposed he must have banged against a window in a wild chase. He was the tamest, most charming of them all. His brothers were rather quiet that day; they called *tsip*, the contact note, more than usual.

In late October Sewall and Eleanor Pettingill drove Constance and me to the A.O.U. meeting in Washington, D.C.* The President of the Union, Dr. Herbert Friedmann of the National Museum, had arranged a symposium on "The Individual versus the Species," and had invited five people to participate. Frances Herrick spoke on this angle in behaviour studies, G. K. Noble on dominance, F. C. Lincoln on migration, Niko Tinbergen (1936) — in America on a lecture tour — on the sociology of the Herring Gull, and I on "The Social *Kumpan* and the Song Sparrow" (1939). The symposium was well worthwhile, Niko's paper being the outstanding one.

I wrote in my chronicle:

Dr. Tinbergen is a delightful man, so unassuming, yet so brilliant. I wished I could have had much more time to consult with him; a week would have been none too long. Bill Vogt and Roger Peterson had breakfast with us, and we discussed problems of Roger's illustrating the *Watcher at the Nest*. A luncheon was devoted to Wilson Club affairs with the Secretary (Sewall Pettingill), the President, and Past-president (Josselyn Van Tyne). You will gather that the A.O.U. meeting was very pleasant and rewarding.

The birds had prospered under Janet's care. Blueboy had been giving loud, short songs, as well as warbling, since October 13; Pucky reached this stage (which I called III) on the 9th of November.

---

*The 56th Stated Meeting of the American Ornithologists' Union, U. S. National Museum, Washington, D. C., October 17-22, 1938.

Blueboy had been the A bird since early October, but now Pucky indulged in loud, short songs in the study whenever Blueboy was in front of the house.

On November 7 I wrote:

A revolution over night. Pucky is a cruel despot to the humbled and fearful Blueboy. Pucky is so relentless that I fear a repetition of the disaster with Redbud.

In the evening, I recorded:

Pucky is now "in bed" in the bamboo cage covered with the black cloth, while Blueboy is resting on newspaper in the transom. He has taken two baths since the light was turned on. He could neither bathe nor eat while Pucky was at liberty. I banished the latter to the kitchen (in the bamboo cage) for hours, but it didn't change the situation when the tyrant returned.

How true was Schjelderup-Ebbe's remark that the unpractised despot is the worst of despots! As, indeed, Sarah and I had also found with our hens.

The next day peace reigned with Blueboy once more the benevolent despot. During the next four days the mastery changed each day; Blueboy warbled but Pucky gave loud, brief songs. On November 11, I noted:

No armistice for poor Blueboy. He seems terrified of Pucky's loud, threatening singing. Escapes into the living room and remains very quiet there.

The next day we witnessed the turning of the tide:

8 a.m. Pucky, although still in the bamboo cage, is master. He warns Blueboy with the threat *jhee*: he sings loud, short songs.

Dr. Hurst Shoemaker of the University of Chicago had just given us a large cage 6 x 4 x 2 feet, since he had finished his studies on hierarchy in Canaries (1939). While Pucky was in the kitchen we installed this cage in the study and Blueboy examined the outside with interest. I then put Pucky in the Shoemaker cage; he flew gingerly from perch to perch. Looked first with one eye, then the other.

8:50 a.m. Blueboy is eager to get in; now on top of cage. Pucky flew to oppose him with spread tail. Both stay there "frozen." In a few minutes Blueboy is boss; he dashes over the top of the cage, while Pucky, terrified, dashes about inside. We drive Blueboy off and Pucky has a chance to get acquainted for a bit with his castle. Blueboy returns to the top; same behaviour from both birds; I shoo Blueboy off.

9:00. Blueboy is on the outside around the base of the cage; Pucky is nervous inside. [Later]: Blueboy lands on top of the cage and Pucky comes up to fight him; he challenges his foe by puffing himself out, waving a wing and warbling.

This display I called the Challenge, "psw," i.e. puff-sing-wave.

Evidently Pucky had been at a disadvantage when put into the strange cage, while Blueboy had become familiar with its outside appearance for half an hour. During the next two weeks dominance shifted now to one, now to the other. Pucky was singing loudly but Blueboy had returned to warbling.

On November 25, Blaine, Janet, and I with Mrs. Amy Baldwin, ardent Chicago bird watcher, drove to the Wilson Club meeting at the University of Michigan at Ann Arbor*, for the fiftieth anniversary of the founding of the society. This was my first meeting as President. It was a wintry day. Soon we ran into ice and snow; a car came cavorting towards us and barely missed us. (The Lynds Jones's had started out from Oberlin but after a near accident had turned back.) At Ann Arbor Janet and Mrs. Baldwin went to a tourist home; Blaine and I to the home of the hospitable Harry W. Hann.

The Wilson Ornithological Club had been founded in 1888 by a small group of teen-age boys, largely in the Midwest, all of whom were greatly interested in the study of the living bird. Notable among the founders were Lynds Jones, later Professor at Oberlin College, Frank L. Burns of Verwyn, Pennsylvania, T. C. Stephens of Sioux City, Iowa, and R. M. Strong. The first two served at one time or another, as president, secretary, treasurer and editor; the third served as president and editor; the fourth as president and treasurer. Dr. Strong (1939) gives special credit to Professor Jones and Stephens:

> The Club would not exist now, if Professor Lynds Jones had not carried the *Bulletin* through the years from 1894 to 1914 or later at considerable financial sacrifice . . . Dr. Stephens [as editor] has been conscientious and highly successful . . . Mr. Percival Coffin as treasurer 1914 to 1916 contributed greatly to the reorganization of the club.

At first all business was carried on through correspondence. The first meeting of the Wilson Club took place in Chicago in 1914. The first publication of the Club was a tiny journal called the *Curlew*; five numbers appeared from October 1888 to April 1889. In March of that year this journal published the names of the 35 members of the Club. Fifty years from its founding the member-

---

*The 24th Stated Meeting of the Wilson Ornithological Club, University of Michigan, Ann Arbor, Michigan, November 25, 26, 1938.

ship had grown to 871 men and women. The struggles and devotion of those founders had born abundant fruit.

This anniversary meeting proved to be the best attended gathering of any of the 24 that the society had held — a total of 261 registrants. In honour of the occasion Dr. Strong spoke on "A History of the Wilson Ornithological Club" (1939), and Sewall Pettingill on "The Wilson Ornithological Club of Today" (1939).

The Symposium on the International Congress went off very well. Dr. Emil Witschi of the State University of Iowa showed us coloured slides of Rouen, of our trips and of a number of ornithologists; Lawrence Hicks gave an interesting talk on "Observations on European Birds," while I talked on "A Month's Study at Altenberg, Austria."

There were four excellent papers involving banding: Amelia Laskey's of Nashville, Tennessee, on her Bluebird studies; Lawrence Walkinshaw's of Battle Creek, Michigan, on his Prothonotary Warblers; and Dr. Hann's on "Longevity of the Ovenbirds (1937)." In this last speech we learned that the survival of his breeding birds averaged 2.57 years, practically the same as I had found with my Song Sparrows while their environment was undisturbed. Rosalie Edge gave two excellent talks — one on "More Wildlife Sanctuaries in the National Parks," the other "Hawk Protection Made Popular." Dr. Charles Kendeigh (1939) from the University of Illinois, Urbana, had made an important contribution with his "Development of Body Temperature Control in the House Wren."

At the banquet, Blaine invited Mrs. Edge to sit at our table and what fun we had! She was a born actress and in response to Blaine's stirring her up, told us most amusing tales of her struggles for militant conservation with obstinate members of the Old Guard among our ornithologists.

After dinner, Sewall* presented splendid movies in colour of everyday birds, and George Sutton gave a magnificent talk on experiences with birds in Mexico, illustrated with his lovely paintings. It was the finest after-dinner entertainment I had ever experienced at a bird meeting.

It had been a wonderful meeting, one of the very best I had ever attended. Teddy Nelson** of Spotted Sandpiper fame, declared it was *the* best in all her experience, and she had been to many A.O.U. meetings. Credit was partly due to the Secretary and the well-planned program, partly to the efficiency of the Local Com-

*Dr. Olin Sewall Pettingill
**Dr. Theodora Nelson

mittee under the chairmanship of Josselyn Van Tyne, and partly to the President's and other presiding officers' untiring efforts to keep the speakers within their time limits on a very crowded schedule.

A frigid welcome awaited us in Chicago, for our furnace boy had allowed the house to become very cold during our three-day absence. The birds had stopped singing and it was not until December 8 that Pucky started to warble again and 11 days later that Blueboy followed suit. On Interpont some of the Song Sparrows might sing till the end of November if the temperatures continued mild, but were silent through December. Singing might start again in late January in response to mild weather. Our hand-raised Song Sparrows had been stimulated to precocious territory activities in the fall by high temperatures and unnaturally long days through artificial light in the evenings.

Christmas was a great event this year for we had twice our normal family with us: Mother, Barbara, Stan and their small son. Malcolm was a lovely baby, 11 months old. He and his great grand-mother were the best of friends; she would sit in the rocker by the big east window, rocking the little fellow and singing to him songs and hymns some of which I did not remember having heard before. Blueboy often joined the party. "Oh, he's on my back!" I once heard my mother exclaim.

On December 31, Pucky burst into adult songs; the next day Blueboy did likewise. Pucky proclaimed territory in the big cage, Blueboy by the east window some 20 yards distant. Blueboy wished to be further from his enemy; he often flew up against the window trying to enlarge his territory. During a blizzard he still busily worked on this problem, despite the wild storm outside.

On February 1, I found him upstairs and caught him on the window sill. I brought him downstairs and showed him to Malcolm. The baby's eyes grew very big and then he smiled in delight. I opened my hand and he looked in wonder as the bird darted out.

The next morning we found Blueboy dead on the floor. We blamed ourselves for not confining him overnight, but it had been impossible to catch him. Pucky was now alone. He sang much. His six songs were typical of the species in their form, length, and timing but not in the quality, and the same had been true of Blue-boy's songs. The brothers had heard no adult Song Sparrow songs in the fall; they evidently had been influenced to some extent by records of British bird songs which we had occasionally played in their hearing in the autumn.

Mr. Whittle, after 14 years of devoted editorship, first of the *Bulletin of the Northeastern Bird-Banding Association*, then of its successor, *Bird-Banding*, felt he had done his duty. To everyone's regret he resigned. No less than eight fellow ornithologists urged me to take the editorship; I appreciated the compliment but firmly declined. James L. Peters, of the Museum of Comparative Zoology at Cambridge, Massachusetts, although absorbed in his great project *Check List of Birds of the World* (1931), was persuaded to accept the task and carried it on for a dozen years. In 1951 E. A. Bergstrom, a birdbander of West Hartford, Connecticut, became the third able editor of this distinguished journal, and, in 1970, he still holds the post.

To return for a moment to my Reviews for *Bird-Banding*, by September 3, 1938, I had composed and typed 51 Reviews in three days — an all-time record. In contrast, on March 10, 1939, I wrote: "One solid week on those wretched Reviews. This lot makes 900 that I've done for *Bird-Banding* in nearly five years." Mr. Peters, however, welcomed the batch of 55 Reviews by me and 12 by Mr. McCabe. He wrote: "You and Mr. McCabe have certainly gone through a tremendous amount of literature and are certainly to be congratulated on your industry and discrimination."

The editor of the *Wilson Bulletin*, Dr. T. C. Stephens, also resigned after 14 years of faithful work. Josselyn Van Tyne accepted the editorship, choosing for associate editors Pierce Brodkorb, a colleague at the University of Michigan, and myself. My duties consisted in giving my opinions and suggestions on many of the papers submitted to the *Bulletin*. I was glad to correct errors before they were published rather than after the damage had been done. Yet that I was appalled at some of the papers is shown by the note in my journal on April 29: "VT keeps sending me awful papers to struggle over." But the editor was appreciative as shown by his acknowledgement: "I am delighted with the splendid help you are giving me on the *Wilson Bulletin* editing. Your promptness and thoroughness amaze me." And again: "Thank you for the splendid critical comments on that paper I sent you. They are just what I needed."

For ten years Dr. Van Tyne rendered distinguished service to the *Bulletin* with his conscientious, dedicated editorship of the journal.

The Watcher at the Nest appeared in the spring of 1939. It was a proud and happy moment for our family. There were many appreciative reviews. The following by T. T. McCabe came out in

Bird-Banding:

Whether in the first half-dozen essays, which are retellings of the epic of the Song Sparrows, and in which the author bodies forth in "real life" the whole range of modern bird psychology, or in the later numbers — earlier memories which must depend in greater degree on sheer description and the charm of the simple and enthusiastic style, the book is *good work*, whether as zoology or as literature.

A letter came from the very successful nature writer, Donald Peattie in Santa Barbara, California:

The Watcher at the Nest is a joy and a delight. I have read it all and am reading it again. Your art of telling it is so good that it conceals how good the science is. My warmest congratulations.

XXVI

Song Sparrows
at Wintergreen Lake

I had learned so much about Song Sparrow behaviour from the three little brothers from Pelham that I was determined to try this summer to raise a member of the opposite sex. Most fortunately for me, kind Miles and Lucy Pirnie invited me to spend June with them for this purpose at the W. K. Kellogg Bird Sanctuary on Wintergreen Lake, near Augusta, Michigan (1948).

Upon my arrival on the first Sunday in June 1939, I was amazed and delighted with the wealth of bird life; there were birds on every hand, from Canada Geese and four species of swans on the lake to Purple Martins in the air and Traill's Flycatchers in the thickets. The Pirnies showed me nests of Killdeer and Spotted Sandpiper, Kingbird and Mallard, Warbling Vireo and Yellow Warbler[1], and Mute and Whooper Swans[2], but they had not yet discovered a nest of a Song Sparrow. Auspiciously enough, I found one that very afternoon, in a most prickly juniper, at the corner of the house. Confiding parents were feeding three chicks, one a Cowbird, about four or five days old. Miles promised to install a blind so that I could take my first motion pictures with his camera.

The next morning I started out with high hopes to find more Song Sparrow nests. Bronzed Grackles[3] had bred in astonishing numbers in the grove of young red pines; their short-tailed youngsters were mostly in the nearby swale and the parents berated me so loudly and so tirelessly that I could appreciate the advantages

---

[1]*Dendroica petechia.* [2]*Cygnus cygnus.* [3]Now called Common Grackle, *Quiscalus quiscula.*

of the semi-communal nesting of this species — any enemy would be glad to retreat.

At last the angry grackles forgot me. I came upon a pair of Song Sparrows and started to beat the surrounding vegetation with a stalk of evening primrose; I soon discovered a nest, white and shining, attached to a briar but toppled sidewise. In it were two tiny, pinkish, white-downed Yellow Warblers. I had nothing in the way of a string but managed to secure the nest by winding a weed around it.

In the afternoon Miles took me to visit two neighbouring estates, and on each we found a nest, one in a privet with a few straws protruding as a name plate, the other in a spreading juniper with dead grass sticking out for all to see. Song Sparrow nests were far easier to locate in the formal plantings on an estate than in the wilderness on the Sanctuary. The first nest was soon robbed, but Juniper-2 proved a useful discovery.

Day after day I searched and continually met with disappointment. What countless times, I thought, I'd searched for Song Sparrow nests — in Ohio, in Massachusetts, and now in Michigan! How many times I had hoped for success, had believed I had learned the pair's secret, and had confidently expected to be rewarded by the sight of a little brown bird scurrying away — only to have my hopes dashed. Had I found a tenth of the nests I had looked for? I doubted it. Next time, I resolved, I would study a bird whose nests are easy to locate.

Friday, Miles came upon *two* Song Sparrow nests, one with three eggs, the other with five. And I, who had studied the nesting habits of *Melospiza melodia* for ten years and had discovered over 200 nests in other states and had worked faithfully for six days, had found nothing independently except the nest by the house.

On the morning of June 10, Miles, his 12-year-old daughter, Cynthia, and I arose at 4:00 and drove into Battle Creek to visit Lawrence Walkinshaw (1939), a wonderful man who achieved an incredible amount of field work despite a busy schedule as a dentist. At that time he had opposite his house a study area with an abundance of Field Sparrows; he mapped their territories, trapped the birds on their nests, colour-banded them, and faithfully followed their fortunes, doing all of these labours in the early mornings and evenings. (Field Sparrows nest in more open situations than do Song Sparrows.) Larry carried on the study for ten years, 1938 to 1947, until his tract became filled with houses. His last published account of his study appeared in 1945, but later he most kindly supplied me with the total figures of success — 593 nests.

The next morning we again made an early start, for Larry had promised to take us to the Crane Marsh. This was a great expanse of marsh hay with a few bulrushes and woolgrass and not one mosquito! On all sides were splendid royal fern and fragrant hay-scented fern, pink meadowsweet, delicate meadow rue and bright blue flag. Best of all were the strange blooms of pitcher plants and the beautiful flowers of *Calapogon* and showy orchis.

Short-billed Marsh Wrens were singing on all sides, while Bobolinks were pouring out their joyous, bubbling melodies, the bizarre males madly chasing their brown mates. Suddenly Larry pointed out the Sandhill Cranes[1] — a parent and two small downy young. We rushed across the marsh, but the family had vanished into the underbrush, and it was in vain that we searched all around for those babies to band. Both parents flew about croaking, showing themselves again and again. At one time a group of five cranes flew about overhead. It was a wonderful experience for me to visit such wild country and so near civilization. Fortunately it is now preserved as the Bernard Baker Sanctuary.

At last my luck changed. On June 10, I found two nests. One, built in a brilliantly blooming rose bush on the work shop, contained four eggs. The other held seven eggs, five of the Song Sparrow and two of a Cowbird. The next day by watching a pair feeding in a tangle of dewberries, I discovered a nest with five young Song Sparrows, the youngest just hatching.

After that, more and more and more searches and nothing gained but health and enjoyment of nature. One morning I did a great deal of whick-whacking with no results but a cottontail rabbit and two dragonflies. It was funny how hard I tried to make such fugitives into Song Sparrows; I wanted them so badly that when any creature hurried out, it seemed as if it *must* be a Song Sparrow. Well, if I couldn't find the nests I needed, at least there was a comforting crop of wild strawberries.

One afternoon we called on the Lee Jicklings; they were interested in banding and had put up many nesting boxes for Bluebirds, Tree Swallows[2] and House Wrens. Now they had nine pairs of wrens and no swallows. One Bluebird they had had for three years; the wrens had just punctured her second set of eggs. Dr. Walkinshaw had found the House Wrens to be serious enemies

---

[1]*Grus canadensis.* [2]*Tachycineta bicolor.*

of the beautiful Prothonotary Warblers nesting in cavities in this region, but down at Reelfoot Lake in Tennessee these warblers have remarkable success, nesting as they do, south of House Wren range. In Michigan Larry reported that 413 eggs in 121 nests of these warblers resulted in 106 fledgelings — 26 per cent of success, while in Tennessee 163 eggs in 36 nests resulted in 100 fledgelings — 61 per cent. I thought of Althea Sherman and her impassioned but disregarded campaign, "Down with the House Wren boxes."

Brown-headed Cowbirds are devoted to Song Sparrows as foster parents for their children, and also to Chipping Sparrows. Three nests of these little rufous-capped birds in a grove of small spruce trees each held an egg of the parasite; one of these hatched along with the Chippies. Six days later I visited them, only to find the nest tilted sidewise and empty, the lining in disarray. On the ground whom did I find but fat Cowbird and tiny Chippy sitting up very straight with their bills wide open. Nearby was Chip No. 2, also hungry and hopeful. I suppose the Cowbird must have overturned the frail nest and precipitated the whole family onto the ground. I fixed the nest more firmly into place and reinstated the waifs. Before long, father came with a cranefly, while mother gathered the trio under her breast.

Next day the Chips begged madly every time I visited them, while Cowbird lay low. I decided to adopt her, to give the Chips a chance. How they appreciated the departure of their guest! Chippychild, as we called her (assuming her femininity from her comparatively light weight, as adult female Cowbirds weigh almost a fourth less than males) was a quiet visitor, pleased with all I gave her — tiny grasshoppers, large damsel flies, hard-boiled egg, and chicken mash.

In the evening we took her to the Nature Club picnic at the Jicklings; she was the hit of the party. I doubt if ever before one of her species had been the centre of attraction for so many human beings, who usually fail to appreciate her kind. The adults saw new beauties in a young Cowbird, and the children fought for the privilege of catching insects for her with my net. Mayflies and one sizable grasshopper were the best finds; most of the grasshoppers were hardly large enough to see without a microscope.

The next day insect hunting continued to be very disappointing. With a net in each hand I industriously swept the grass in each halfway favourable-looking locality, but all I got for my labour was a large collection of daisy fleabane heads with a few demoralized flies and a miscellaneous set of very small creatures; these I picked out with care and served, a half-dozen at a time, to my eager pet. But even so, Chippychild, two days after her adoption, had lost, rather than gained weight. So I took her back to the spruce, transferring the family to a strong and ample Song Sparrow nest with which I replaced the original flimsy structure; the three filled the new nest comfortably.

At noon a fine batch of mealworms from Carl and Marjorie arrived in the mail. When I went to the spruce, Chippychild seemed so restored by her six-hour visit home, while the little chips seemed so oppressed by her presence, so hungry and so squashed, that I extracted the Cowbird, who fat and full, cowered as her famished foster brothers stood upright, shrieking for provender. I offered her a bite from the forceps; she gaped, and I said, "Come with me."

The next day I took the two youngest from the Dewberry Song Sparrows, one to keep, the other to exchange with the Juniper-2 family; I felt sure from previous experience that the parents would not be troubled at the change in their family. We banded the chicks with red, blue and yellow, and six-year-old Susy Pirnie and I decided to call them Scarlet, Flax and Goldilocks.

Disaster had overtaken many of our nests, while others still had eggs, so that only one nest now contained small young. I should have adopted some of these, but, since my first attempt at taking motion pictures — at the nest by the house — had proved disappointing, we put up a blind at this nest and I took movies of both parents feeding the young and finally of the babies leaving. As Goldilocks, the smallest of the Juniper-2 family, had not thriven well in the house, I had added her to this household and the parents cared for her as one of their own.

When Dewberry, Flax, and Scarlet were two weeks old, it was time for me to go. I was sad to leave the beauty and peace of the Sanctuary, the songs of the birds in the daytime, the amazing flights of young Starlings coming to roost in the buttonbushes, the intriguing night sounds from the lake — shouts of Whooper Swans, insistent drone of Fowler's toads, the pebbly tinkle of the cricket frogs, and deep boom of the bullfrogs.

It had been a happy month for me with the charming Pirnie family, with the guidance of Miles in photography, delicious meals prepared by Lucy Pirnie, the contacts with other bird people, and the wealth of bird life.

The little birds made the journey by car. On our arrival at Chicago, Pucky who had been alone since February, was much excited; he came over, tail spread, perched first on one cage, then on the other, and examined the newcomers for some minutes. Interestingly enough, although Chippychild begged at him, the Song Sparrows did not. We gave Pucky a mealworm, and soon we noticed that he was carrying it about. At length he ate it, and we gave him another. This he worked in his bill and again carried about for a long time, approaching Dewberry several times. If the Song Sparrows had only begged, he might have been able to carry out his parental impulse to feed them; they gave their location call, meaning "I'm here. I'm hungry," but did not open mouths, wave wings, and call *zee-zee-zee*. To our disappointment Pucky finally ate the second worm.

For four days Pucky carried mealworms about — once for 18 minutes, but always ended by eating them himself. Due to his hostility to the newcomers I shut his cage door when they were out of their cages, but the little innocents would not learn that he was dangerous. They would perch on top of the large cage; he would sneak up and peck a foot or pull out a bunch of feathers; the victim would squeal *but remain*. For instance, when Dewberry was 20 days old, I noted:

Y (Pucky) fighting D who is perched above him; D fights back. Y puffs, sings, waves his wing. Pecks D and pulls out feathers; D squeals but *still* stays.

Similar happenings took place between Pucky and the two little Junipers.

When Chippychild was 23 days old, she flew to the top of Pucky's cage and begged down to him. "He attackes her. She squeals and remains. He returns towards her; she looks down and begs and begs."

Two days later Chippychild was left for the afternoon in Janet's care; unfortunately I had not warned her against over-feeding the enthusiastic beggar. Upon my return Chippychild seemed stupified and our attempts to cure her may have brought on her death. This was a keen disappointment, as Cowbirds, belonging to a social species, have been reported to make most interesting pets.

By this time, thanks to Pucky's behaviour, Flax had only a few tail feathers left and Scarlet none at all. Janet remarked, "At least she's *neater* that way than with only one feather," while the next day Constance observed, "It's a help in distinguishing the babies since Scarlet has no tail, Flax has one feather and Dewberry has a tail." Two weeks later Dewberry had only two tail feathers left.

My friend of Columbus days, Charles Walker, then assistant at the State Museum, later professor of Zoology at the Ohio State Stone Laboratory on an island in Lake Erie, had invited me to give two lectures on "The Role of Territory in Bird Life" (1941). In preparing the lectures my reviews in *Bird-Banding* proved to be of the greatest help. The trip to Put-in-Bay was a delight in every way. Charles met me at Sandusky and drove to the boat which took us to the laboratory.

My talks came Saturday evening and Sunday morning. People were much interested, and we had long discussions afterwards. I enjoyed the students and faculty very much. One of the boys — Dale Jenkins — had graduated from Ohio State University and was coming to the University of Chicago on a Ridgway Fellowship in the fall*. Another student — Loren Putnam — had a charmingly trusting hand-raised Cedar Waxwing; he made a fine study of this species (1949) and later was called to teach at Ohio State University. Here he lived on the edge of Interpont.

As for *The Watcher*, in April I had been proud to receive a pre-publication payment of $80.00 from the publisher. In July, however, instead of another cheque, came a notice that they had over-paid me to the tune of $41.60! Unfortunately for my book, Bill Vogt had left the country early in 1939 to study the ecology of the Peruvian guano birds. The publicity put out by the publisher had been poor, and the book had not gotten off to a good start. The second pay cheque, sent in January 1940, amounted to $79.24.

A quick trip was made to Grey Rocks, largely to admire Marjorie's seven-months-old son, Hugh — a fine sturdy baby. Grey Rocks had suffered greatly from the 1938 hurricane; many of its great trees had been uprooted. In New York we saw Dr. Noble and David Lack from England, and wished we could have talked longer with them.

Back in Chicago I found the four Song Sparrows somewhat subdued, for all were moulting. They had established a straight-line peck-order: Pucky, Dewberry, Scarlet, Flax. I had cherished a faint hope that Scarlet might be my much desired female, as "she," in contrast to Dewberry and Flax, had never been heard to warble. Yet "her" ferocity appeared to contradict this opinion. Once again I had apparently raised three males! On September 3 I noted, "I can't work in the evenings for the birds fight so much if the light is on."

On the morning of September 19 Scarlet was found dead on the floor and the same was true of Flax two days later. Post-mortems confirmed that both were males. "Well," I consoled myself, "with no female at all, there'll be less to write."

*Oil had been found on Robert Ridgway's home grounds at Olney, Illinois; returns from these wells financed a yearly fellowship at the University of Chicago, which had charge of the Sanctuary.

XXVII

At Last,
A Lady Song Sparrow

A friend of ours in Columbus, William Schantz, wrote me that he could give me a young female Song Sparrow he had raised by hand from the age of eight days, as well as two Goldfinches, hand-raised from the age of two days! Bill was a gifted, ingenious, shy young man, a birdbander and intense nature lover. Lawrence Hicks brought these birds with him in late November, 1939, to the Wilson Club* meeting at Louisville, Kentucky; they rode in a handsome two-compartment wire cage constructed by their foster-father and donated to us.

It was a fine W.O.C. meeting, the second largest in our history. We went over the 1,000 mark in membership, nearly 200 members more than ever before. The program was full yet there was time for discussion of most of the papers. Mine, on "The Development of Song Sparrows and a Cowbird," lasted 30 minutes and was illustrated with lantern slides and my motion pictures. When the projector was turned on, the film proved to be in backwards! I didn't mind; during the rewinding I kept talking about Chippychild. Seven of the 37 papers were motion pictures in natural colours, all of them good and two of them magnificent — Peter Koch's of Spoonbills in Florida and Cleveland Grant's of Ruffed Grouse and Baltimore Orioles.

---

*The 25th Stated Meeting of the Wilson Ornithological Club, Louisville, Kentucky, November 24-26, 1939.

I wrote to my mother:

Many people were shocked and grieved that I was not to continue as President. It has been an honor and an opportunity, and with the help of excellent fellow-officers we have been able to achieve a number of important things. Of one new feature I am especially proud — the establishment of the Wildlife Conservation Committee. (This became a permanent feature of the society, I am happy to say.)

Lawrence Hicks became the new President, while Sewall Pettingill continued as a most efficient Secretary. At the close of the meeting Blaine remarked to me, "One of the best things you have from your bird work is your host of friends." Truly my career in studying birds has been an adventure in friendships.

Home again with our precious lady Song Sparrow. Jewel elicited a moderate amount of interest from Dewberry but little from Pucky. The Goldfinches were ignored by all three Song Sparrows.

Only scattered songs had been heard from Pucky between September 15 and October 6, none later. Yet he had been consistently dominant over Dewberry throughout the autumn. On December 17 Pucky was suffering from a mild case of diarrhea, so I shut him in the big cage with a tonic in his drinking water. The same day Dewberry warbled rather loudly by Jewel's cage, waving his wings. She retired to the back of her cage. He then flew to Pucky's cage, warbling more and more loudly, his wings waving. Pucky at once went into a perfect ball, both wings up, and singing softly. Dewberry raised his crest; Pucky rushed at him and drove him off.

On the 19th Dewberry started to sing short songs. Three days later he sang loud, short songs, intimidating Pucky who flew back and forth in his cage with crest raised in alarm. Dewberry, puffed up and wings vibrating, sang very loudly. Ten minutes later he started to *tchunk*, a sure sign of dominance, then flew to the cage and repeated the challenge with loud singing instead of the typical soft utterance.

The course of song development, from the first appearance of short songs when fighting, to the firm establishment of the adult repertoire, had lasted 88 days with Blueboy and 81 with Pucky. Yet Dewberry's song development had been telescoped into *six* days! I believe that the chief factor lay in Pucky's temporary lack of vigour which allowed Dewberry to gain the mastery.

On January 9 and 11 I recorded and studied Dewberry's songs, discovering five the first day and a sixth the next day. I looked up my notes on Pucky's songs, made on March 2 and May 24 in 1939 and was amazed to find them practically the same as Dewberry's.

On January 17, 1940, I wrote in my Chronicle:

Great adventures in the study today. Pucky burst into singing; he and Jewel must have had 50 fights through the wire and at last Jewel is getting somewhat intimidated; Dewberry is completely cowed and had to be taken out into the kitchen. One thrilling discovery is that he has four of "Dewberry's songs" and maybe a fifth.

Our good friend, Dorothea Ewers, working at the University of Chicago for her Ph.D. in psychology, at different times borrowed Dewberry and Pucky and recorded their songs. She corroborated the situation that each bird had six songs and that each song of Dewberry's matched one of Pucky's — something I had never found in the field. Dewberry must have become imprinted on Pucky's repertoire from hearing the latter sing a small amount in late September and early October. The crowding of the establishment of his repertoire into six days had left him no time in which to practise variations on the models he had heard in the fall.

Emmet Blake, assistant curator of birds in the Field Museum kindly lent me a handsome mounted Barred Owl so that I could test the responses to it of my inexperienced hand-raised birds. All of them, including the Goldfinches, showed strong alarm at the sight of the mount, especially when Dewberry on four occasions and Pucky on six, discovered it on the piano in the living room. The piano evidently acquired an "owl tone," for it was viewed with distrust even after the mount had left our house. After four months absence at Mrs. Ewers' in the summer Pucky, on his return home, at once showed strong alarm with crest and tail raised as he kept his eyes on the empty end of the top of the piano.

As for Jewel, she had been a pleasant occupant of the study, holding her own when threatened by the males. Most of the time she was alone in the big cage, while one male was in the bamboo cage and the other free, except when visiting the Ewerses. She was a quiet bird, only occasionally threatening either male with a *zhee*. Throughout February I heard whispered, faint warbles from her. On February 28 and 29 and also on March 2, she was very restless, flying back and forth in the cage, giving the call *tsip*. I wondered whether this behaviour might be due to migration restlessness. She had been hatched in central Ohio where I had found most of my female Song Sparrows migratory.

The members of the American Physiological Society were to

meet in March in New Orleans and we utilized the occasion for a trip to see the countryside. There were no signs of spring in the Chicago region when four of us bird watchers — Dr. and Mrs. Alfred Lewy, Blaine, and myself — started south in our car on the morning of March 8, 1940. Roadside pools were frozen; vegetation was brown. A Herring Gull in Jackson Park and House Sparrows were our first birds. In the country we met a few flocks of crows and many flocks of starlings. The two Prairie Horned Larks which were sighted were probably on their nesting territories.

In central Illinois grass was greening and we met our first spring birds — a Meadowlark, a Red-winged Blackbird and a Loggerhead Shrike, as well as hawks — Cooper's, Marsh[1], and Sparrow Hawk. In southern Illinois all but the Redwing and Cooper's Hawk were met in larger numbers; five Marsh hawks and 16 Sparrow Hawks, besides two Red-tailed Hawks and our first Turkey Vulture. Exciting spring birds were two Purple Martins, a robin, a bluebird, and finally, near the Mississippi River, three Mourning Doves. Scarlet maples were in bloom.

On crossing the river into Missouri at Cape Giradeau, and continuing south we found cotton fields, mules, mistletoe and our first great flocks of blackbirds — Brown-headed Cowbirds, Bronzed Grackles, Red-winged Blackbirds, and Starlings. Spending the night in a tourist court at Blytheville, Arkansas, was a treat to us city-dwellers; in the clear air in the evening we saw Venus, Jupiter, Mars, and Saturn, and in the early morning the songsters were roosters and a zealous robin. As we pursued our southern course through the northern edge of Arkansas the next morning, it was the extraordinary numbers of grackles that impressed us most. It was here that we met our first cypress trees and heard our first Mockingbird of the trip.

Recrossing the Mississippi at Memphis, we followed Route 51 down through the state of Mississippi past woods of oak and yellow pine, and past eroded farms with hungry-looking cows. It was painful to see the great gullies on the hillsides; we hoped that soil conservation would be speedily adopted for its beneficial results from many standpoints. The practice of strip cropping and of protecting woods from grazing has doubled the bird population in some regions. Elms and maples were in bloom and a weeping willow was in leaf. After the hordes of migrating blackbirds in the flood plain of the Mississippi, the scarcity of birds in the uplands

---

[1]*Circus cyaneus.*

was striking. Shrikes, perched on telegraph wires, intently studying the ground, and Turkey Vultures, circling in the air, were the commonest birds.

In central Mississippi we were delighted to see daffodils, forsythia, and pansies in bloom. Just north of Canton we met our first Spanish moss, hanging on a cypress; this is not really a moss but a member of the pineapple family. The plant is not a parasite of the tree, which it utilizes merely as a perch. Our first wild flower of the year proved to be a star lily (*Nothoscrodum*), a favourite of ours in Oklahoma. In southern Mississippi we found loblolly pines, a few maples in leaf, Japanese quince, and camellias in bloom, as well as our first Purple Martin since Illinois, and our first and only robin in Mississippi, making one robin for each state.

We spent the night in Hammond, Louisiana, centre of the strawberry industry. The town was fascinating to us with its great willow oaks, its blossoming roses and peach trees, and its singing Mockingbirds. We were told that the spring was late and that the winter had been the coldest in thirty years; there had actually been *snow*, and that people had driven up from New Orleans to see it.

The next day we made our way in leisurely fashion to New Orleans, for it was a strange world in which we found ourselves. On each side of the road were bayous flanked by forests of cypress and gum which, draped with masses of grey moss, looked like ghost trees. There was no green except in the undergrowth, which consisted entirely of the exotic-looking dwarf palmetto. Against the grey-black of the moss-draped cypress the flaming beauty of the scarlet maple in seed made a breath-taking sight. They might symbolize the tragedy and the glory of life, which come together, neither complete without the other. Life is pictured in its darkest and brightest colours, the contrasts between its sorrows and its joys; its frustrations and its achievements.

New Orleans, despite the frosting of the palms and palmettos, was brilliant with magnolias, roses, redbud, camellias and its Floral Trail of azalias. Each morning we were awakened by a Mockingbird. In Audubon Park we saw our first Boat-tailed Grackles[1] and were impressed by the immense, moss-covered live oaks. A pair of tame White Storks in the flying cage were adept at catching peanuts thrown to them.

Our trip into the delta region the following day took us through a flat, monotonous country of truck gardens, corn fields, pear

[1]*Quiscalus major.*

orchards in full bloom, and finally orange groves. One of the most abundant of the native shrubs was a relative of the bayberry, the wax myrtle, from which the commonest winter warbler in Louisiana takes its name. White clover was in bloom and we heard our first frogs of the season.

It was on this trip that we saw our first Black Vultures; Turkey Vultures were abundant. Marsh Hawks, Kingfishers, Mockingbirds, and Loggerhead Shrikes were characteristic birds of the roadsides and prairies; a few Martins and Tree Swallows were noted and several flocks of Redwings. The predominant bird, however, was the Boat-tailed Grackle; numbers of males perched in trees facing the wind, while greater numbers walked over the plowed fields. At a lake we saw gulls, cormorants[1], and Common Egrets.

The gravel road came to an end at Venice. Leaving the car we walked along a dike above a bayou and had a splendid view of an Anhinga that perched for long periods at a time near the top of a tree. A Red-shouldered Hawk carried prey to its nest. Caspian Terns[2] flew over the water, while out in a field Lesser Yellowlegs[3], Little Blue Herons[4] in adult and immature plumage, and Snowy Egrets[5] waded in a brook. The most amazing sight to us Northerners was a Brown Pelican[6]; this extraordinary, prehistoric-looking creature sailed about with head drawn back, then suddenly dashed head first into the water.

On March 16 the Lewys joined friends on their way to Florida, and Blaine and I drove north on our somewhat roundabout route to Chicago. The colours in the woods were softer than the week before with more green in the maples, willows, and cypress; the gums were in bloom and the maple seeds more orange and salmon than before. The country changed little as we passed through St. John the Baptist Parish, St. James Parish, and Ascension Parish; there were cane fields, wax myrtle, palmetto, willow oaks in bloom, and the gorgeous scarlet maples against the background of cypress and gum swathed in funeral garments. Birds were not numerous – a few hawks, Turkey Vultures, shrikes, and Mockingbirds and a few flocks of redwings and cowbirds were all that we recorded. In one place we met seven robins in a group. Gradually we lost the south and with it, spring.

---

[1]Double-crested Cormorant, *Phalacrocorax auritus.* [2]*Hydroprogne caspia.* [3]*Tringa flavipes.* [4]*Hydranassa caerulea.* [5]*Egretta thula.* [6]*Pelecanus occidentalis.*

There was a sudden change in the character of the country when we crossed the Red River at Alexandria; we left the cypress swamps in the flood plain for uplands covered with yellow and loblolly pines and blackjack oaks. Spanish moss became scarce; it draped itself on pecans and other trees in the stream valleys, but before long we saw it no more. There was a small amount of cypress, not yet in leaf. Shortly before we reached Shreveport we saw three Purple Martins at a box and many large flocks of blackbirds, apparently mostly grackles and cowbirds.

We slept in a tourist court near the Red River and next morning were happy to hear the melodious coo of the Mourning Dove. A 260-mile drive across the northeastern corner of Texas brought us to the Red River once more and to the border of Oklahoma. Here fragrant sand plums were in full bloom and redbud was beginning to come out. There was much mistletoe on the scrubby oaks; elms were in bloom and in seed. We explored a creek bed in hopes of meeting some of our old friends; to our delight juncos and Cardinals sang, Hairy and Red-bellied Woodpeckers were in evidence, a goldfinch took a bath, a robin scolded and our beloved Harris' Sparrows gave snatches of their sweet songs.

In Carter County we met a flock of some 80 Starlings, the first we had ever seen in Oklahoma. This species was first recorded in the state in November 1929, two years after we had left. In a small pond we found Pintails[1], Gadwalls[2], Baldpates[3], Green-winged Teal, scaups, and Coots. On the shore were Killdeer and a Wilson's Snipe; Meadowlarks quarrelled in the pasture, while two redwings proclaimed territory on the broken-down cat-tails. The ground was pitifully dry and flowers were scarce; we found only single examples of old favourites — spring beauty, anemone, and bluet.

Highway 77 passes across the Arbuckle Mountains and beautiful Turner's Falls may be admired at ease. Twenty years before, we had trundled over the rocky pastures from our camp at Price's Falls, a long and jolty drive to visit what was then an unspoiled bit of wilderness. It was near here that Constance had found the first nest for Oklahoma of the Rock Sparrow (now Rufous-crowned). We were hoping to get a glimpse of this interesting bird that lives only in rocky, broken country in Mexico, Texas, and Oklahoma. To our joy two, and later three, Rock Sparrows appeared just below the lunchroom opposite the falls; they allowed us to

[1]Common Pintail, *Anas acuta.* [2]*Anas strepera.* [3]American Wigeon, *Anas americana.*

approach within eight feet as they walked and hopped and scratched the ground. In contrast to their volubility in the nesting season, at this time they were silent. They have evidently become semi-domesticated in this spot, picking up crumbs from visitors' lunches. I do not suppose that one in a thousand of the people who stop for the view realize what a rare treat they are offered in seeing this bird.

Other notable events in Oklahoma were the lovely songs of the Western Meadowlarks on the farm of Blaine's brother in Kingfisher County and a Roadrunner perched in a scrub oak. In northeastern Oklahoma we once more met great flocks of migrating blackbirds.

On March 20 we again traversed Illinois. In the southern part of the state hordes of redwings, grackles, and cowbirds impressed us; they had moved north during our absence. Meadowlarks and shrikes were present in southern and central Illinois; Sparrow Hawks were migrating, as we noted three in southern Illinois, nine in central Illinois and five in northern Illinois. As to Marsh Hawks one was recorded in southern and five in northern Illinois.

As we neared Joliet all signs of spring vanished, and soon to our amazement we came upon snow and ice. The only roadside birds that we saw besides two hawks were Crows and Starlings. We stopped at McGinnes Slough where the lake was nearly covered with ice; our list here consisted of 15 Canada Geese, 100 Black Ducks[1], 60 Mallards, 15 Pintails, 2 Baldpates, 200 Herring Gulls, one *Buteo*, 20 Crows, 2 Redwings, 10 Starlings, 3 Juncos, and 8 Tree Sparrows.

We had driven 3,312 miles and seen 105 species of birds. We had returned just in time; the next day it snowed all day and for a week winter reigned. Our fascinating experience of spring seemed like a dream.

A scattering of grackles and redwings had reached the Chicago region before our start. Others had come during a short spell of warm weather in our absence — a few robins, Mourning Doves, Meadowlarks, Killdeer, and Song Sparrows. A visit to McGinnes Slough on March 29 showed no geese and fewer ducks than on the 20th with about the same numbers of crows and gulls. But the snow was gone and spring was in the air; we heard the songs of Mourning Doves, Meadowlarks, Redwings, Cardinals, and Song Sparrows.

---

[1] American Black Duck, *Anas rubripes*.

And how had our little aviary at home thriven during our fine trip? Alas, three days before our return both Jewel and Dewberry had died through accident. Post mortems showed the following: The male's measurements were: wing 65mm; tail 68mm; weight 19.8 grams; the female's were: wing 62mm; tail 59mm; weight 24.5 grams. The diet of the two birds had been the same; Jewel's heavy weight lent support to my theory that she had been preparing for migration. It is possible, if she had lived, that she might later have shown some specifically female behaviour.

Once again, Pucky was our only Song Sparrow.

XXVIII

Jan Joost Ter Pelkwyk, Naturalist[*]

One afternoon in early May 1940, a tall young biologist arrived at our home on his circuitous way from Holland to Dutch Guiana, where he planned to study wildlife and collect specimens for the University of Leyden for his doctor's degree. Two days later his country was invaded, and all his plans were changed.

For several weeks he stayed with us, and he and I continued on Pucky experiments on enemy recognition that I had begun in February. We used various mounted birds and other animals, including the Barred Owl lent by Mr. Blake, as well as cardboard models of the same, varying in their degrees of completeness. These were constructed by Joost (pronounced Yost), who was a skilled artist as well as a keen naturalist, with wide and thorough experience. As each model was shown him, Pucky, by his vocalizations, gave us a numerical standard by which we measured his degree of disturbance. In a detailed paper (1941), Joost and I reported that:

Adult hand-raised male Song Sparrows showed strong alarm to the stationary model of an owl, and fear to moving models.

We concluded that

We think that owls are recognized by Song Sparrows in Nature by an inborn pattern, hawks through fast movements, and cats and probably Cowbirds after conditioning.

Pucky, belonging to a species that is only slightly gregarious, was an independent creature, not hand-tame as in his early youth.

*See M. M. N. in *The Chicago Naturalist*, Vol. 9, pp. 26-35.

JAN JOOST TER PELKWYK
1914-1942

Joost had amused me once by exclaiming, "I think the Song Sparrow is the *worst* pet!"

Joost made sketches of Pucky in different attitudes for our article and for my book on *The Behavior of the Song Sparrow* as well as sketches for various papers I was writing on European experiences. For *Bird-Banding* he wrote an article on the ancient art of "Fowling in Holland" (1941 a), and also a review of a Dutch paper on orientation behaviour in birds. His boundless enthusiasm for all aspects of nature made him the best of companions on field trips. He loved the flowers on the unbroken prairies, and when we showed him his first Scarlet Tanager, he exclaimed, "That is the most splendid bird I have seen in America!"

The University of Chicago awarded him a Ridgway Fellowship; he was to work out his thesis under Dr. Allee on a problem connected with the behaviour of fishes, thus continuing with studies he had undertaken in Leyden with Niko Tinbergen (1937).

During the summer he lived at International House at the University of Chicago where he served as librarian, "a very pleasant kind of work," and had "a regular disciple to teach German", he took courses with Dr. Carl R. Moore, the endocrinologist, and Dr. Alfred Emerson, writing for the latter a paper on "Sex Pairs of Fishes as Cooperative Units" that contained a vast amount of information.

In the fall the Netherlands Government in Exile appointed Joost ichthyologist at the Fishery Research Station in Batavia. On the way to Java he visited Yellowstone Park and several government fishery stations on the West Coast; with David Nichols of Berkeley, California, he took a Christmas census in Nevada where he found "the cactus desert perfectly exciting." It was with great regret that he left "this *dear* country," and he often wrote of his intention of returning. In Java, while one biologist experimented on improved methods of salting fish, Joost's task was to find new fishing grounds and new methods of capture. This work involved travelling to many islands, where he saw "daily the most amazing creatures and the most fascinating scenery."

Joost's letters from the East Indies gave vivid descriptions of what he saw. I will give quotations from them, as he wrote them. "English spelling is still witchery to me, as is sometimes gramar," he once wrote me.

On April 16, 1941, he wrote his family from Batavia:

In spite of everything we are and we will stay optimistic here. Whatever happens, I will be gratefull that I have had an opportunity to see so much of this beautifull world. Moreover it gives me satisfaction to know that I am doing my duty . . . The happy life of the fisherman and the fascinating sailing business – the world I spend my time at now – are still more a fairy tale to me than a reality. So you see, I have a very good time indeed. The idea is that practically all of my work will be more or less purely scientific. This is fine, for then I will keep a way open for further work.

On the same day he wrote to me:

You will be surprised to hear that there are fishes here with "Territorial

Songs" they really *sing*, though it doesn't sound very pleasing to our ears . . . Lovely are the flocks of noisy paraquits[1]. In Borneo I have seen on the same day Proboscis monkeys and Rhinoceros birds[2]. Smaller monkeys are quite common and of course, I love them! Everywhere in the rice-fields of Java you may see hundreds of herons, night herons, egrets and small passerines.

By the way two days ago I did an observation you will be interested at. In a tree in the garden a terrific noise made me curious; 45 sparrows (*Passer montanus malaccensis*)[3], two or three orioles (*Oriolus chinensis*)[4] and 15 rice birds (*Padda oryzivora*)[5] made alarm notes in chorus. I expected to see an owl in the tree so I looked and looked with my glasses but did not see a thing. I just had stated that they might be crazy or something as I observed one of the "branches" of the tree moving slowly. It was a small *Python reticulatis* that had caused so much excitement! Some native boys went into the tree to kill the harmless snake; they disturbed a nest of wild bees; were bitten and ran away, the hive following them with great ferocity. The birds had gone during all this excitement and the snake remained for the rest of the morning unobserved.

On April 26 he sent a charming letter, illustrated with pen and ink sketches:

To my bird-friends, New York,
Dear Friends!
Would you like to go birding here? OK, take a bicycle and come along. A bicycle is here the best means of transportation and like everywhere the early morning is the best time for birding. Then the temperature is very pleasant too. We leave at half past five or quarter to six. My one-room house is in the garden city of Batavia. Batavia, a half-million city, is rather large and has the most unusual shape being nearly ten times as long as broad. Wherever you live, you are relatively near to the fields. The city offers a great variety of "Habitat" for human beings — and birds. The roads in the neighbourhood are excellent for bicycles, except after a shower, which comes nearly every afternoon. But then we will be home again. In the tops of the trees, as silhouets against the clear sky, small thrush-like birds are singing in chorus. These are golden vented bulbuls (*Pycnonotus aurigaster*)[6]. They sing more or less like robins, and live everywhere near human dwellings. An other 'city bird' is the gray backed shrike (*Lanius schach*)[7] very much like the California shrike, but with a nice orange colored breast and very tame indeed. On a lawn in front of one of the larger houses, six or eight starlings are walking, pecking industriously in the

---

[1]Psittacidae. [2]Rhinoceros Hornbills. [3]Malaccan Tree Sparrows. [4]Black-naped Orioles. [5]Java Sparrows. [6]Sooty-headed Bulbul. [7]Black-headed Shrike.

grass. These rose-colored starlings (*Sturnogaster contra*)[1] are perhaps one of the most popular cage birds, kept by the native population. Keeping of cage birds is an ancient tradition and no bird-protecting law has the power to deprive the people of their hobby. However the starlings are plentyfull and tame notwithstanding many are caught and sold. The other, may be still more popular cage bird is a little dove (*Geopelia striata*)[2]. Nearly every native home has its "perquutut" in a dome shaped cage sometimes attached to a long pole to give the little favorite a maximum of fresh air. A small woodpecker is making a terrific machinegun-noise in top of an antenna (*Dryobates analis*)[3].

We are in the fields, just after dawn. The air is clear and bluish green in color. Far away you may see clearly the outline of two big blue volcanoes. In front, flooded rice fields. Early in the morning those fields remind to ancient church windows. All shades of colours from the rising sun are reflected in the separate parts of water, bordered by irregular narrow strips of black dikes, forming an interesting pattern over the scenery. In the water with its regular dots of bright green rice plants, hundreds of herons are fishing. During the flooded period the fields yield an additional crop of fish, but certainly not every little fish planted out will be found back afterwards! There are many different herons in Java and they are all rather common too. On a single trip you may see the great blue, and purple herons, three egrets, night herons, bitterns[4], and two little 'pond herons' (*Ardeola*)[5]. It is a marvelous vieuw to see a big heronnery in a huge Ficus-tree on the middle of the market place in a native village. Of course you may expect some rails in the rice fields. One of the most beautiful birds I know, is the native coot (*Porphyrio albus*)[6].
Between the yellowish green of the rice you suddenly see a coot with a bright red bill and purple all over.

Between the fields you see many little "woods." Please don't suppose this were tropical jungles! They are but villages with gardens of all kinds of fruit trees. The thing that fascinates me is that these trees look all the time as if it were spring. They don't have the dull green colors of our trees in summer, but look like oaks in early June. Some trees, or branches of trees however look very winter-like indeed. A flight of noisy paroquets (*Psittacula alexandri*)[1] has stripped all the leaves. Many singing golden orioles make me think of my own garden in Holland.

---

[1] Asian Pied Starling, now called *Sturnus contra*. [2] Zebra Dove. [3] Spotted-breasted Pied Woodpecker, now called *Picoides macei analis*. [4] Probably the Cinnamon Bittern, *Ixobrychos cinnamoneus* and Schrenk's Bittern, *Ixobrychos eurhythmus*. [5] Javan Pond Heron, *Ardeola speciosa* and Chinese Pond Heron, *Ardeola bacchus*. [6] Purple Swamphen. [7] Red-breasted or Moustached Parakeet.

It was surprising to find a pale colored edition of the ordinary European Great Tit (*Parus major*)[1] here. They look like mounts that have been preserved for half a century or so in a show, not far from the window. Two other interesting birds are the fan-tailed flycatcher (*Rhipidura albicollis*)[2] and the magpy-colored Straits robin (*Copsychus saularis*)[3], which however is certainly not named after your robin, but after the British one.

Real jungle may only be found here on the slope of the volcanoes. Don't forget that Java is one of the most densely populated spots of the world. Over fifty million people live together in an area the size of Florida. If you realize that, it is surprising how much is left for a naturalist here. It seems unbeleavable that tigers, rhynocerosses, wild bulls and crocodiles can live in such an anthill of human beings. But they do, thanks to the rather well arranged nature protection and (if nothing unforseen happens) they will be safe for an indefinite period of time. Along the coast however there is a strip of very much jungle like woods; partly flooded woods with trees on stilt-roots, partly a kind of secondary or tertiary jungle, that has a definite value as a producer of fire wood. We might best go there to spend the rest of the morning. We might just as well go to the mountain slopes to see wild orchids and rhinoceros birds, but we can do so a next time. In the coast-woods we are sure to see lots of my favorites: the monkeys and birding is generally easier there. We have got to wade through brooks and swampy thickets. You may feel at home while hearing the rattle of the American kingfisher. However the noise is produced by *Rhamphalcyon capensis*[4], the stork-billed kingfisher, who has about the size of the American and the brilliant colors of the European kingfisher[5]. There are many kingfishers here and you see them near every little brook or stream. Some are bigger, others are smaller but all have the most brilliant colors and color-patterns. An other bright bird that we will see without doubt is the bee-eater[6], (not beef-eater, though that is a brightly colored animal too). They are considered to be migrants here though they stay all the year round. But nobody has ever seen them breeding and they will have to reproduce somewhere.

There are lots of migrants here: in Winter from Asia and in Summer from Australia. The barn swallows are leaving just now for China. All the time you hear the monotonous call of cuckoos. One of them has the disagreeable name of "brain-fever" because of the sound (and the effect) of its call (*Cacomantis merulinus*)[7]. An other cuckoo, crow-pheasant (*Centropus sinensis*)[8] is big and heavy and if he calls, it is, if a drum is beaten. It will not last long before we

---

[1]*Parus major cinereus.* [2]White-throated Fantail. [3]Oriental Magpie-Robin. [4]Stork-billed Kingfisher, now *Pelargopsis capensis*. [5]*Alcedo atthis.* [6]Probably the Blue-throated Bee-eater, *Merops viridis.* [7]Plaintive Cuckoo. [8]Greater Coucal.

see the first monkeys. Sometimes you notice them far, far away because of their screaming noises. Often, especially at the middle of the day you observe them suddenly overhead, sitting quietly and making faces at you. They are rather tame, and will certainly stay, if you keep quiet. There are two kinds that are by far the most common: a gray one with a very human expression and a slender black one (*Macacus cynomolgus* and *Semnopithecus maurus*). A remarkable creature that is quite common here is the "dragon," a little lizard that sails through the wood like a glider-plane on the skin, expanded between the ribs. There are many species of them and most have a very nice color. Between the roots of the trees all kinds of little noises are heard, produced by armies of crabs. At the edge of a brook or in the top of a palm tree a groop of birds, more or less sparrow-like, is flying about in a very busy manner. It is a colony of weaverbirds. There are three kinds of them here, all with different types of nests, the most remarkable being *Proceela hypoxanta*[1], a rather common zoo-bird, I believe. The bright Java sparrow, the munias[2] and field sparrows are the most common finches. They feed in huge numbers on the ripe rice fields.

Between the sea and the land often fish ponds have been laid out. They are more or less like the famous salt pans near Salinas (Monterey), only they are filled with brackish water instead of brine. All kinds of shore birds are to be found there: golden plovers (*Charadrius apricarius*)[3], curlews (*Numenius phaeopus*)[4], snipes (*Capella stenura*)[5] and sandpipers (*Eriola ruficollis*)[6], for instance, make you think of Long Island. In a sandy pool however a groop of very official Adjutant-birds[7] remind you of the fact that you are birding in the far east.

Because of my job, I spend most of my time on or near the Java Sea. Now you might think that I will have a fine opportunity for watching birds. It is a great shame that real sea birds are scarce here. Joe Hickey will be disappointed indeed for we don't have any gulls here to give them colored bands. He will have to spend all his time at peregrine falcons, that are only slightly different from the American ones. There are many more 'hawks' here. Exceedingly common everywhere along the coast is a chestnut-colored Brahminy kite[8]. Far from rare is a sea-eagle (*Haliaetus leucogaster*)[9], that makes me think of your quarter and half dollars. They come down in the fish-markets to steal fish! But as a whole, the sea is rather desolate. Except for a few terns and one or two frigate birds[10] or boobies[11], very little distracts my attention from the

---

[1]Asian Golden Weaver, now *Ploceus hypoxanthus*. [2]*Lonchura*. [3]Eurasian Golden Plover, now *Pluvialus apricaria*. [4]Whimbrel. [5]Pintail Snipe, now *Gallinago stenura*. [6]Red-necked Stint, now *Calidris ruficollis*. [7] Lesser Adjutant Stork, *Leptoptises javaicus*. [8]*Haliastur indus*. [9]White-bellied Sea-Eagle, *Haliaeetus leucogaster*. [10]Andrews or Christmas Island Frigatebird, *Fregata andrewsi* and/or Lesser Frigatebird, *Fregata ariel*. [11]*Sula*.

fishes. I wish that all of you, or at least one of you, will come here in the next future to go with me on a real bird-trip. I hope it will give you as much joy, as birding around New York has given to me.

— — Pelk — —

On May 10 he wrote to me from Batavia, lamenting the lack of a good ornithological library:

Next week we are going to found an Ornithological Club. About 50 people all on the archipeligo have announced their cooperation. May be we even are going to publish a little paper but for time being we will spend most of our time writing a booklet with field characters of Javanese birds. There is only one, very expensive book made in Japan, that is rather good (Price $50).

Anton de Vos, formerly Curator at the Museum of Zoology at Buitenzorg, now at the Ontario Agricultural College at Guelph, Canada, told me that the journal was founded; it was called "Irena" and two numbers appeared; the handbook with field characters and Dutch names was prepared, but had not been published.

On August 27 Joost wrote me:

About three weeks ago I left naval service; now back in fisheries again. Next Tuesday I will leave for Somabaya. From there by way of Makassar to Manada right near the Philippines in the north of Celebes. Then to the Moluccas and may be to New Guinea. I certainly have an interesting time here; moreover the heat does not yet bother me a thing. Nevertheless the fine letter of Dr. Allee made me a little homesick for quiet and peaceful laboratories where you can do just what is interesting from the viewpoint of biology. I feel very fortunate that you brought me in contact with this wonderful man.

After mastering some elementary Malay I am tackling now some Chinese too. The Chinese are the great fish-merchants here. It is funny to come in fisheries villages and to find small relicts of ancient China where the trade is concentrated. Chinese certainly is an interesting language. [He gives the characters for wren, goldfish, ornithology, Chicago, Utrecht, and mob-psychology.] Everything seems so much more beautiful and pittoresque than in our dull western tongues . . . Last week end I observed my first Sacred Ibises[1] nesting in the middle of an egret and cormorant colony.

It was not until December 16, 1941, that he wrote again, this time to Joe Hickey:

I should have written you long ago but the last few months have been full of tension and of hard work under great pressure. In the clear knowledge that

---

[1] *Threskiornis aethiopicus.*

things might become a little upset by this time, we have been extremely busy. I am now ready to leave for the navy as soon as I am called.

First I went to Manada and the Sangir Islands in the north of the island of Celebes. Then to the south (Makassar) and the south east (Boeton) and to a number of small coral-islands in the Flores-sea. On a next trip I went to Bali, Madoera and East Java. You bet it has been interesting! I like the eastern part of the Indies better than the West. The climate has stronger extremes, more rain, longer dry periods; the people are much more energetic and best of all: the sea is richer in the amount and variety of creatures.

The last letter was written January 22, 1942, from Palembang, Sumatra, and sent to his New York friends:

It is a shame that I did not write more during the past weeks. More than ever before my mind is with you, but I have to tell so much and I get so little chance to sit down and write that it seems a hopeless job to keep up with our correspondence. Since the outbreak of the Pacific war my work is in South Sumatra. You may understand that it is but 1 per cent biology and 99 per cent of every other occupation you possibly can imagine. I often think of those old traders that went out to America to bring fur to Europe. In a rather similar way we gather fish for Java. Because of the vital importance of that smelly stuff I have not yet been called in active service.

East Sumatra is about just as different from Celebes and Madura where I spent most of the autumn as Florida is from Nevada. It is about the wildest jungle you can think of, a regular 'green Hell,' with all the odd attractions of a place that is despised by the majority. The city of Palembang, the plantations and the oilfields are of course very civilized but there I rarely come. Where I spend my time, only fishermen and hunters and rather primitive agriculturists reside. The coast is shallow: mudflats with adjutant-birds and egrets. In the rhizophore woods white-breasted eagles, fishkites and bee-eaters have their nests. The swampy woods more inland make you think of discriptions of those ancient carboniferous woods. I can't help to look in vain for giant dragonflies and trilobites. You should see those majestic rivers: broad and quiet, very much like the Mississippi near Dubuque. Those floods around Harrisburg are nothing as compared to the terrific floods that come back every year in the rainy season, which is at its highest right now! Herons are walking slowly in the deep green swampy meadows on the banks. The water is brown and reflects as a perfect mirror every little detail of the monotonous wooded background. At daytime you hear but the annoying song of insects and invisible birds. Purple and green kingfishers[1] form a delightful

---

[1] *Alcedinidae* sp?

contrast to the green and the brown of trees and water. At night the horrible roar of a crocodile breaks the monotonous songs of toads and frogs. Flying foxes make you think of night-herons that have lost their tails. Rather often a big lizard shows its neck and head in front of the boat. Black and gray monkeys laugh at those stupid human creatures that strive day and night to gather food for somebody else. I finally may get my chance for a skin of a tiger. The regeon is very rich in wildlife but elephants, tapirs, tigers and rhinos are not the way bears and Bisons are in Yellowstone Park. Proportionally you see very little. Moreover Jacques' gun got another destination: in the homeguard.

Every time I come back to civilization I hear the news. The news is not worse than I have expected ever since I decided to go hither and to take it. Still there is very much that makes me very sad. I never realized that I loved this country until the war reached its borders. The occupation of the Minahassa was to me, after my wonderfull time there, hardly three months ago, about just as horrible as the occupation of our country in Europe. It will be free once, if peace comes. You hardly can imagine how we are looking at you, at the aid America promised. There may be no doubt that America will win in the long run but to us it is most important that it wins in time, before this wonderfull country is destroyed. Our native servant is sure that Java, the center of civilization, will never be hurt. He reasons: as soon as the Japs come with planes, the bombs will go back and destroy the very plane that released them, for Allah will never allow that his garden becomes a ruin. Our servant is a wise man; maybe he is right.

In the summer of 1941 Joost had received some naval training, but returned again to fishery problems. When war enveloped the Indies we heard no word of him. "We always imagine Joost living on some forgotten island," his sister wrote me. In the spring of

1946 we at last learned his fate. On March 1, 1942, a small motor-boat left Batavia for Australia with a staff of officers, and Joost of his own free will accompanied them as one of the sailors. Early the next morning they ran into a group of Japanese boats that immediately started shooting. Joost was one of the first to be killed.

At my request, Mr. G. A. Ter Pelkwyk, Bourgomeister of Utrecht, wrote me something of the childhood and youth of his son. Joost was born at the Hague, October 24, 1914; he was a sturdy boy, but his years at school were difficult. With his independence and his passion for the outdoors, the dry subjects of the school curriculum made little appeal to him.

The love for traveling he possessed already as a young boy. He came to know early all the beautiful spots of his country which he searched for animals, plants and mussels. His bedroom was his laboratory. The difficulties this caused in his home may be imagined.

His mother wrote me,

I remember that once I was very happy when the smell in his room was too bad for himself.

His father continued:

One of his favorite tours was to the peninsula "de Beer," a nature monument at the mouth of the River Maas, opposite the Hook of Holland, a place rich in plants and animals. To reach this place he crossed the river in a canoe in any kind of weather. He knew no danger. In the dunes he discovered pottery fragments and coins from the Romans, which he took to the School Museum at the Hague.

In 1933 he went to Greenland, as a reward from his father for passing the entrance examinations for the University. Here he visited Niko Tinbergen and made sketches for the latter's "Behavior of the Snow Bunting in Spring" (1939).

That journey was a glorious one for him. He visited Iceland and its geysers, lived in Greenland among the Eskimos, made long trips across glaziers and learned to move about on sea in a kayak.

During his years at Leyden (where he became assistant to Dr. Tinbergen), Joost worked hard and traveled much. With slight means he went off alone or joined excursions. His own country he got to know extremely well. He travelled in Germany, England, Denmark, Norway and Sweden, in Switzerland, Spain, Italy, North Africa and the Balkans. From all these journeys he brought home drawings, and sketches and he sent articles on his experiences to magazines and professional papers.

Disguised as a seal, he more closely studied the life of these animals. Long hours he spent hidden in a shelter to observe the life of birds. Whenever a whale or a big fish had been cast on the shore, he immediately went there and the most disgusting smell could not frighten him from dissecting these animals . . . Jan Joost had his friends amongst fishermen, farmers and hunters. He was known to all circles of friends of nature and was a popular leader of excursions of members of the Netherlands Youth Corporation for Nature Study.

Because of his interest in fisheries Joost received a commission, which was thus described to my by his friend, Dr. Luuk Tinbergen, brother of Niko:

Since its enclosure in 1932 the shallow Zuyderzee, formerly a brackish inland sea, soon became a freshwater lake. The marine fishes (herring, flounder, shrimp, etc.) disappeared within a few years. For the eel, however, (which always had inhabited the Zuyderzee) environmental conditions improved, but the future supply was endangered because the larvae could no longer enter upon their arrival from the Atlantic. Pelk (Joost) was asked by the "Service of the Zuyderzee Works" to solve the difficulty. He found that the eels, once they arrived in coastal waters, are directed by a positive rheotaxis, which is released by a decrease in the salinity of the water and by darkness, and that the larvae are capable of swimming only against rather weak currents. He planned a system by which the eels were first attracted by fresh leak water currents from the closed 'great sluices' (i.e. those sluices which are not used for the passage of ships, but only for draining off the enormous amounts of superfluous water). Subsequently when a great number of eels is concentrated before these sluices, the larvae are locked through as if they were ships in a lock. This system proved successful, enormous numbers being lured into the Zuyderzee with very little trouble, and it is still in use.

Joost's father wrote of his son's interest in photography, modelling and drawing; with some difficulty he persuaded him to take lessons from the artist, Dirk van Gelder, and a warm friendship sprang up between teacher and pupil. "Van Gelder saw Joost as a person of lively talent and a fierce, almost poetical interest, with a passion for drawing, which is that of the artist and which one rarely finds with young people."

Dr. Allee wrote to Joost's mother:

He was one of the most promising of the many excellent young people who have been associated with me. He was an interesting combination of maturity of judgment, outlook and ability combined with his full share of youthful enthusiasm . . . I admired your son, appreciated his abilities and personality and am sorrowed by this final news of his death.

In *Birds Across the Sky* (1942), Florence Jaques writes of him: "I have never seen a youth so absorbed by nature and so brilliantly informed in all its aspects."

What I remember best about Joost is his eagerness, his friendliness, his keen awareness of nature, his passionate love for the "gallant glory of the World." His welcome to a baby of his friends, named for him, well represents his own attitude: "I hope he will learn to love this world, which is large and good and which shelters immense values in every little corner."

XXIX

The Writing of SS II.

During the summer of 1940 at Grey Rocks each of the three birds I was raising showed a different picture. There were two Song Sparrow brothers and a Cedar Waxwing (1941).

The Song Sparrow, Turquoise, marked with a blue band, was a true pet; from the age of 23 days he would come to me as I rested on the bed, hop onto my feet or shoulder, and lie down on top of me. He would tweak at my hair, and, perched on my finger, he would stretch, yawn, preen, and shake himself. He reminded me of my Bobwhite, Loti, of Clark University days. Also at this extraordinarily early age he showed incipient copulatory behaviour, fluttering toward my hand, toward his brother, Amber, and toward the Waxwing. The Song Sparrows raised in 1938 in Pelham had not shown this activity until the ages of 75, 92, amd 95 days. Unfortunately, when 28 days old, this charming little bird suddenly died, evidently from digestive troubles.

Amber was a contrast in every way; stunted, mute and slightly crippled, from the age of 20 days he was as scary as a deer, whereas all the others of his kind had remained trustful till the age of independence, at about four weeks or a little longer.

Waxwing was adopted the day it left the nest; it at once took blueberries from me but, like the Cuckoo in Altenberg, it treated me as a mere food counter and insistently begged with its large open mouth directed toward the Song Sparrows. I had hoped that the Waxwing, as a highly social animal, would become devoted to me but, instead, it and Amber became attached to one another. They lay in the sun together, preened at the same time, ate at the same time, and roosted side by side on the same picture frame. Amber was quicker in his actions than his companion; wherever he flew, Waxwing was sure to follow.

The greatest admirer of the birds was 18-month-old Hugh, who at that time had not yet begun to talk. I wrote home:

Hugh is adorable. He shouts so at the poor birds that they seem quite dumbfounded. I told him that the seeds were their food; he picked some up, went as near to them as he could get (they were safely perched on top of a picture frame) and held out the seeds to them, shouting loudly. Then he sampled the food himself.

On September 3 I released the Waxwing, trusting it would find a flock of its friendly fellow-species. Amber I took with me, stopping on the way home at the A.O.U. meeting* in Boston and Cambridge, Massachusetts. As always, the meeting was friendly and stimulating. I reported on Joost's and my "Experiments on Enemy Recognition in the Song Sparrow (1941 b). It was a special pleasure to visit with my old friend, Hubert Clark, whose *Birds of Amherst* had so greatly helped me in my youth.

In October my beloved mother died. She had been a wonderful woman. With remarkable energy and executive ability she had managed her household of seven children and rendered invaluable aid to my father. Yet she was a power for good in the community, both for her hospitality in our home and through outside activities. She worked zealously for woman suffrage; she had been President of the Hampshire County Mount Holyoke Club, of the Amherst Womens' Club, and Amherst Indian Association, an institution founded and engineered by herself. She had had a long and active life for 85 years, full of doing for others. It was a rich life and largely a happy one.

In November Lawrence and Thyra Hicks drove Constance and me to the Wilson Club meeting* at Minneapolis, Minnesota. Southwestern Wisconsin was new to us – a region of low, level, wet land covered with aspens, the home of Prairie Chickens and Sharp-tailed Grouse[1], its sandstone hills weathered into grotesque shapes. At the University of Minnesota we had a fine meeting, the outstanding

*The 58th Stated Meeting of the American Ornithologists' Union, Boston and Cambridge, Massachusetts, September 9-15, 1940.

*The 26th Stated Meeting of the Wilson Ornithological Club, Minnesota Museum of Natural History, Minneapolis, Minnesota, November 22, 23, 1940.

[1]*Pedioecetes phasianellus.*

event being a symposium under the leadership of the noted ecologist Aldo Leopold, of the University of Wisconsin on "What is Wildlife Management in Practice?" (1949). My charming friend, Doris Speirs of Toronto, talked on the Evening Grosbeak[1] of which she was making an exhaustive study (1968). For the second time I gave the same paper in one year as I had at A.O.U., a talk which I privately called "Scaring Pucky." After two years as vice-president and two as president, I found it restful to have no responsibilities. I was a little taken aback, however, by the query of a new acquaintance, "Is this your first Wilson Club meeting?"

No less than nine splendid films in natural colour were shown; the most impressive were Sewall Pettingill's "Bright Feathers of the Prairies," in which we saw Avocets brooding and hundreds of Eared Grebes[2] fleeing from their nests; and Earle Wright's (of the Chicago Academy of Sciences) "Wildlife of the Southwest," that featured scorpions, snakes, ground squirrels, butterflies and birds.

This winter we had only the two Song Sparrows in Chicago; one was always caged while the other was free. Pucky had greeted the arrival of Amber with the puff-sing-wave (described in Chapter XXV) and Amber had responded in alarm by raising his crest and compressing his body feathers. Amber's wing measurement indicated that he was a male. In February he started to warble. Remembering that Jewel had warbled during the previous winter, we wondered whether Amber might possibly be a female, despite these measurements. So on February 20 Constance suggested a romantic experiment; under our strict supervision she put Pucky into Amber's cage. Pucky made one dash for Amber, then sat quiet; Amber was nearly frightened out of his wits, tearing back and forth with a crest as pronounced as a Cardinal's.

So Amber was another male after all. He never progressed in singing beyond the warbling stage. In June Blaine released him at the Nice family farm in southern Ohio, where he showed a slight inclination toward people by hanging around the farm house throughout the summer.

I was now President of the Chicago Ornithological Society, succeeding Rudyerd Boulton of the Field Museum. With the help of the Secretary, Harold O. Wales, and the Chairman of the Field Trip Committee, the devoted bander Karl Bartel, we planned and mimeographed fine programs for each of the two years: nine speeches and seventeen trips for 1939-40, ten speeches and ten trips for 1940-41.

---

[1] *Hesperiphona vespertina.* [2] *Podiceps nigricollis.*

On May 10 and 11, 1941, the Illinois Audubon Society held a field meeting at Quincy, Illinois, on the Mississippi River. This town is famed ornithologically for the pioneer Bluebird Nest Box Trail established by T. R. Musselman. Three species were found nesting in large numbers: Bank Swallows in two great colonies; many Bluebirds (and a Black-capped Chickadee family) in boxes and finally Prothonotary Warblers in smaller boxes in the valley of the Illinois River. Here Ocean Trail Park offered us three choices for dinner: fish or turtle dinner for 60 cents; frog legs for 25 cents. Remembering the tasty feast prepared for us by Blaine in Pushmataha County in Oklahoma, 21 years earlier, I decided to choose turtle. Blaine, however, advised fish as a safer bet. I was glad that I had followed his counsel as the catfish turned out fairly good, but a number of unfortunate birdwatchers reported the turtle as cold, leathery, and tasteless.

We found warbler nests in many of Dr. Musselman's boxes, some just finished, others with varying numbers of eggs and one with a mother on it. This bird Dr. Musselman caught and banded. A male Prothonotary sang just outside the lunchroom, giving us a fine view of his golden plumage.

The last of May we took a trip with the Michigan Audubon Society to Higgins Lake in northern Michigan. The country there was fascinating with its evergreens — jack, red, and white pines, hemlocks, larches, arbor vitae, spruces, and balsams. In the woods around the lake spring peepers and Whip-poor-wills sang at night, while during the day we heard Robins, Veeries[1], and a number of warblers.

A caravan of 28 cars made a pilgrimage to find Kirtland's Warblers[2], one of the rarest warblers in the world. It winters in the Bahamas and nests only in a few counties in northern Michigan among jack pines of a certain age — about ten feet in height. It was a notable event to see and hear this famous bird, which is yellow below and grey above and sings a fine loud song. It must have been a funny sight — the company of bird-lovers, kneeling breathless in the woods, hoping for a glimpse of the rarity as he flew about in low branches.

There were Juncos there too and an abundance of Chipping Sparrows in the woods. Other exciting birds were an Olive-sided Flycatcher[3], pretty Prairie Warblers[4] and intriguing Clay-colored

---

[1]*Catharus fuscescens.* [2]*Dendroica kirtlandii.* [3]*Nuttallornis borealis.* [4]*Dendroica discolor.*

Sparrows whose song is scarcely more than a squeak. We were shown a nest of this species with greenish-blue eggs, speckled with brown. Constance found a Field Sparrow's nest with chicks and Blaine a Chipping Sparrow nest on which the brave little mother sat unmoving while I lifted a branch two inches away.

In late November 1941, Dr. and Mrs. R. M. Strong drove Blaine and me to the Wilson Club* meeting at the University of Illinois at Urbana. Both the Strongs were ardent conservationists. Dr. Strong was a remarkable man, then 69 years of age, founder of the Wilson Club and Chicago Ornithological Society, and at this time President both of the Illinois Audubon Society and of the Chicago Conservation Council. His greatest scientific contribution lay in his monumental four-volume *Bibliography of Birds* (1939-46).

Friday and Saturday were as busy as could be with meetings and open houses from 9 a.m. to 11 p.m. Papers of special interest to me were Harry Hann's "The Cowbird at the Nest" (1941), Hurst Shoemaker's "Color Vision in Canaries" (1942), Larry Walkinshaw's report on Sandhill Cranes (1949), and Mrs. Edge's talk on Hawk Mountain. Dorothy Ewers contribution was unique: recordings of Pucky's and Dewberry's identical songs, as well as warblings of the Goldfinches and of the two hand-raised Bobolinks we had kept for some months for Sewall Pettingill while he was in Mexico. My own talk was on "Song in Female Birds." We saw movies of baby Wood Ducks jumping out of nesting boxes and bouncing up from the ground beneath; some of the boxes were 30 feet up. We met many good friends but, as usual, did not have time enough to visit with them. George Sutton was elected as the new President, and Maurice Brooks of West Virginia as the new Secretary, Sewall retiring from this arduous post after five years of distinguished service.

Meanwhile my chief writing was on the *Behavior of the Song Sparrow and Other Passerines* (1943). In contrast to the first volume (on population), which except for notable advice from Ernst Mayr, was largely worked out independently by myself, for this volume I needed help on theoretical aspects of animal behaviour. Here I received suggestions from a number of people of whom I am most indebted to Konrad Lorenz and Wallace Craig.

In the fall of 1939 I had made a good start on working up the study, but in 1940, due to a multiplicity of activities, I had made little progress. It was in 1941 that I really concentrated on the

---

*The 27th Stated Meeting of the Wilson Ornithological Club, University of Illinois, Urbana, Illinois, November 20-23, 1941.

task. I will quote from my Plans Books X and XI that tell of some of my ups and downs in this project:

Jan. 29, 1941. A great day. Started again on SS II.

Feb. 26. I have a colossal array of materials. It tires me just to think of it.

Apr. 20. SS II is a ball and chain. (But later in the day): Really got into the spirit of it this week; found it absorbing.

May 2. SS II is getting me down.

June 8. This everlasting plugging is showing results.

July 17. SS II is a nightmare. It is the last — I hope — big task — rather — enormous task. I've achieved hard things before. I cannot fail now.

Sept. 18. I have the outline before me and my heart sinks. I do not have a feeling of mastery before it — just one of discouragement.

Oct. 8. I am eager to do great deeds on SS II and I am working freely and happily. Most of the debris has been cleared away. And I am alone all day except for Pucky. This is fun, excitement, joy.

Nov. 29. I feel crushed by SS II. Why did I ever leave it so long?

Nov. 30. I grew quite fascinated by the work yesterday and hated to leave it at noon. It's largely a matter of organization now. I feel quite encouraged and intend to go on from 'Victory unto Victory.'

Dec. 18. Several new ideas are sizzling . . . New ideas are very upsetting and time-consuming.

Dec. 30. A grand day on SS II yesterday . . . Oh, how eager I am to start typing! Janet has been typing for me during her Christmas vacation from Ohio University.

Jan. 8, 1942. Working 6-7 hours a day, typing it and revising as I go.

Jan. 10. The best week I've ever had — 51 hours on ornithology, 43 of them on SS II.

Jan. 12. Tired this morning; have worked at too terrific a pace.

Jan. 21. SS II has been going splendidly — way ahead of schedule.

Feb. 20. Four days off for Reviews.

Feb. 21. At last I begin again on beloved SS II.

March 13. SS II (the main body of it) went off to Dr. Craig, Ernst and Joe Hickey!"

All sent criticisms but for the most part bestowed praise. In September 1943, it was published. It was dedicated to my husband "for his unselfish encouragement of my ornithological labors during the last 23 years."

I will quote from two of the many appreciative reviews:

Ernst Mayr wrote in *Audubon Magazine* (1944):

This treatise is far superior to anything of the kind that has been previously attempted. Many of the chapters . . . are complete treatises in themselves with enough meat in them to fill separate volumes . . . This book is a "must" in the library of every serious bird student.

In his splendid *Guide to Bird Watching* (1943:231), Joe Hickey characterizes the book thus: "No other life-history study combines such rich scholarship with such keen field work."

It was a proud moment when I learned that I had been awarded the Brewster Medal for the two Song Sparrow volumes. This is the highest honour given by the American Ornithologists' Union. On one side of the bronze medal is a profile of William Brewster with his name and the legend, "Awarded by the A.O.U."; on the other stands an American Indian on a ledge, watching the rising sun, while above him flies a V of wild swans. On the rim it says "Margaret Morse Nice Life History of the Song Sparrow." Along with this beautiful medal came an emolument of $386.00.

As for *The Watcher* my third pay cheque had dropped to $25.00. In August 1942 the book was sold at remainder. One thousand and six books — half the edition — had been sold; my remuneration had amounted to $206.00.

About this time Pucky developed a lump beneath his bill. We took him to a veterinary surgeon who accidentally brought about his death. So ended the career of this courageous and enduring individual, who had proved to be the key figure of the hand-raised Song Sparrows. For four years he had greatly helped me in my studies on the behaviour of his species.

The writing of *The Behavior of the Song Sparrow and Other Passerines*, the composing of some 1800 Reviews in nine years, the editing of contributions to the *Wilson Bulletin* — this program had proved too much for my health. I firmly resigned from the Reviews, and Dr. Donald Farner, an excellent linguist and later professor at Washington State University at Pullman, became the Review editor of *Bird-Banding*. Dr. Van Tyne lessened the editorial labours for the *Bulletin* and I took life easily for a few years.

Indeed, I had no choice, for as John Cowper Powys had so truly written:

There is such a thing as a desperate pursuit of "Truth"; a pursuit fierce, relentless, absorbing, which is even more destructive than warm sociability to any peaceful self-realization . . . a furious intensity that leaves all personal human life a thing of shreds and patches.

XXX

Late Spring in Arkansas

After three months in a hospital with heart difficulties, I came home to a long convalescence. Now I had a sense of leisure, a chance to read literature, and to listen to classical music on our FM radio. For bird work I finished a number of small articles on experiences on Interpont and in Europe; these were published in the *Chicago Naturalist* (1940, 1944, 1945, 1946) and the *Bulletin of the Illinois Audubon Society* (1940, 1944).

In September 1944, we moved three blocks to the east from our large, old-fashioned house on Kenwood Avenue to a smaller, less old-fashioned one on Harper Avenue. This was an opportunity to reduce possessions; I gave away about two-fifths of my ornithological library to the Wilson Club Library, and to various friends, chiefly Joe Hickey and Bill Elder, who were both doing research in Chicago during the War. Dr. Elder, Wild Life Conservationist, later became professor of zoology at the University of Missouri; his wife, Nina, daughter of Aldo Leopold, at this time was a research assistant in the zoological laboratory at the University of Chicago. Joe and Peggy Hickey, Bill and Nina Elder, were most welcome visitors at our home; the last two regularly came to lunch with me each week, they bringing sandwiches, I supplying soup and ice cream.

One advantage of our new home was its proximity to Jackson Park, in those days a good place in which to follow spring and fall migration, and even in 1949 and 1950, affording me opportunities for small nesting studies on two of my favourite birds – Red-eyed Vireo and Wood Pewee. We discovered that the Duneside Inn at the Indiana Dunes State Park was a happy place for short visits.

With either Janet or Constance I spent a few days to a week there in spring and fall, rejoicing in the warblers and thrushes, the flowers and the brilliant fall colouring.

An adventure for me in this interim period of uncertain health was a six weeks visit to my friend, Ruth Thomas, in Little Rock, Arkansas (1950). For 13 years Ruth had been writing a weekly nature column for the *Arkansas Gazette*, the best nature column of any I knew. On March 13, 1946, I wrote to my family in my Harper Chronicle:

Ruth Thomas writes in her column:

Spring's gold is scattered over the earth — in the jonquils, the jasmine and the forsythia. Spirea is flecked with white, a memory of winter snow, and like a pledge of summer is the fire of the burning bushes.

It must be fascinating there in Arkansas.

Ruth was living alone since the death of her husband, Rowland Thomas, nearly a year earlier. I developed a great longing to visit my good friend, an idea she cordially welcomed.

In mid April, I travelled south by train just as the trees were greening and redbud and wild plum were in bloom: I woke the next morning to what seemed like June. Illinois had been too culti-vated, so clean-farmed that hardly a sprig was left under which a Bobwhite might hide. It was a delight to find in Arkansas, woods and underbrush and wild land with Common Egrets silhouetted against cypress trees.

Past blooming roses and honeysuckles, red buckeye bushes and lavender chinaberries, we drove out from Little Rock to Crip's Hill with its post oaks and black jacks, its shrubs and rose bushes, its wealth of bird houses and feeding shelves. Everywhere there were birds, most of them banded with numbered aluminum rings, while many had in addition coloured celluloid bands for sight recognition.

Instead of the noises of civilization — trains, automobiles, House Sparrows, and Starlings — I listened to sounds of nature. At dawn came the exquisite chorus of White-throated Sparrows, the spirited song of the Cardinal, the outpourings of the unmated Brown Thrasher to the west; throughout the day there were the ringing calls of the six-year-old Carolina Wren who sought a wife, the measured melody of the Mourning Dove, the husky warble of Lincoln's Sparrow, the lonely call of the Tufted Tit that had lost his mate, the mad, gay twitterings of the Chimney Swifts, and always a soft undertone of insect voices. After nightfall we heard the concert of the swamp tree frogs and the musical utterance of

Chuck-will's-widow, endeared to me from camping days in Oklahoma.

I was eager to see Crip, the famous ten-year-old Brown Thrasher, chief character of Ruth's weekly "Country Diary"; he had broken his wing six years before and could fly only with difficulty. He and his three-year-old mate had a nest in the silver moon rose bush near the house; when she left the eggs, he took her place, each bird singing softly upon the arrival of its mate. The north garden belonged to another pair of thrashers — Red and Greta — each five years old. Greta had been Crip's mate for two seasons, but the third year Crip returned late to his hill and found wife and territory in possession of his neighbour.

In this haven where birds were attracted with skill and devotion, and where many of their enemies — cats, House Sparrows and some of the snakes — were eliminated, the population was remarkably stable and many of the inhabitants were old acquaintances of Ruth; for instance, wintering Whitethroats that came three, four and six years in succession, Red-bellied Woodpeckers three years old, an Orchard Oriole seven years old, and a male Cardinal at least ten years old. The trapping of a bird was always an occasion of excitement; perhaps the captive was an old friend, while with the nesting birds, where male and female look alike, sex could often be determined by examination for the brood patch, a large, granulated bare place on the abdomen of an incubating bird; we found it in females in the titmice, chickadees, wrens, and jays, and in both sexes of the woodpeckers.

On April 19 Ancient , the mature Carolina Wren, won a bride, a newcomer to Crip's Hill. Without delay they started nest-hunting and Ruth cleverly lured them to a grape basket, partly covered with a shingle, on the sleeping porch. On Sunday morning — the 21st — both birds worked with furious zeal; from 8 to 10 o'clock the bride brought 104 loads and Ancient 205, the fastest building rate I remembered having seen with any species. After that Ancient let his wife finish lining the nest. She even continued to bring wisps of hair when she came each morning half an hour after sunrise to lay an egg, and later occasionally while she was incubating. Ancient sang and guarded, and every once in a while brought his wife a tidbit. He scolded at Blue Jays and chased the unmated Bewick's Wren[1] who was building nearby.

Leaving our oak hilltop, we were driven by the Terrel Marshalls

---

[1] *Thryomanes bewickii.*

to their cottage at Lakeside, 24 miles northwest of Little Rock. It was a different world with cypress and sweet gum, short-leaved and loblolly pines, willow, water, and southern red, oaks, brake, and royal fern. Anhingas live on the lake and Red-cockaded Woodpeckers in the pine woods. White waterlilies were in bloom, cricket and bullfrogs were vocal, while Prothonotary and Sycamore Warblers (now called Yellow-throated) sang. From the cottage porch we watched Kingbirds over the lake, saw a White-breasted Nuthatch feed his mate and a beautiful Summer Tanager take a bath, while Chipping Sparrows came for crumbs. Deeper in the woods at the cabin of Glen and Ann Hoke we listened to the absurd song of the White-eyed Vireo and to the lovely notes of the Wood Thrush. We heard Tufted Tits calling in a different dialect from those on Crip's Hill, and were happy to find a Blue-gray Gnatcatcher on its exquisite nest.

Another trip — 24 miles east this time — took us through rice country to the "World's Largest Fish Hatchery" at Lonoke. On the way, fields of vetch were noisy with Dickcissels, while Hill's Lake was a joy to behold with its wealth of cypress, not draped, as in Louisiana, with Spanish moss. The hatchery is landscaped with weeping willows which give an exotic effect. Warbling Vireos[1], Yellowthroats, grackles and redwings were all abundant; graceful Black Terns[2] coursed over the water and a Bell's Vireo gave his earnest song.

We wandered about, admiring great dragonflies and the prettiest baby Cumberland tortoises. In one pond we noticed myriads of tiny black tadpoles that acted like no tadpoles we had ever seen before, for they *schooled*. Presently a large catfish appeared, swimming slowly about. This made us wonder: were they really tadpoles? We caught one and could just make out tiny whiskers and diminutive fins. It was fascinating to watch these baby fish, as they separated, then rejoined and milled about in an extraordinary writhing black ball. Father Catfish returned and hovered over one school, but the other group divided itself into three balls and benefited from no parental interest as long as we watched. It was a glimpse into a new world for us.

On a picnic at Boyle's Park, of 230 acres with splendid oaks and sweet gums and sycamores, just outside the city of Little Rock, Tufted Tits and Blue Jays shared our lunch. Here we heard, besides Wood Thrushes and Prothonotary Warblers, three vireos — White-

---

[1] *Vireo gilvis.* [2] Common Black Tern, *Chlidonias niger.*

eyed, Red-eyed, and Yellow-throated. On our way home we learned that Red-headed Woodpeckers had been driven from their hole in a telegraph pole by a pair of "short-tailed, yellow-billed blackbirds" that had raised a family themselves. This was the first time Ruth had heard of Starlings nesting in Little Rock. This alien was extending its range to the southwest, breeding at this time in scattered towns throughout the northern half of Arkansas.

By the end of April winter birds had left Crip's Hill, but each day brought new visitors, most of them to pass on, a few to stay. The haunting melody of the Gray-cheeked Thrush[1], heard for ten days from April 29, compensated in some measure for the loss of those sweetest of singers, the whitethroats. As to summer residents, Orchard Orioles and Ruby-throated Hummingbirds visited the cups of sweetened water, Crested Flycatchers whooped and fought each other and the bluebirds, while the catbird, after his arrival May 6, sang very early and very loud. Strangely enough, we heard not one song from the two pairs of robins nesting near the house until May 5, when both pairs had young a few days out of the nest.

It was bird watching deluxe to study the Carolina Wrens' nest from our beds on the sleeping porch. Ancient wakened us early each morning with his spirited songs; Serena incubated her five eggs for very long periods (averaging an hour and a half in length) and left them for half an hour at a time. After the babies hatched, Ancient brought most of their food at first, while Serena brooded. As they grew, she became more and more enthusiastic over feeding them, swinging in under the porch roof with crane fly or caterpillar so often that Ancient spent most of his energies playing policeman on the nearest oak, *churring* at the jays who paid him not the slightest attention.

Our longest trip was to Petit Jean Mountain, 65 miles northwest. We drove through pleasant countryside, past picturesque Pinnacle Mountain, past woods and hilly pastures. Petit Jean (pronounced Petty Jane), lying between the Ouachitas to the south and Ozarks to the north, is a very ancient flat-topped peak rising abruptly 800 feet above the Arkansas River; it extends 30 miles in the shape of a great horse shoe. The top is level, partly farmed and partly covered with second growth forest. We visited Dr. and Mrs. T. W. Hardison who have lived on the mountain for many years. A magnificent view of the Arkansas Valley, of Petit Jean and more distant mountains spread out before us, while beside us sang a Pine Warbler

---

[1] *Catharus minimus.*

and a Summer Tanager. Dr. Hardison, who had been largely responsible for the mountain having been made into a State Park, showed us treasures he had found here: Indian relics, as well as an immense stem of a fossil tree fern 50,000,000 years old, and strange, pecan-like seeds of another tree fern that grew here 200,000,000 years ago.

We drove and clambered about, enjoying great ledges, spectacular falls, curious turtle-shaped rocks, splendid short-leaved pines, curious little sundews, and masses of golden coreopsis. There were many birds, among them Black-and-white Warblers and Yellow-breasted Chats and, right by the Lodge, a heavenly Wood Thrush. We watched the sunset from in front of the Lodge, a marvellous view of deep valley between high cliffs. The Chuck-will's-widow gave its eery chant; two Black Vultures flapped their way silently overhead, then came to rest in a pine. On the opposite side of the canyon three Turkey Vultures landed in a dead tree. Venus shone and then Jupiter and a little later Mars and Saturn, Spica and Arcturus, Regulus, Castor and Pollux. Beauty to be remembered as a charm against the petty cares of every day.

On Crip's Hill, on May 26 the baby wrens were two weeks old. Ancient came several times to the basket without food, looked in and flew off, then gave loud songs from the nearest oak. Four babies scrambled up on the edge. Serena arrived, scolded, and fed the baby inside; she scolded again and all the chicks disappeared inside. But the next minute three clambered up again; she went into the box without food and all followed her. Ancient started to sing once more in the oak; three young appeared and two flew to the eaves of the porch. Serena brought food and with coaxing notes got some of the brood back into the nest. But when one baby flew wildly and landed on the floor, Serena gave up trying to get her children back home and, like Ancient, tried to get them out and away. She brought food but did not surrender it, leading the hungry children into the garden. Soon the whole family had started down the hill and into the woods.

Two days later, on my last morning in Arkansas, there was still adventure on Crip's Hill. Just 46 days earlier Ruth had noticed Blue Jays starting to build in the post oak by the porch; since then all had been quiet in the tree, but today two engaging, stubby-tailed babies were ready to explore the world and came tumbling to the ground.

Crip was followed to the feeding shelf by his two large children, hatched 31 days before; he fed them, but their mother ran at them.

Red came with no fewer than four fine youngsters; one of them begged from Crip who made a jab at it. The two then made the mistake of begging from Mrs. Crip; she rushed at them. As we drove away, we heard Crip singing from the top of an oak in his finest tones, loud and clear, a fitting ending to a richly rewarding experience.

Credit: Life

JANET, MARGARET AND CONSTANCE NICE

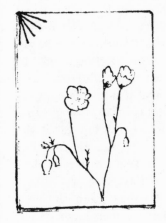

XXXI

The Aftermath of World War II

In the fall of 1946, I found out that I could sketch after a fashion. Niko Tinbergen had spent a week with us; he told us that in the hostage camp to which the professors of Leyden University were sent because of their refusal to allow their institution to be nazified, one of the projects had been a class in portraiture, and almost all of the men had done well. "The Dutch seem to have special ability in drawing," he said. When I spoke of this to another Dutch biologist, Anton de Vos, a friend of Joost, he answered: "I do not believe that. I think it is that they are taught it is important." Well, thought I, if any one can draw, then I will. Following suggestions of William J. Beecher (who was to become the very able Director of the Chicago Academy of Sciences) as to books to read and techniques to follow, I made a start. Sketching simple things became a delight to me as well as the greatest of helps in my study of plants and of birds and beasts.

During the next fall I discovered the Plant Kingdom. This happened during Janet's and my week at the Indiana Dunes from September 9 to 13, 1947. The first morning I was the only pupil of T. P. Amadie, Park Naturalist, on his nature walk; he told me much about the trees, especially the various oaks, and he named all the flowers for me.

In my notebook devoted to Plants, I wrote:

Sept. 8. I've just drawn my first Lizard's Tail. The plant delights me with its unique leaves and flower stalk. Also the fact that it is the only representative of the Saururaceae in temperate North America.

Sept. 9. Agrimony. Yesterday Mr. Amadie pointed it out to me — with its long spikes of tiny yellow flowers. A queer intriguing name I had heard before but never had connected it with the little round burs on my clothes. The dictionary says "The common agrimony of Europe and America was formerly of much repute in medicine." In the evening I gathered a plant in order to draw it. Its leaf arrangement amazed me — between each pair of large leaves there sprouted a pair or two of tiny ones! To think that all my life agrimony had been at my feet and on my skirts and never until now had I seen its extraordinary structure. An example of what Joost's father had called the "mightiness of the smallest things."

Lion's Foot, Rattlesnake Root (*Prenanthes alba*). This is a common plant in the woods, not yet in bloom. It intrigues me with its strange and striking leaves, with their amazing variability in form. And to think that never before had I noticed it! Certain leaves have a great appeal to me; their designs deeply stir me. Of all the new plants, lion's foot has made the greatest impression on me: five pages in my sketch book are devoted to its astonishing leaves.

Sept. 28. I ponder over the shapes of leaves, their infinite variety, their strangeness, their beauty. Why shouldn't they be all alike, or nearly alike? Birds need distinctive plumage and voices for species recognition. Plants need different flowers, pollen, etc., but it isn't clear why there should be a necessity for such a charming variety in leaf forms.

The trees and other plants are my friends now that I can call them by name. It is an awakening somewhat like that of 1919 to the bird world. The woods and fields are abounding in life and when we are aware of it, it flows into our spirits, enriching us. Certain trees inspire me like noble architecture — beeches, the different oaks, some of the conifers.

Oct. 10. My trip to the Dunes by myself. The colours are unbelievable: the crimson of the shining sumach and the gold of the tulip tree; the orange, gold, and green of the sassafras; carmine and scarlet of the pepperidge and pin oak; deep red of dewberry; purplish-scarlet brown of the ash. The world is too beautiful to believe. Witchhazel — rather disappointing with its small, solitary, drooping flowers — is in bloom and so is my lion's foot. It is a wonderful new world for me, now that my eyes are opened to my brothers the plants.

The Second World War had started on September 1, 1939, and had lasted for nearly six years. After a while ornithological journals from Europe no longer reached us, and we heard little news of our friends abroad. On May 7, 1945, Germany surrendered to the Allies.

The aftermath of the war brought great suffering to the people in Europe. Gradually we were able to help the ornithologists. Our family had started in 1945 sending food and clothing to Dutch friends, but the credit for undertaking to help a great number of ornithologists goes to Joe Hickey, who persuaded the A.O.U., and the Wilson and Cooper Clubs to appoint committees for European Relief. He wrote to Dr. Stresemann and Dr. Gustav Kramer for names and addresses of needy families and passed them on to donors.

Most credit of all goes to Frances Hamerstrom of Plainfield, Wisconsin. Expert in the use of the German language, she did a wonderful piece of work, writing to Europe for names of unfortunate families, for their special needs, and the ages and sexes of their children, then relaying all this information to people in this country. It is almost incredible what she accomplished.

Faithful workers in the eastern part of the country were the John Emlens who took charge of assigning contributions for Care packages, Theodora Nelson, Ellen Amman, and Ernst and Gretel Mayr; while on the West Coast Mrs. Jean Linsdale and Mrs. Laidlaw Williams, among others, worked zealously for destitute ornithologists. Many other women worked most unselfishly in gathering and packing food and clothing and many denied themselves that their distressed colleagues might have a little comfort.

One scheme of Fran's* was to have European artists among the ornithologists send bird paintings to us; these were auctioned at bird meetings, resulting in over $1,500 for the artists.

The herpetologists, ichthyologists, and mammalogists all sent relief to their colleagues. All of us busied ourselves sending reprints, journals, and books to the scientists in the devastated countries.

From the multitudes of grateful letters we received I will quote from a few.

A Dutch ornithologist who had lost his home and all his library wrote, "I do not know if we are happier to wash ourselves with one of the pieces of your soap or to drink a delicious cup of your tea."

From Hungary we heard from Dr. Keve that the Hungarian Ornithological Institute was destroyed with all its collections and library and other valuables; the Germans had used it for a fortress for three weeks and probably the last SS man burned it. On reaching Budapest after the War, Dr. Keve found only ruins of his home. "I have lost all . . . My library is quite burned. We are thirsty for American science."

My hostess in Budapest in 1938 described in brief her experiences after the Russian troops took over the city in February 1945. (Fortunately she had sent her 12-year-old daughter to her sister in Switzerland.)

---

*Dr. Frances Hamerstrom

We have been in the cellar (of the apartment house) for about three months and were afraid that in the end we will not have enough food; in the beginning we ate once a horse from the street but later we had only beans and no lard and no bread and the worst of all no water to drink. Only when there was snow and somebody was so brave and fetched some during the night we could melt it . . . First the terrible bombing and shooting was frightening; all the balconies were in the garden or on the street; the 3rd, 4th and 5th floors broke down. It was terrible. Later we were robbed; my trunks were taken away, packed as they were; first they found all the jewels and then they took away my underwear. I can miss the gold, and I have got a few things to change; the main things is that we live.

She speaks of a parcel from her parents in America:

I was terribly happy with it. You cannot imagine, to possess coffee and tea, that is like to be in paradise . . . I had to sell half of my coffee (to pay a dentist's bill) because coffee costs here $3 one pound.

She tells of a park where "hundreds and thousands of soldiers lay; they were buried in three big holes and we women had to carry them to one place! We will look forward to a better future and forget all the evil past."

Happily she and her daughter were able to come to this country the following year.

A very great thank-you came from an obscure Austrian ornithologist for a package of clothes and food — a *Wunder-packchen der Caritas.*

Weeping, my wife thanked on her knees for this providence. She is pious, and will never forget your goodness. Everything was there that had been brought together by a sisterly, loving hand. Receive, good lady, our deepest thanks with the assurance that God will mark this great-hearted deed in His book.

Konrad Lorenz had served as a physician in the War; for a long time after the fighting stopped his friends heard no word of him. At last the good news came that he was still alive, a prisoner in a Russian camp where he served as a specialist in neurology. Margarete Lorenz wrote me in May 1946 that soldiers returning from that camp told her that "he is always full of jokes and hope. He is a comfort for all the others." At this time she was living alone in Lorenz Hall, Konrad's father and old nurse, Resi, having died. During the War she had operated on many patients, but later had to give up her professional work due to lack of a car.

In October she thanked me for two big Care packages. (The children were with her):

Agnes is such a good help for me. She is better than a grown-up and she is beaming with joy every hour . . . We live in a part of the house. There are five more families here but we live in good contact and there is no quarrel . . . Agnes and I are working the whole day and late in the evening, but the house and garden are kept very well and we feel rich and comfortable.

At length, one wonderful day, Konrad was released.

From Germany, early in 1947, came a joyous letter from an ornithologist with two little boys; a Care package and a clothes package had arrived at about the same time. The baby was an "Amerikaner" in a creeper donated by one of our neighbours, while the four-year-old pranced around in blue trousers calling himself "Merikaner." Their father was very happy with one of Blaine's suits and a pair of his shoes; no longer would he be ashamed to go out in the street.

Later, his wife, herself an ornithologist, wrote:

From morning to night we are on the hunt for food. Standing in line for hours for bread and other food. This month I have at least ten times stood for 4 to 6 hours, only to find everything sold when it came my turn . . . You cannot imagine what endless joy you have brought us with your packages.

Elderly Dr. Alfred Laubmann, formerly Curator of the Natural History Museum in Munich, was forced to do heavy factory work and not allowed to visit his Museum where all of his own library was housed. I wrote him a friendly letter in March 1947, telling him we had ordered a Care package for him. He answered:

Many hearty thanks for your kind letter which for a long, long time was the first sign of human kindness and professional interest from America. When the Care package arrived, it was as if the Christ Child Himself had come to us. You can have no idea with what excitement we all opened the parcel and took out the so unexpected and valuable treasures — it was simply like a fairy tale. We will never, never in all our lives forget what you have done for us.

He begged for reprints, "I burn after scientific nourishment." Before long he was released from his factory job and from restrictions on his movements.

My good friend, Ernst Schüz, Director of the Museum of Natural History at Stuttgart, wrote me:

What an enormous surprise, your wunderful new parcel! You should have heard and seen the nearly endless rejoicing of old and young. All, that to eat and that to wear, is a very great gift.

As to the coloured bands, he planned to use them on titmice and Starlings.

Dr. Otto Koehler, Professor of Zoology at the University of Freiburg, wrote me in 1947:

There are two electric bulbs in the Institute, one in the ceiling of the warm room, one on the table for 20 and more micriscopes sitting around it. For warming that furnace and my furnace at home I have worked seven days in the forest to make wood, and my boots are quite rotten now.

[As to his students] : They hunger badly, they have no boots, no warm room; I cannot show them much in the lesson, but the little I can, they scrutinize with quite more zeal than other more lucky generations did in the times of pre-war years. They are good-hearted most of them; he who has anything he will divide and give to those who have not.

For a Care package from Harold and Josephine Michener of Pasadena, California, Professor E. V. Holst wrote from Heidelberg:

If you could have seen the excitement and jubilation of my three children and my wife, that would have been a better thanks than this letter! That there are people like you who unselfishly do a kindness to a member of a nation which people of the world scorn, enables one to believe again in the goodness of man, and this moral help is as great as the material one.

And, finally, an editor of a German ornithological journal wrote:

We are full of the most heartfelt thanks to our American colleagues: their friendship lets us believe once more in the future, which otherwise lay before us in frightful darkness.

By the end of 1949 Fran writes me, over 3,000 boxes had been sent by over 1,000 donors to European ornithologists in 15 countries: Germany, Austria, Hungary, Belgium, Poland, Finland, Bulgaria, Czechoslovakia, Yugoslavia, Italy, Rumania, Greece, France, Holland, and England. There were rich rewards for us in the touching gratitude of the recipients and firm friendships were formed between people who had never seen each other. These efforts had brought the devastation wrought by war very vividly to us in America.

XXXII

My Second Bird Life

For five years my health had fluctuated up and down to the perplexity of the doctors. I owe an incalculable debt to our good friend, the heart specialist, Dr. Emmet Bay. On March 21, 1947, after examining my electrocardiograms taken in 1942, he told me that I had not had a real attack of coronary thrombosis; that my difficulties were due to a labile sympathetic system and too many drugs. "Take up your bed and walk," said he.

So I most thankfully dropped the drugs and in time regained my strength. The wrong diagnosis of the other physicians had not been wholly without benefit, for it had rescued me from the impossible schedule I had set myself of research, reviews, and editing.

In the quarter century since my Emancipation Day, there have been rich experiences and significant achievements.

In the summers from 1951 through 1954 Constance and I were "visiting investigators" at the Delta Waterfowl Research Station in Manitoba at the invitation of the genial and gifted Director, artist and writer, and Brewster Medal recipient, Albert Hochbaum. Here we watched, from hatching, many birds, mostly precocial species (1953). The ducklings we returned to the hatchery after a few days, while other young birds we kept till independence. Our chief aim was to study the stages of behaviour development in precocial birds in order to compare them with the course taken by altricial species. There were exciting experiences. The research station is beside the great marsh and its waterfowl, so vividly described by Dr. Hochbaum (1944, 1955). The friendly, eager atmosphere of staff and students, engaged in the study of waterfowl life, and the visits of biologists from the Old and New Worlds — all these were truly stimulating.

The scientific aspects of our studies were published in 1962 as *Development of Behavior in Precocial Birds*; Transactions of the Linnaean Society of New York, VIII:1-212. I dedicated the work "To Albert Hochbaum without whom this book would never have been written." There are 18 tables, and 19 pages of sketches of the baby birds drawn by myself. In contrast to some of my other books, with this one I owe a great debt to my friend, the editor, Anne Wachenfeld of Orange, New Jersey, whose devoted labours and eagle eyes caught all errors in the manuscript and eliminated them before publication.

My other chief project was an investigation into the sources of the many errors published as to length of incubation periods of birds. This started in November 1951. Doris and Murray Speirs had invited me to join them at their home in Pickering, Ontario, near Toronto, whence we had driven to the A.O.U. meeting in Montreal*. After the meeting we had driven through the city of Quebec to Cap Tourmente to see the mighty congregation of 40,000 Greater Snow Geese[1], assembled on their southward migration to Chesapeake Bay.

At the Speirses' home I was shocked to find in several of their new bird books many incubation periods stated that were greatly at variance with well established ones. I spoke to Joe Hickey about my findings and he suggested I should write it up for the *Auk*. "Oh," said I, "it would take two weeks," and I didn't want to spare the time from my labours on precocials. Actually it took the better part of two years.

I had long been aware of problems concerning length of incubation periods, because in 1931 Dr. Heinroth had sent me a reprint of his classic paper on this subject (published in 1922). Besides giving the incubation periods of some hundred species, based on eggs hatched in incubators, the author discusses underlying principles. He points out that incubation is prolonged where the brood is little endangered, as in most hole-nesting species, in petrels in their burrows, as well as with birds of prey.

Fortunately for me, Chicago has two fine ornithological libraries,

---

*The 69th Stated Meeting of the American Ornithologists' Union, University of Montreal, Montreal, Quebec, October 8-11, 1951.

---

[1] *Chen caerulescens atlantica.*

adequate for the investigator in the history of science — the Field Museum and the John Crerar Library. I started to trace the errors in American bird books from Bergtold (1917) through Burns (1915) to Bendire (1892). I could find no earlier American book that gave many incubation periods except Gentry (1876, 1882) and his figures were so ridiculously short (from 8 to 10 days for small birds to 21 for Great Horned Owl and Red-tailed Hawk) that no one had bothered to quote him.

Evidently Major Bendire must have been the source of incubation periods in our country. Where had he got them? Not from observation in his busy life campaigning against Indians and amassing an "immense collection of eggs," or they would have been different. He had come to this country from Germany in 1852 as a lad of 16 and undoubtedly had brought the European viewpoint with him.

Heinroth had referred to the excellent studies of William Evans in the *Ibis* in 1891. This Scottish naturalist had hatched eggs of 79 species in an incubator or under hens, pigeons or canaries. He also had combed the literature and quoted 251 incubation periods with their sources, the earliest reference being that of F. Tiedemann in 1814. (Evans's list ironically enough, even though he had pointed out many of the most fantastic figures, served to perpetuate a number of these very guesses, that were subsequently quoted by careless compilers as reliable observations!)

Tiedemann, Professor of Zoology at the University of Heidelberg, had given 99 incubation periods in his book *Zoologie*; most of these were far too short. Although he mentioned no authorities for these periods, he did cite Aristotle's statement that incubation in hens last 25 days in winter and only 18 in summer. On looking up this reference I discovered what this great biologist of antiquity had said on incubation periods in his *Historie Animalium*, Book 6, Chapter 6:

The eagle incubates for about thirty days. The incubation period is about the same with other large birds, such as the goose and the bustard. With middle-sized birds it lasts about twenty days, as with the kite and the hawk.

So here were the original too-short incubation periods for the birds of prey!

Aristotle (1910) had assumed from the situation in the barn yard that incubation with large birds would follow the pattern of the domestic goose, while those of middle-sized birds would match that of the hen.

In reality, eagles hatch their eggs in about 45 days, the kite and hawk in four to five weeks. The Great Bustard, related to the Crane, on the other hand, hatches her eggs in 24-25 days! This initial attempt to assign length of incubation according to size of bird was a signal failure.

Here, then, I had found a beginning for the abbreviated periods for birds of prey, but could it be possible that these mistakes had been transmitted for 22 centuries? Or did the ornithologists of the 19th century hit upon them independently?

So my search through the libraries continued with renewed zeal. In this enterprise I found my smattering of foreign languages indispensible. German, French, Italian, and Latin I used contantly and Greek occasionally, while even a few words of Swedish and Portuguese were enough to tell me what, if anything, was said about incubation periods of the various species, designated as they were, by their scientific names.

I discovered that the great naturalists and great compilers in the past — Pliny in the first century A.D. (see Plinius, 1855), Albertus Magnus (1596) in the 13th, Gesner (1555) in the 16th, Aldrovandi (1610) in the 17th, and Buffon (1770-86) in the 18th century — *all quoted Aristotle's incubation periods.* Moreover, they all omitted the original qualifying "about" the stated number of days.

The succession is clear through 2,000 years from Aristotle (about 350 B.C.) to Buffon (1770). At the end of the 18th century, two Germans, J. M. Bechstein (1791-1795) and J. A. Naumann (1795-1803), branched out in new paths; both published sets of books in which they supplied *all their birds* with incubation periods manufactured according to size of species. Bechstein was clearly Tiedemann's model. Books by the Naumanns — father and son — and their followers, had a great vogue; were reissued and translated with all their mistaken incubation periods until at least 1923. It was to these books that Evans had traced the confused state of opinions on incubation periods in Great Britain in the 19th century.

This pursuit through the libraries had given me a fascinating course in the history of ornithology so far as life-history matters were concerned. It resulted in four papers.

I will quote the last paragraph of the last paper (1954 b):

Three kinds of people have been concerned with incubation periods: Guessers, Copyists, and Investigators. The history of statements on incubation periods has been largely a copying of assumptions by such important people as Aristotle, Bechstein, Naumann, and Bendire. Sixty years ago ornithologists in the Old World were set on the right path by the first great investigator in this field — Evans — and 30 years later they were again stimulated by the second great investigator — Heinroth. In the New World, however, we were led astray by a great "Guesser" — Bendire — and many of us still believe him. For the most part the 2300 years during which men have recorded their thoughts on incubation periods of birds make a sad story of the blind leading the blind.

And although bird students are more aware now than previously of the complexities involved in length of incubation periods, still some are misled by trusting in older compilations of the birds of North America, for example, Forbush's *Birds of Massachusetts* (1925-29) and Bent's series through 1940.

As to other papers, a new field was entered in a comparison of behavioural development between precocial and altricial mammals; the sequence of appearance of behaviour patterns appears to be much the same in both. Both categories show markedly different rates of development that have evolved in different orders and in families and in response to different external conditions.

A time-consuming project was finishing a paper on the Purple Martin (1952), started by a student of Dr. Van Tyne, Robert W. Allen, who had lost his life in New Guinea during the War. In "Nesting Success in Altricial Birds," he summarizes from 29 published studies the fledging success of 21,951 eggs in open nests (46 per cent), and that from 33 studies of 94,400 eggs in nests in holes (66 per cent).

A report on experiences with a hand-raised Eastern Meadowlark (1962 a) imprinted on me as his mate, describes his courtship and nest-invitation displays, as well as his rich and varied singing.

I have assisted the different Review Editors of *Bird-banding*, contributing an average of 54 reviews a year from 1943 through 1968, in contrast to the average of 187 reviews a year from 1934 through 1942, the total coming to 3,280 reviews in 35 years. In the early days the field was modest, but now it has grown gigantic. A total of serials with avian content cited by *Biological Abstracts* came to 335 from 34 countries, ranging from 1 to 137 (U.S.A.) per country. During the early 1960s more than 1,000 serials published material on avian biology.

There have been great advances in techniques in serious bird study, for instance, the use of mist nets in capturing birds for banding and in the rich field of recording bird songs on tape and reproducing them for study and playback as sonograms and oscillograms.

Unfortunately, especially in the United States, it has become the fashion to write up researches so stiffly, matter-of-factly, and technically that all feeling and atmosphere have been banished from too many of them.

DR. BLAINE NICE, MRS. MARGARET NICE, CONSTANCE NICE
Delta, Manitoba, Canada
Summer, 1953
Photographed by H. Albert Hochbaum

XXXIII

In
Conclusion

In the last quarter of a century I have not realized my long cherished ambitions of journeying to the Tropics or the Arctic, to Africa or Australia.

Family duties and Father Time have both curbed such high ambitions. However, I attended three International Ornithological Congresses: one in Oxford, England, in 1934; one in Rouen, France, in 1938, and the third in Ithaca, New York, in 1962. There was one trip to Florida, several journeys to the Southwest and Far West of the United States, as well as many to Canada. I was able to enjoy nine A.O.U. meetings and the same number of W.O.C. (now Wilson Ornithological Society), making in all 22 assemblies of each of these in 60 years — from A.O.U. in 1908 to W.O.S. in 1964*. At the majority of these meetings (from 1920-1964) I gave a paper.

I will mention a few of the most outstanding trips.

In late February 1948 I travelled by train to Arizona and California. In Tucson I was most hospitably entertained by the Anders Andersons, specialists on the life history of the Cactus Wren (1957-1963), and by Mrs. William Foerster and her son Allan Phillips, authority on the birds of Arizona (1964). These ornithologists took me to see birds in the Santa Ritas, Santa Catalinas, and elsewhere. In these fascinating surroundings I saw many birds new to me; I also learned the names of the most striking plants and enthusiastically sketched them. In Los Angeles I became

*Annual Meeting of the Wilson Ornithological Society held at Western Michigan University, April 30 — May 3, 1964.

acquainted with my daughter Barbara Thompson's three little sons, and later had delightful visits with Laidlaw and Abby Lou Williams at Carmel, and with Jean and Mary Ann Linsdale at the Hastings Natural History Reserve. Finally I stayed with my sister Sarah in Piedmont. The crown of this visit was the week at the end of April in a cabin at the Yosemite National Park. Here with the help of the Park Naturalists we identified the noble great conifers and we marvelled at the scenery, the birds, and the flowers. Before we left, a heavy snowstorm gave the Park a new, unforgettable glory.

Seven years later, Blaine and I spent a happy spring in Oklahoma where the W.O.C. met at Stillwater*. On the field trip to the Salt Plains Wildlife Refuge we saw ducks, geese, and, sailing overhead, 200 magnificent White Pelicans[1].

Business affairs in Norman occupied Blaine for some weeks, while my chief task lay in helping fight the efforts of the U.S. Army that planned to take over for a guided missile centre the very best of the wilderness areas in the Wichita Mountains Wildlife Refuge. Richard Westwood, dedicated editor of *Nature Magazine,* had asked me to write an article for his journal on this outrageous scheme (1955). Three times at two-week intervals we camped out in this wild, rocky refuge, loved by us from our first visit 35 years earlier. At each successive visit in 1955 there were new birds, new flowers, and new frog voices.

Our second trip there that spring was with the annual meeting of the Oklahoma Ornithological Society, founded in 1950, and five years later numbering some 300 members*. This meeting coincided with a dust storm — our first experience with this disagreeable phenomenon. It was strange while eating our picnic lunch to have to hold on to our utensils and to find our food coated with dust.

My paper, "Wichita Mountains Wildlife Refuge in Peril" appeared in *Nature Magazine* in May 1955. Mr. Westwood generously donated 1,000 reprints and these were sent far and wide.

On May 18 I wrote to Mr. Westwood:

We feel hopeful that right will win. More and more indignation is being

---

*The 36th Stated Meeting of the Wilson Ornithological Club, Stillwater, Oklahoma, April 7-10, 1955.

---

[1] American White Pelican, *Pelicanus erythrorhynchos.*

---

*In contrast to the known half-dozen earnest bird watchers in the state in 1923, by 1968 this society had grown to a membership of 530 people, some 60 times greater in 45 years!

stirred up in Oklahoma. We conservationists all worked together and encouraged one another. It was Mrs. Lovie Whitaker who had alerted the Oklahoma Outdoor Council to the danger two-and-a-half years ago. If it had not been for her, the Army might have succeeded in its first pincer movement designed to engulf the whole refuge.

In this battle the conservationists finally defeated the Army!

Two other trips in Oklahoma that spring were of special interest to me. On May 4 Jean Graber drove Lovie Whitaker and me 50 miles west of Norman to Caddo County to the canyon where she was studying Black-capped Vireos for a Ph.D. thesis under George Sutton, professor at the University of Oklahoma since 1952. This canyon was a remarkable place of red cedars and oaks with Poor-wills[1] nesting on top and Chuck-will's-widows nesting in the depths. Such fascinating birds and flowers! But rough terrain to scramble over, especially in the hot sunshine. Jean had had excellent returns from her adult banded Black-caps. Two nests had been built this spring but no eggs had yet been laid. Cowbirds are a great burden to these rare little birds; it is difficult for the vireos to raise any of their own progeny!

Two days later another student of Dr. Sutton took us to a ranch two miles north of Norman, where he had found four singing Cassin's Sparrows, those birds with exquisite songs that normally nest at the end of the Oklahoma Panhandle. The drought of several years' duration had induced them to extend their range temporarily to the east. It was indeed a joy to hear them once more — as well as to see gorgeous prairie flowers, to watch Dickcissels establishing their territories, and to find a Scissor-tailed Flycatcher on her nest with her mate perched nearby.

In later years the conservationists again defeated the Army in their plans to take over the wooded island in Jackson Park in Chicago for a dwelling place for the officers of the Fifth Army. We also helped save Dinosaur National Monument, some of the California redwoods, and part of the Indiana Dunes, as well as other unique wilderness areas. But we have been ignominiously defeated in our struggles against wholesale poisoning of the world with death-dealing pesticides. It is a constant battle to keep gains that protect a little of the earth from the hands of greed. The situation is ever worsening due to the irresponsible, appalling increase of the human race.

My bird studies have brought me many fine friends, both men and women. Of the latter I will mention five.

[1]Common Poorwill, *Phalaenoptilus nuttallii.*

I have already told of my happy visit with Ruth Thomas in Arkansas. Amelia Laskey of Nashville, Tennessee, is a tireless investigator and defender of wild life; she has done outstanding work on her Bluebird Trails (1939), on Cowbirds (1950), and on other species. Winnifred Smith, of Two Rivers, Wisconsin, is a most eager worker, spreading the gospel of nature study in the schools. Doris Speirs of Toronto, Canada, is full of zeal and love, not only for nature but for people too; her special study has been the Evening Grosbeak (1968). Finally, there is Louise de Kirilene Lawrence, of Rutherglen, Ontario, who lives with her husband in a charming log house in the north woods where she has watched with sympathy and understanding the life around her. She has written two distinguished books — one of woodpeckers, the other — *The Lovely and the Wild* — a fascinating narrative of the wildlife about her home (1967, 1968).

All of these are gallant women, undaunted by difficulties and sorrows, rejoicing in the beauty of the earth and sharing that joy with others.

In Toronto, as in some cities of the United States, the one ornithological club was (and still is) restricted to men. Doris Speirs determined to found a club for women who were serious students of birds. This she did in 1952 and it was named the Margaret Nice Ornithological Club. It numbers twelve Active Members in the Toronto region, and seven Corresponding Members in other parts of Canada (see Appendix # 2).

In answer to my recent question as to what the Club has meant to its members, Doris answered:

The twelve of us are mostly very busy women, and our day each month means a tremendous amount to us, to get outdoors, to look at nature, to listen and record the birds, to observe innumerable details of wilderness, from skunk cabbage to baby Yellow Warblers.

And they have been able to contribute over $600.00 to the Dorcus Bay Federation of Ontario Naturalists' Reservation on the Bruce Peninsula of Ontario.

It has been gratifying to receive the honorary degree of Doctor of Science, both in 1955 at my 50th reunion at my Alma Mater, Mount Holyoke College, and again, seven years later, from Elmira College, Elmira, New York. Two sentences in the 1962 citation, composed by the dean, Richard Bond, particularly pleased me:

She used the outdoors near her home as her laboratory and common species of birds as her subject. In so doing, she joined the ranks of the eminent ornithologists of all time, who saw so much in what appeared common to so many.

My beloved Song Sparrows have again come into my life. A race of this species in Mexico was named *Melospiza melodia niceae* by Robert Dickerman who wrote, "I take pleasure in dedicating this subspecies to Mrs. Margaret M. Nice in recognition of her contribution to the literature of, and affection for, the Song Sparrow.

I am happy that three of my books have been reprinted in paperback by Dover Publications, Inc., New York: two in 1964, the other, three years later. By mischance I did not receive Hayward Cirker's letter concerning the two volumes of the *Life History of the Song Sparrow*, so had no opportunity to eliminate typographical errors in Volume II, nor to give advice as to the covers, one of which pictures an olive-green Song Sparrow and the other a bright red one! Mr. Cirker assures me that these matters will be set right in the next printing.

The Watcher at the Nest, on the other hand, is most attractively set up and contains a note, which tells of Amelia Laskey's important study of "Cowbird Behavior," which corrected my conclusions on the marital relations of this species.

For the opportunity to follow my career, which has involved much more outlay of money than income derived from it, I am deeply indebted to a most understanding and sympathetic husband, who earned the living for us and who shared in many trips to see birds and attend meetings. I am also grateful to four enthusiastic and helpful daughters, and I rejoice in our seven fine grandsons. Finally, my brother Ted*, with his editorial experience, and his enthusiasm, has given me fresh courage as I struggled on with this story of my life with birds.

Although in my long life, I have visited only a fraction of this wonderful world, yet I have been able to see many choice things and to study some of them, intensively.

It is true that I deplore much in the present situation in the world — basically due to overcrowding — yet for many of the features of civilization I am profoundly thankful: for instance, the comparative freedom of women, the advances in medical science, the availability of classical music over FM radio, the great improvements in photographic techniques, paperback books printed in America, electric refrigerators, electric and gas stoves, frozen foods,

---

*Edward S. Morse

and for transportation — the convenience of the automobile, and the marvellous experience of flying over the earth.

The study of nature is a limitless field, the most fascinating adventure in the world. I feel that ornithology is a splendid pursuit in which strong sympathy and fellowship reign among the majority of serious participants; we are friends, and we are glad to help one another.

We who love nature, who see and try to understand and interpret, are following the true goal. We have a talisman against the futility of the lives of many people. We must try to open the eyes of the unseeing to the beauty and wonder of the earth and its wild life.

Appendix

APPENDIX # 1. Professor Dr. Konrad Lorenz explains:

Margaret Morse Nice's thorough understanding of ethology and its cardinal questions became effective in still another way. Her wide reading, and her faculty to analyze what she had read, led her to an important discovery: she realized that Charles Otis Whitman on one side of the Atlantic Ocean and Oskar Heinroth on the other, without knowing each other, had come to absolutely identical conclusions concerning the evolution as well as the physiological nature of "instinctive" behaviour.

This realization was not at all as easy as it appears to be in retrospect. Quite apart from the fact that the two scientists were writing in different languages, their personal modes of expressing themselves were as different as possible. As a matter of fact, Margaret Morse Nice only began to read Whitman and Heinroth after she had become acquainted with the work of Wallace Craig who was a pupil of Whitman, and of myself, who am a pupil of Heinroth. Thus she discovered a clear case of convergent evolution of two schools of behaviour study, each developing on one side of the ocean. Also she realized that the Whitman school in America and the Heinroth school in Germany and Austria were quite unaware of each other's existence.

It is a deplorable fact that the outstanding pioneer work of Charles Otis Whitman has so long remained unknown, not only to European scientists, but to American psychologists and behaviour students as well. After Margaret Morse Nice had taken a hand, and, through her agency, I had come to know Whitman's and Craig's work, I took pains to ask every American psychologist who came to visit my psychological teacher Karl Bühler in Vienna, whether he or she knew Charles Otis Whitman and his work. Karl Bühler was well known in the States and there were many visitors from America to his Institute, but among them there was not one who had even heard Whitman's name; his own son, whom I happened to meet years later, knew about his father only, that "he was crazy about pigeons."

The great discovery which was made independently by Whitman in pigeons, and, a few years later, by Heinroth in waterfowl, can be explained in very few words. They both found that certain sequences of movements — now called "fixed motor patterns" — are as constant characters of a species, a genus, a family, an order or even of a much larger taxonomic unit, as are any bodily characters, such as the morphology of teeth, feathers or bones. Both demonstrated irrefutably that the concept of homology is equally applicable to behaviour patterns as it is to bodily structures. It is no exaggeration to say that this discovery constitutes the archemedic point from which the new branch of science, now called ethology, has arisen.

The full recognition of Charles Otis Whitman's merits might have remained in abeyance for many years if Margaret Morse Nice had not taken action, which she did very simply by bringing Wallace Craig and myself into contact. He became one of my most important and certainly one of my most influential teachers. As Whitman had been older than Heinroth, so Wallace Craig was older than myself and he certainly had advanced much farther than I had along the path of understanding animal behaviour on which we were both travelling, when we made each other's acquaintance.

I was still a devout believer in Sherringtonian reflex theory, caught up in its doctrine all the more inextricably as I felt that it was an undesirable concession to vitalism, if one assumed that fixed motor patterns were not chains of reflexes. It was largely due to Wallace Craig's influence that I began to pay attention to the spontaneity.

In retrospect, it seems quite incredible with what stubbornness I clung to the reflex theory even though I was fully cognizant of the facts contradicting it. I still remember how conviction dawned upon me on reading one very simple sentence in a letter from Wallace Craig: "It is obviously nonsense to speak of re-action to a stimulus not yet received."

It was as simple as that, but it was needed to start me on a train of thought which later brought me into contact with physiologists such as Erich von Holst, Paul Weiss and others, who had exploded the physiological basis on which all stimulus-response psychology is built up.

I hope to have made it clear what an immense amount of gratitude I, personally, owe to Margaret Morse Nice. It is to her that I owe one of my most influential teachers, one who helped me to surmount the most difficult mental obstacle I encountered in my life.

Konrad Lorenz

APPENDIX # 2

Cobble Hill, 1815 Altona Road,
Pickering, Ontario, Canada.
L1V 1M6. January 31, 1975...

Mr. Edward S. Morse,
Under Mountain Road,
South Londonderry,
Vermont 05155. U.S.A.

Dear Mr. Morse:

In my letter to Constance I expressed something of what your precious sister, Dr. Margaret Morse Nice, meant to me. She was one of the most helpful friends that ever blessed my experience — I was a young amateur when we met an an AOU meeting in Washington, D.C. (1938, was it?) and she a most distinguished and already famous ornithologist. Yet she questioned me on my research with evidently a sincere and even keen interest, as though I could really contribute to her knowledge of bird behaviour by my observations. Her simplicity, her deep humility and sense of awe and wonder before the marvelous revealings of the natural world were evidences of her greatness. Like the Elephant Child in Kipling's Just-So story, she had an insatiable "curtiosity". This led her to discover much before undescribed in bird behaviour, and to faithfully publish the results of her arduous and penetrating researches.

You ask me if I will tell you of the founding of the Margaret Nice Ornithological Club. It happened in this way:

On January 10, 1952, my husband and I had dinner in Toronto with a distinguished Hungarian ornithologist and his wife, Miklos and Maud Udvardy. He was preparing a lecture to be given at the University of Toronto and Murray was helping him with the English wording. After dinner Murray announced that he was taking Dr. Udvardy to the monthly meeting of the Toronto Ornithological Club at Hart House, U. of T. "Aren't the ladies coming?" asked Miklos. Murray explained that the Toronto Ornithological Club was for *men* only. "Is this the 14th century?" queries Miklos in surprise. Then he had a suggestion. "Why don't you start an ornithological club for *women* only?" So the seed was sown.

Less than a week later, on January 17th, Mrs. Henry H. Marsh and I were invited to Mrs. Joseph W. Barfoot's to luncheon. All three being ardent bird lovers, we discussed seriously the idea of founding a bird club for women only, and before Margaret and I left Olive's for home, the club was organized.

We decided to limit the membership to twelve kindred spirits. Our first minute book reads:

The Margaret Nice Ornithological Club was organized in January, 1952, and affiliation with the Federation of Ontario Naturalists followed immediately. The aims of the club are: to gain a better knowledge and appreciation of bird life through a study of the birds in the field; a further understanding of the bird's habitat or environment; to record all species of birds observed and numbers seen on each field trip and also phenological data. The club makes possible the meeting of ornithologists at regular intervals, for mutual encouragement and a certain joyous fellowship. We discuss, review and report on topics of natural history interest and ecological significance furthering a more scientific understanding of ornithology.

The club honours in its name Dr. Margaret M. Nice, internationally famous ornithologist who is especially known for her study of the Song Sparrow. I would like to quote from a letter she wrote to her club from her home in Chicago, Illinois, on January 30, 1952:

"The study of nature is a limitless field, the most fascinating pursuit in the world. I feel that the study of ornithology is a wonderful game in which strong sympathy and fellowship reign between the serious participants: we are friends and glad to help one another. We have high standards for our science and we want beginners to realize this.

"We must *see clearly, record fully and accurately,* and *try to understand.*

"Emerson wrote: 'I am impressed with the fact that the greatest thing a human soul ever does in this world is to see something and tell what it saw in a plain way. Hundreds of people can talk for one who can think, but thousands can think for one who can see. To see clearly is poetry, philosophy and religion in one.'

"We who love nature, who see and try to understand and interpret, are following the true goal. We have a talisman against the futility of the life of most people. We should try to open the eyes of the unseeing to the beauty and wonder of nature.

"*'Blessed is he who has gained knowledge in nature.*
. . . *who observes the ageless order of immortal nature.*
How it is constituted and when and why:
To such the practice of base deeds never cleaves.'"

Euripides.

Sincerely yours,
(Signed)   Margaret Morse Nice

With such a goal and such inspiration, the club forged ahead. Mrs. Nice sent us reprints of many of her articles and also autographed copies of her books: "The Watcher at the Nest," "Studies in the Life History of the Song

Sparrow," I and II, etc. These were the nucleus of an MNOC library.

Dr. Margaret Morse Nice passed away in June, 1974, at the age of 90. I have a large file of her letters: very precious. One year we were able to take her to the Annual Meeting of the American Ornithologists' Union in Montreal. Another year my husband and I took two of the MNOC members (Olive Barfoot and Irma Metcalfe) to meet her at the Annual Meeting of the Wilson Ornithological Society in the Great Smokies. We gave a dinner in her honour at the AOU Meeting in Denver, Colorado. We were able to drive her north to Rutherglen to meet Louise de Kiriline Lawrence (a corresponding member of MNOC) with whom she had been in close touch. Then and there they became fast friends.

The present (1975) active members of MNOC are:

1. Mrs. Olive Barfoot, past president of the Toronto Junior Field-Naturalists' Club, which meets at the Royal Ontario Museum. Olive is a sculptor in terra cotta, of gulls and terns, grouse, ptarmigan, and, especially, and most delightfully, of owls. Her Starling appeared at Stratford, her Water Buffalo in the Royal Ontario Museum. She is a Founding Member.

2. Mrs. Janet Goodwin, another Torontonian. Janet is an Associate of the Photographic Society of America (APSA). She exhibits in international and club salons, has done regional work across Canada. While she enjoys photographing birds, she specializes in wild flowers and fungi.

3. Miss Sylvia Hahn, Myrtle, Ontario. Sylvia is the muralist of the Royal Ontario Museum. She has illustrated many books with her wood engravings, including "A Naturalists' Guide to Ontario" by W. W. Judd and J. Murray Speirs: "Carolina Quest" by Richard M. Saunders and "The Forehead's Lyre," poems from the Swedish of Lars von Haartman, translated by Doris Huestis Speirs. She has made a special study of the Barn Swallow and has given talks in the ROM theatre on her findings, illustrated by her own drawings. She is also a poet.

4. Mrs. Ida Hanson of Toronto. Ida is the Membership Secretary of the Toronto Field Naturalists' Club, following her retirement from the staff of the Federation of Ontario Naturalists. She was made an Honorary Member of the Federation at its 41st Annual Meeting "in recognition of outstanding service promoting the objectives of the Federation." Her cottage in the Georgian Bay is a special delight to this keen naturalist, and she has been able to share its loons, whip-poor-wills and rare prairie warblers with MNOC members.

5. Dr. Katherine Dawson Ketchum of Toronto. Since the passing of her husband and retirement from the staff of the Women's College Hospital, Katherine has been able to travel and to add many species to her list of the birds of the world. In 1967 she visited Scotland, Holland and France: in 1968, Poland, Hungary and Romania: in 1969, East Africa; in 1970, Texas and

Mexico. That same year she was up in Churchill to see the nesting shorebirds. In 1972 she visited West Mexico: in 1972, East Mexico, Trinidad and Spain: in 1973, Panama, Guatemala and Peru (including the Galapagos Islands). This year she went to Venezuela, the Amazon and Argentina. On her return from trips she writes the highlights of her birding adventures for the Newsletter of the TFNC, and shares with the MNOC her lovely slides.

6. Mrs. Naomi Le Vay of Toronto. Naomi heads the Records Committee of our club. She has a summer cottage by Lake Ontario and Cranberry Marsh. She has kept a careful record of her bird observations there for a number of years, and consequently has been able to contribute many records to the J. Murray Speirs' series of the "Birds of Ontario County, Ontario". Many of our field trips are held at the LeVays. As a result of this we have been able to send to the proper authorities the reasons why we thought that the Cranberry Marsh should be a Bird Sanctuary. We have urged this with enthusiasm, coupled with the supplying of much data. Therefore, it is most gratifying to the club to be able to report that the Central Ontario Conservation Authority has purchased the Cranberry Marsh and acreage leading to it, and it is well posted. We were able to send this glad news to Dr. Nice. Naomi is not only a good conservationist, she is also a poet.

7. Miss Grace Malkin, Thistletown, Ontario. Grace's photographs of wild flowers are now on exhibition at the Herbarium of the Botany Building, University of Toronto. For many years she wrote for the Junior Red Cross Magazine, illustrating her articles with her own nature photography. She has been a guest speaker on nature at the Royal Ontario Museum Theatre. In 1938 her "Story Book of Nature" came out in three volumes. In 1965 she took part in Treasure Tours' ornithological trip around the world. She visited a research station in the Ukraine, and on her return told the club of the bird life in the Orient, in Japan and India, as well as in eastern Europe.

8. Mrs. Margaret Marsh, "Hedgerows," Cobourg, Ontario. Margaret is a Founding Member of the MNOC. She is the wife of the Right Reverend Henry H. Marsh, the former Bishop of the Yukon. Since his retirement they have been living in lovely rolling country near Cobourg, where they maintain an active bird-feeding station. Recently they returned from the Holy Land. Margaret gives many talks to church and naturalists' groups, illustrated by her remarkable slides. She has worked hard in her region protecting the environment from pollution and exploitation. She has a deep love and understanding of the Indian people and made many friends in the Yukon, at Whitehorse and Old Crow. She is a joyous student and photographer. She writes well.

9. Viola Whitney Pratt, D. Litt. S., of Toronto. Viola is the widow of the great Canadian "Poet-Laureate," E. J. Pratt. She founded, and for twenty-six years edited, a children's magazine called "World Friends". A collection of her stories and editorials from this publication is called: "Journeying with the

Year". She is also the author of a book on three famous Canadian doctors, Sir Frederick Banting, Sir William Osler and Dr. Wilder Penfield — "Canadian Portraits". (This is now also in paperback.) Dr. Pratt is past president of the University Women's Club. She is a gifted speaker and her club was charmed on hearing her talk on "The Birds of the Bible". She has a beautifully mounted collection of bird stamps from all over the world which have been on view at the Royal Ontario Museum. Poems on the birds, which she has selected from both famous and lesser poets add to the uniqueness of this collection.

10. Mrs. Doris Huestis Speirs of Pickering, Ontario. Doris is Founding Member of the MNOC. She followed Olive Barfoot as president of the Toronto Junior Field Naturalists' Club in the 1950s. Since the club was founded she has represented the MNOC at Directors' meetings of the Federation of Ontario Naturalists. The Cobble Hill feeding station for birds welcomes bird students from all over the world. Doris' special study has been the Evening Grosbeak, and she has contributed the life histories of the Eastern, Western and Mexican subspecies of *Hesperiphona vespertina* to the Arthur Cleveland Bent life histories of North American Birds.

11. Mrs. Rose Speirs of Toronto. Rose knows the scientific names of most garden plants and is an expert at designing beautiful gardens and fostering the birds that visit them. Her European travels have introduced her and her husband, Rae, to many new species. Indoor meetings in winter are a joy as she shares with the members their slide collection.

Note: Two of the original members who joined in 1952 have passed on: Irma Metcalfe of Thistletown and Marjorie Lawrence Meredith of Bolton.

Irma was an all-around naturalist, knew all the local birds but was also the club's authority on the identification of ferns, mosses and lichens. She and her husband were rock-hounds and had a large and elegant collection of rocks and minerals. Most summers were spent in the north, digging for more of the earth's treasures. On winter evenings the stones were polished, and, set in hand-crafted silver, became rings, cuff-links, earrings and pendants.

Marjorie wrote a nature column for the Bolton newspaper, gave illustrated talks on birds and conservation to the schools, and sponsored bird-house-building campaigns. For a few years she was the pianist in a musical ensemble. She was also a skillful painter in both oils and watercolour and exhibited internationally.

Both these women quickened our awareness of nature's ever-unfolding wonders and so enriched our lives. And both loved the Margaret Nice Ornithological Club and honoured its patron saint, Margaret Morse Nice.

(signed) Doris Huestis Speirs

Literature Cited

ABBOTT, Clinton G.
    1911   The home life of the osprey. London, Witherby & Co. 54 pp. 32 pls. Bird Lovers' Home Life Series.

ALBER, J. W.
    1846   On the upper Arkansas and through the country of the Comanche Indians in 1845. U. S. Sen. Doc. I, 438 Sess., 29 Cong., Vol. VIII: 75 pp.

ALBERTUS Magnus, Bishop of Ratisbon (1193-1280)
    1596   Albertus Magnus de Falconibus, Asturibus, & Accipitribus, Ex libro ejus XXIII De Animalibus. Frederick II, *Emperor of Germany*, Reliqua Librorum Friderici II. De arte venandi cum avibus, &c.

ALDROVANDI, U.
    1610   Ornithologiae. Hoc est de avibus historiae. Bologna. Libri XII.

ALLEE, W. C.
    1938   The social life of animals. Boston, Beacon Press. 233 pp.

ALLEN, Robert W. and Margaret M. NICE
    1952   A study of the breeding biology of the purple martin (*Progne subis*). Am. Midland Naturalist, 47: 606-665.

ALTUM, Bernard
    1868   Der Vogel und sein Leben. Münster.

AMERICAN ORNITHOLOGISTS' UNION
    1910   The A.O.U. check-list of North American birds. Third Edition, revised: 1-430.
    1957   The A.O.U. check-list of North American birds. Fifth Edition: i-ix: 1-691.

1973   Thirty-second Supplement to the American Ornithologists' Union check-list of North American birds. Auk, 90: (2): 411-419.

1976   Thirty-third Supplement to the American Ornithologists' Union check-list of North American birds. Auk, 93: (4): 875-879.

ANDERSON, Anders Harold

1957   Life history of the cactus wren. Pt. I. Winter and pre-nesting behavior. Condor, 59: 274-296.

1959   Pt. 2. The beginning of nesting. Condor, 61: 186-205.

1960   Pt. 3. The nesting cycle. Condor, 62: 351-369.

1961   Pt. 4. Development of nestlings. Condor, 63: 87-94.

1962   Pt. 5. Fledgling to independence. Condor, 64: 99-212.

1963   Pt. 6. Competition and survival. Condor, 65: 29-43.

ARISTOTLE

1910   Historia animalium. Trans. by D. A. W. Thompson. Vol. IV of Works of Aristotle. Oxford. Edited by J. A. Smith and W. Ross.

AUDUBON, John James

1827-38 Birds of America. 435 coloured plates.

AUKLET

1922   Dix Cissell: "Evolution of deecnomialism" Vol. 1: (2): 1-3. "Song sparrows of the Thousand Islands" Vol. 1: (2): 8.

BAILEY, Florence Merriam

1902   Handbook of birds of the western United States . . . Boston and New York. Houghton, Mifflin & Co. xc + 512 pp.

BAILEY, Florence Merriam

1928   Birds of New Mexico. Sante Fé, N. M. Dept. Game & Fish: xxiv + 807 pp. 80 pls., 136 figs. 60 maps, 2 diagrams.

BARDE, Frederick S.

1912   Field, forest and stream in Oklahoma. Okla. Game & Fish Dept. Ann. Rept.

BECHSTEIN, J. M.

1791-95 Gemeinnützige Naturgeschichte Deutschlands nach allen drei Teichen. (Vögel). Leipzig. 3 vols.

BEEBE, Charles William

1918-22 A monograph of the pheasants. London. Witherby & Co. 4 quarto vols. pls. (part col.) maps.

BENDIRE, C. E.

1892-95 Life histories of North American birds. U.S. National Mus., Special Bull. 2 vols.

BENT, Arthur Cleveland
1919-68   Life Histories of North American Birds. U.S. National Mus. Bulls. 113, 135, 142, 162, 167, 170, 174, 176, 178, 179, 195, 196, 197, 203, 211, 237.

BERGTOLD, W. H.
1917   A study of the incubation periods of birds, what determines their length? Denver, Colo. McKendrick-Bellamy Co. 109 pp.

BRAND, Albert R.
1935   A method for the intensive study of bird song. Auk, 52: (1): 40-52.

BUFFON, G. L. L. de
1770-86   Histoire naturelle des osieaux. Paris. 10 vols.

BURNS, Frank L.
1915   Comparative periods of deposition and incubation of some North American birds. Wilson Bull., 27: 275-286.

BUTTS, Wilbur K.
1930   A study of the chickadee and white-breasted nuthatch by means of marked individuals. I. Bird-Banding, 1: 149-168.
1931   II. Bird-Banding, 2: 1-26.

CARTER, T. C. and O. J. TRENTON
1908   Thesis on Oklahoma birds. The Northwestern (Apr., 1908)

CHAPMAN, Frank M.
1895   Handbook of the birds of eastern North America. D. Appleton & Co. 581 pp.

CHAPMAN, Frank M.
1903   Colour key to North American birds. New York. Doubleday, Page & Co. vi + 312 pp.

CHAPMAN, Frank M.
1922   In memoriam; Joseph Asaph Allen. Born July 19, 1838 – died August 29, 1921. Auk, 39: 1-14. pl. 1

CHIGI, Prince Francesco
1933   Methods of capturing birds at the ornithological station of Castel Fusano. (Translated from Italian into English by Margaret Morse Nice.) Bird-Banding, 4: (2): 59-67.

CLARK, Hubert L.
1883   Butterflies of Amherst. The Amherst Record.

CLARK, Hubert L.
1887   Birds of Amherst and vicinity. An artificial key to the birds of

Amherst. Amherst, Mass. J. E. Williams. (In three parts.)
1906   Birds of Amherst. Second edition, revised.

CLARK, Hubert L.
1947   How I became an ornithologist and how I fell from grace. Bull. Mass. Audubon Soc. (Jan., 1947)

CRAIG, Wallace
1908   Voices of pigeons regarded as a means of social control. Am. Journ. Sociology, 14: 86-100.

CRAIG, Wallace
1926   The twilight song of the wood pewee. A preliminary statement. Auk, 43: 150-153.

CRAIG, Wallace
1943   The song of the wood pewee. New York State Museum, Bull. 334: 186.

DAWSON, William Leon
1923   The birds of California. San Diego, Los Angeles, San Francisco. South Moulton Co. 4 vols. 2121 pp. 30 photogravures, 120 duotone pls., 110 colour pls., 44 drawings, over 100 photos.

DELACOUR, Jean
1935   Les élevage f. de Clères en 1934. (The ornithological collections of Clères.) L'Oiseau, 5: 145-149.

DELACOUR, Jean
1937   Review of: "The population study of the song sparrow" by Margaret Morse Nice. L'Oiseau, 7: 655-656.

DELACOUR, Jean
1938   First rearing of Pittas in captivity. Proc. VIII International Ornithological Congress (Oxford, Eng. July, 1934): 717-719.

DELACOUR, Jean
1947   Birds of Malaysia. New York. Macmillan Co. 382 pp.

DICKENS, Charles
1853-54 A child's history of England. Bradbury & Evans. 3 vols. Frontispiece by S. W. Topham.

DROST, Rudolph
1939   Über den Einfluss von Verfrachtungen zur Herbstzugszeit auf den Sterber (*Accipiter nisus* L.) zugleich ein Beitrag zur Frage nach Orientierung der Vögel auf den Zuge ins Winterquartier. C. R. 9ème Congrès ornithologique international (Rouen, 1938): 503.

EATON, Elon Howard
   1910   Birds of New York. Univ. New York State, Educ. Dept., Mus.
            Mem. 12, pt. 2. Illustr. by Louis Agassiz Fuertes.

EDWARDS, Ernest Preston
   1974   A coded list of the birds of the world. Sweet Briar, Va. Ernest
            P. Edwards 174 pp. Map.

EMERSON, Ralph Waldo
   1867   May Day and other pieces. Boston Ticknor & Field.

EVANS, William
   1891   On the periods occupied by birds in the incubation of their eggs.
            Ibis, (6)3: 52-93.

FISHER, Albert Kenrich
   1893   The hawks and owls of the United States in their relation to
            agriculture. U. S. Dept. Agr., Div. Orn. & Mamm., Bull. 3.

FORBUSH, Edward H.
   1910?   Bob White. National Assoc. Audubon Societies, Leaflet No. 47.

FORBUSH, Edward Howe
   1925-29   Birds of Massachusetts and other New England States. Mass.,
            Dept. Agr. 3 vols. Illustr. by Louis Agassiz Fuertes & Allan
            Brooks.

FRIEDMANN, Herbert
   1929   The cowbirds, a study in the biology of social parasitism.
            Springfield, Ill. & Baltimore. Md. C.C. Thomas xvii + 421 pp.
            73 photos, 9 maps, 4 graphs.

GENTRY, T. G.
   1876   Life-histories of birds of eastern Pennsylvania. Philadelphia.

GENTRY, T. G.
   1882   Nest and eggs of birds of the United States. Philadelphia.

GESNER, C.
   1555   Historia animalium. Liver III. Zurich.

GESNER, C.
   1574   Bibliotheca instituta et collecta. Zurich.

GESNER, C.
   1585   De natura avium. Frankfurt.

GESNER, C.
   1600   Vogelbuch, oder ausführliche Beschreibung . . . aller und jeder
            Vögel. Franfurt. Trans. & ed. by R. Heüsslin.

GILBERT, Humphrey Adam

1925   Secrets of the eagle and other rare birds. London Arrowsmith 196 pp.

GILLESPIE, Mabel
1930   Suggestions for a revised bird-banding terminology. Bird-Banding, 1: (1): 14-19.

GILMAN, Charlotte Perkins Stetson
1898   Woman and economics. Boston Small, Maynard & Co. 2nd Ed. 1899. 3rd Ed. 1900. Also 1966 Ed.

GRANT, John B.
1891   Our common birds and how to know them. Scribner's.

GREENE, Frank C.
1927   Notes on the Pteridophyta. Am. Fern Journ., 17: (4): 125-127.

GRINNELL, J. and H. S. SWARTH
1924   Review of: "The birds of Oklahoma". Condor, 26: (3): 115.

GUERNSEY, Lucy
1860   Jenny and the birds. Philadelphia Am. Sunday School Union.

HALL, Granville Stanley
1923   Life and confessions of a psychologist. New York D. Appleton 622 pp.

HANN, Harry Wilbur
1937   Life history of the ovenbird in southern Michigan. Wilson Bull., 69: 145-237.

HANN, Harry Wilbur
1941   The cowbird at the nest. Auk, 37: 295-297.

HEINROTH, Oskar
1922   Die Beziechungen zwischen Vogelgewicht, Eigewicht, Gelegegewicht und Brutdauer. Journ f. Ornith., 70: 172-285.

HEINROTH, O. and M.
1924-33   Die Vögel Mitteleuropas. Berlin-Lichterfelde. Bermühler. 4 vols.

HENSHAW, Henry Wetherbee
1875   Report upon the ornithological collections made in portions of Nevada, Utah, California, Colorado, New Mexico and Arizona during the years 1871, 1872, 1873, and 1874. Ann. Rep. Geogr. Geol. Expl. Surv. West 100th Mer., Zool., 5: 133-507.

HERRICK, Francis H.
1924a   An eagle observatory. Auk, 41: 89-105.
1924b   Nests and nesting habits of the American eagle. Auk, 41: 213-231.
1924c   The daily life of the American eagle: late phase. Auk, 41:

389-422; 517-541.

1924c   Family life of the American eagle. Nature Mag., 4: 33-140.

HERRICK, Francis H.
1929   The eagle in action. National Geogr. Mag., 55: 635-660.

HERRICK, Francis H.
1932   Daily life of the American eagle. Early phase. Auk, 307-323; 428-435.

HERRICK, Francis H.
1933   Daily life of the American eagle. Early phase (concluded). Auk, 50: 35-53.

HERRICK, Francis H.
1935   Wild birds at home. New York. D. Appleton — Century Co., Inc. xxii + 345 pp.

HICKEY, Joseph J.
1943   A guide to bird watching. London, New York, Toronto, Oxford Univ. Press xiv + 262 pp.

HOCHBAUM, H. Albert
1944   The canvasback on a prairie marsh. Washington, D.C. Am. Wildlife Inst. xii + 207 pp.

HOCHBAUM, H. Albert
1955   Travels and traditions of waterfowl. Minneapolis Univ. Minn. Press x + 301 pp. Illustr. by author.

HODGE, Clifton F.
1902   Nature study and life. Boston Ginn & Co. 514 pp.

HODGE, Clifton F.
1910   The bobwhite. Nature Study Review.

HORNADAY, William T.
1913   Our vanishing wildlife, its extermination and preservation. New York Charles Scribner's Sons 411 pp.

HOWARD, H. Eliot
1920   Territory in bird life. London Murray 308 pp.

HOWARD, H. Eliot
1929   An introduction to the study of bird behaviour. Cambridge Univ. Press 135 pp.

HUXLEY, Julian
1938   Threat and warning colouration in birds, with a general discussion on the biological functions of colour. Proc. VIII Intern. Ornith. Congr. (Oxford, July, 1934): 430-455.

IRVING, Washington
1835   Crayon miscellany. Revised edition 1861. New York Putnam 250 pp.

JAMES, Edwin
1823   Account of an expedition from Pittsburgh to the Rocky Mountains, performed in the years 1819, 1820 ... under the command of Maj. S.H. Long. In Thwaites' early western travels, XVI, 1905: 133-191, 251-291.

JAQUES, Florence (Page)
1942   Birds across the sky. Illustr. by Francis Lee Jaques. New York and London. Harper 240 pp.

JENSEN, Jens
1939   Siftings. Chicago Ralph Fletcher Seymour 110 pp.

JOURDAIN, F. C. R. (Ed.)
1938   Chapter XVII. Proc. VIII Intern. Ornith. Congr. (Oxford, England, July 2-6, 1934).

KENDEIGH, S. Charles
1939   The relation of the metabolism to the development of temperature regulation in birds. Journ. Experimental Zool., 82: 419-438.

KINGSLEY, Charles
1863   The water-babies. A fairy tale for a land baby. London and Cambridge Macmillan and Co. 350 pp.

KLUIJVER, H. N.
1933   Bijdrage tot de Biologie en Ecologie van den Spreeuw (*Sturnus vulgaris vulgaris* L.) gedurende zijn Voorplantingstijd. Versl. en Med. Plantenziektentk. Dients. Wageningen, 69: 1-146.

LASKEY, Amelia Rudolph
1939   A study of nesting eastern bluebirds. Bird-Banding, 10: (1): 23-32.

LASKEY, Amelia
1940   The 1939 nesting season of bluebirds at Nashville, Tennessee. Wilson Bull., 52: (3): 183-190.

LASKEY, Amelia
1950   Behavior of the cowbird. Wilson Bull., 62: 157-174.

LAWRENCE, Louise de Kiriline
1967   A comparative life history study of four species of woodpeckers. Ornithological Monographs, 5: 1-156.

LAWRENCE, Louise de Kiriline
1968   The lovely and the wild. Drawings by Glen Loates. New York,

Toronto, London, Sydney MacGraw-Hill Book Co. 228 pp.

LEOPOLD, Aldo
1949   A Sand County almanac and sketches here and there. New York. Oxford Univ. Press xiii + 226 pp.

LEWIS, Walter E.
1925   Cinnamon teal and black brant in Oklahoma. Auk, 42: (3): 441.

LOCKLEY, Ronald M.
1942   Shearwaters. London J. M. Dent & Sons xi + 238 pp. pl.

LORENZ, Konrad
1932   Betrachtungen über das Erkennen der arteigenen Trieghand lungen der Vögel. Journ f. Ornith., 80: 50-98.

LORENZ, Konrad
1935   Der Kumpan in der Umwelt des Vogels. Journ. f. Ornith., 83: 137-213; 289-413.

LORENZ, Konrad
1937   The companion in the bird's world. Auk, 54: 245-273.

LORENZ, Konrad
1938   A contribution to the comparative sociology of colonial-nesting birds. Proc. VIII Intern. Ornith. Congr. (Oxford, July, 1934): 207-218.

LOW, Carmichael
1924   The literature of the Charadriiformes. London H. F. & G. Witherby xii + 220 pp.

MARCUS AURELIUS ANTONINUS (121-180 A.D.)
1898   Marcus Aurelius Antoninus to himself. (The meditations of Marcus Aurelius.) Am. reprint. Gerald H. Randal.

MARTIN, Martha (Evans)
1935   The friendly stars. Introduction by Harold Jacoby. New York and London Harper & Bros. (1st Ed. 1907)

MAY, John B.
1935   The hawks of North America. New York National Assoc. Audubon Societies ix + 140 pp. 41 pls. 33 maps.

MAYR, Ernst
1935   Bernard Altum and the territory theory. Proc. Linn. Soc. N.Y., Nos. 45-46: 24-38.

MAYR, Ernst
1944   Review of: "The behavior of the song sparrow and other passerines" by Margaret Morse Nice. Audubon Mag., 46: (1): 60.

McATEE, W. L.
1935 Preface to "Fish-eating birds" by Ellsworth D. Lumley. Emergency Conservation Comm., Cons. Ser., Teaching Unit 4.

McCABE, Thomas T.
1937 Review of Dr. Friedrich's paper: "Observations and investigations of the biology of the herring gull (*Larus a. argentatus* Pontotopp.) on the bird island of Memmeertsand" in Journ. f. Ornith., 85: 1-119. Bird-Banding, 8: (3): 132-134.

MERRIAM, C. Hart
1894 Laws of temperature control of the geographic distribution of terrestrial animals and plants. National Geog. Mag., 6: 229-236.

MILLER, Olive Thorne
1896a Four-handed folk. Boston and New York Houghton, Mifflin and Co.
1896b Tommy-Anne and the three Hearts. Boston and New York Houghton, Mifflin and Co.

MORSE, Katherine
1951 Three volumes of poems: Assyrian sword and Spanish chalice. 56 pp. Deep root the elms. 48 pp. I saw a city. 48 pp. New York The Paula Press.

MORSE, Margaret
1896 Fates and fortunes of Fruit-acre birds. Booklet.

MORSE, Margaret
1897? Bird families (climbers, fruit lovers, seed eaters, flycatchers, ground builders, pensile nests, tinys, larges, cannibals). Manuscript.

MORSE, Margaret
1908 Letter refuting a correspondent's attribution to the House Sparrow as a great consumer of weed-seeds, instead of to the Tree Sparrow. Springfield Republican (Oct. 22, 1908). "first item in my ornitholigical bibliography".

MOUNTFORT, Guy
1962 Portrait of a river. Illustr. by Eric Hosking. London Hutchison 207 pp. Coloured Frontisp., 111 Monochrome Photos.

MOUSLEY, Henry M.
1924 A study of the home life of the northern parula and other warblers at Hatley, Stanstead County, Quebec. Auk, 41: 263-288

MOUSLEY, Henry M.
1926 A further study of the home life of the northern parula and of the yellow warbler and ovenbird. Auk, 43: 184-197.

MOUSLEY, Henry M.
1928   A further study of the home life of the northern parula warbler. (*Compsothlypis americana usneae*). Auk, 45: 475-479.

NAUMANN, J. A.
1795-   Naturgeschichte der Land und der Wasservögel des nördlichen
1803   Deutschlands und angränzenden Länder. Koethen. 4 vols.

NELSON, Theodora
1930   Growth rate of the spotted sandpiper chick with notes on nesting habits. Bird-Banding, 1: 1-12. 8 photos. 2 graphs.

NICE, L. B. and M. M. NICE
1920   Christmas census from Norman. Bird-Lore, 22: 41-42.

NICE, L. B. and M. M. NICE
1921   The roadside census. Wilson Bull., 33: 113-123.

NICE L. B. and M. M. NICE
1932a   A study of two nests of the black-throated green warbler. Bird-banding, 3: 30-31.
1932b   A study of two nests of the black-throated green warbler. Part II. Chronicle of the August nest. Bird-Banding, 3: 157-172.

NICE, L. B.; Martha LINDSAY and H. L. KATZ
1932   The changes in the specific gravity and in the chemical elements in the blood after emotional excitement. XIVth Intern. Physiological Cong. (Rome, Aug. 30-Sept. 3): abstracts: p. 193.

NICE, Margaret M.
1910   Food of the bobwhite. Journ. Econ. Ent., 3: (3): 295-313.

NICE, Margaret Morse
1915   The development of a child's vocabulary in relation to environment. Pedagogical Seminary, 22: 35-64.
1919   A child's imagination. Pedagogical Seminary, 26: 173-201.
1921a   Late nesting of mourning doves. Proc. Okla. Acad. Sci. (Feb., 1920). 1: 57.
1921b   Some experiences with mourning doves in captivity. Proc. Okla. Acad. Sci. (Feb., 1920) 1: 57-65.
1921c   Nests of mourning doves with three young. Condor, 23: 145-147.
1922   A study of the nesting of mourning doves. Auk, 39: 457-474.
1923a   A study of the nesting of mourning doves (continued). Auk, 40: 37-58.
1923b   What is a game bird? Daily Oklahoman.

NICE, Margaret Morse and Leonard Blaine NICE
1924   The birds of Oklahoma. Univ. Okla. Bull., New Ser. No. 20

(Univ. Studies No. 286): 1-122. 2 pl. 2 photos. map.

NICE, Margaret Morse

1924   Nesting records from 1920 to 1922 from Norman, Oklahoma. Proc. Okla. Acad. Sc. (Feb., 1923). 3: 271.

1925a   Changes in bird life in Amherst, Massachusetts in twenty years. Auk, 4: 594.

1925b   A child who would not talk. Pedagogical Seminary and Journ. Genetic Psychol., 32: 105-143.

1925c   Length of sentences as a criterion of a child's progress in speech. Journ. Educational Psychol., 16: 370-379.

1926a   Christmas census from Norman. Bird-Lore, 28: 48-49.

1926b   Study of the nesting of the magnolia warbler. Wilson Bull., 38: 185-199.

1926c   On the size of vocabularies. Am. Speech, 2: 1-7.

1926d   Nesting of mourning doves during September, 1925 in Norman, Oklahoma. Auk: 43 (1): 94-95.

1927   A child's vocabularies from fifteen months to three years. Proc. Okla. Acad. Sci., 6: (2): 317-333.

1929a   Some observations on the nesting of a pair of yellow-crowned night herons. Auk, 46: 170-176.

1929b   Some weights of mourning doves in captivity. Auk, 46: 233-234.

1930a   Observations at a nest of myrtle warblers. Wilson Bull., 42: 60-61.

1930b   A study of the nesting of the black-throated blue warbler. Auk, 47: 338-345.

1931   The birds of Oklahoma. Revised edition. Univ. Okla. Press. 3 (Biol. Surv. No. 1): 1-224. 2 maps. 1 diagram.

1932   Observations on the nesting of the blue-gray gnatcatcher. Condor, 38: 18-22.

1933a   Zur Naturgeschichte des Singammers. Journ. f. Ornith., 81: 552-595.

1933b   A child's attainment of the sentence. Journ. Genetic Psychol., 42: 216-224.

1933c   The theory of territorialism and its development. A.O.U. Fifty Years Progress of American Ornithology (1883-1933): 89-100.

1933d   Some ornithological experiences in Europe. Bird-Banding, 4: 147-154.

1933e   Review of: "Bijdrage tot de Biologie en Ecologie van den Spreeuw (*Sturnus vulgaris vulgaris* L.) gedurende zijn Voorplant-ingstijd." by H. N. Kluijver. Bird-Banding, 4: (4): 209-211.

1934   Zur Naturgeschichte des Singammers. Journ. f. Ornith., 82: 89-100.

1935a   Edmund Selous – an appreciation. Bird-Banding, 6: 90-96.
1935b   Review of: "Der Kumpan in der Umwelt des Vogels." by Konrad Lorenz. Bird-Banding, 6: (3): 113 and 6: (4): 146-147.
1936a   Cowbird as a subject of study (abstract). Wilson Bull., 48: (1): 60.
1936b   Review of: "Social behaviour of birds." by T. Schjelderup-Ebbe. Bird-Banding, 7: (2): 94.
1936c   The way of a song sparrow. Bird-Lore, 38: (4): 256-264.
1936d   The nest in the rose hedge. Bird-Lore, 38: (5): 337-343.
1936e   Uno and Una return. Bird-Lore, 38: (6): 421-428.
1936f   Translation from German of "The life history and migration of the stork. The white stork as a subject of research." by Ernst Schüz. Bird-Banding, 7: (3): 99-107.
1937   Studies in the life history of the song sparrow. I. A population study of the song sparrow. Trans. Linn. Soc. New York, 4: 1-247. (Reprinted by Dover in 1964.)
1938a   The biological significance of bird weights. Bird-Banding, 9: (1): 1-11.
1938b   Territory and mating in the song sparrow. Proc. VIII Intern. Ornith. Congr. (Oxford, July 2-6, 1934): 324-338.
1939a   The watcher at the nest. New York Macmillan 159 pp. Illustr. by Roger Tory Peterson.
1939b   The social kumpan and the song sparrow. Auk, 56: (3): 255-262.
1939c   What determines the time of the song sparrow's awakening song? Proc. IX Intern. Ornith. Congr. (Rouen): 249-255.
1940a   Golden orioles. III. Audubon Bull., 36: 1-5.
1940b   Birds of an Hungarian marsh. Chicago Naturalist, 3: 79-85.

NICE, Margaret M. and Joost ter PELKWYK
1940   "Anting" in the song sparrow. Auk, 57: (4): 520-522.

NICE, Margaret Morse
1941a   Observations on the behavior of a young cedar waxwing. Condor, 43: 58-64.
1941b   The role of territory in bird life. Am. Midland Naturalist, 26: (3): 441-487.
1943   Studies in the life history of the song sparrow II. Trans. Linn. Soc. New York, No. 6: 1-328. (Reprinted by Dover, 1964.)
1944a   In search of the reed bunting. Chicago Naturalist, 7: (1): 6-10.
1944b   Fall in Interpont. Chicago Naturalist, 7: (3): 51-55.
1944c   Spring comes in January. Bull. III. Audubon Soc., 49: 1-5.
1944d   The robins of Interpont. Bull. III. Audubon Soc., 50: 1-5.
1945   Seven baby birds in Altenberg. Chicago Naturalist, 8: (4): 67-74.

1946 Jan Joost ter Pelkwyk, naturalist. Chicago Naturalist, 9: (2): 235.

1948 Song sparrows at Wintergreen Lake. Jack-Pine Warbler, 26: (4): 143-151.

1953a Incubation periods of birds of prey, a historical review. Die Vogelwarte, 16: 154-157.

1953b The question of the ten-day incubation period. Wilson Bull., 65: (2): 81-93.

1953c Some experiences in imprinting ducklings. Condor, 55: (1): 33-37.

1954a Problems of incubation periods in North American birds. Condor, 56: 173-197.

1954b Incubation periods throughout the ages. Centaurus, 3: 311-359.

1955 Wichita Mts. Wildlife Refuge in peril. Nature Mag., 48: 292-294.

1962a Displays and songs of a hand-reared eastern meadowlark. Living Bird, 161-172.

1962b Development of behavior in precocial birds. Trans. Linn. Soc. New York, 8: 1-211 incl. 19 illustr., bibliography, two indices.

NICHOLSON, E. M.
1938 Review of: "Population study of the song sparrow." by Margaret M. Nice. British Birds, 31: (8): 276-277.

NICKELL, Walter P.
1965 Habitats, territories and nesting of the catbird. Am. Midland Naturalist, 73: (2): 433-478.

OBERHOLSER, Harry C.
1974 The birds of Texas. Univ. Texas Press 2 vols. 1069 pp.

PALMER, George W.
1897 Self-cultivation in English. New York and Boston T. Y. Crowell 32 pp.

PEARSON, T. Gilbert
1917 Birds of America. New York The University Society 3 vols. Illustr. by Fuertes.

PELKWYK, J. J. ter and N. TINBERGEN
1937 Eine reizbiologische Analyse eineger Verhaltensweisen von *Gasterosteus aculeatus* (L.) Z. f. Tierpsych., 1: 193-201.

PELKWYK, Joost ter
1941 Fowling in Holland. Bird-Banding, 12: (1): 1-8.

PELKWYK, Joost ter and Margaret M. NICE
1941 Enemy recognition in the song sparrow. Auk, 58: 195-214.

PETERS, James L.
1931   Check-list of birds of the world. Vol. I. Cambridge, Mass. Mus. Comp. Zool. xiii + 345 pp.

PETTINGILL, Olin Sewall
1939   The Wilson Ornithological Club today. Wilson Bull., 51: (1): 52, 54.

PHILLIPS, Allan R.; Joe MARSHALL and Gale MONSON
1964   The birds of Arizona. Tucson Univ. Arizona Press xviii + 212 pp.

PLINIUS, C.
1855   The natural history of Pliny. London. 6 vols. (Trans. by J. Bostock and H. T. Riley)

PUTNAM, Loren S.
1949   The life history of the cedar waxwing. Wilson Bull., 61: (3): 141-182.

REED, Chester A.
1906   Bird guide. Land birds east of the Rockies, from parrots to bluebirds. Garden City, N.Y. Doubleday viii + 228 pp.

REED, Chester A.
1906   Bird guide. Water birds, game birds and birds of prey east of the Rockies. Garden City, N. Y. Doubleday 240 pp.

ROBERTS, Thomas S.
1932   The birds of Minnesota. Minneapolis. Univ. Minn. Press Vol. 1: xxii + 691 pp. 49 pls. Vol. 2: xv + 821 pp. pls. 50-90.

RÜPPELL, Werner
1939   Planbeobachtung und Beringung von *Larus ridibundus* in europäischen Winterquartieren. C. R. 9ème Congrès Ornithologique International (Rouen, 1938): 271-278.

1940   Neue Ergebnisse über Heimfinden beim Habicht. Vogelzug, II: 58-64.

1944   Versuche über Heimfinden ziehender Nebelkrähen nach Verfrachtung. Journ. f. Ornith., 92: 106-132.

SAGE, John Hall and Louis B. BISHOP
1913   The birds of Connecticut. State Geological and Natural History Survey, Bull. No. 20: 370 pp.

SAUNDERS, Aretas Andres
1924   Recognizing individual birds by song. Auk, 41: 242-249.

SCHJELDERUP-EBBE, Thorlief
1922   Beiträge zur Socialpsychologie des Baushuhns. Zeitschrift für Psychologie, 88: 225-252.

SCHÜZ, Ernst
1936   The white stork as a subject of research. Bird-Banding, 7: (3): 99-107. (Trans. from German by Margaret Morse Nice.)

SEMPLE, John Bonner and George Miksch SUTTON
1932   Nesting of Harris' Sparrow (*Zonotrichia querula*) at Churchill, Manitoba. Auk, 49: (2): 166-183.

SHANNON, Charles W.
1913   The trees and shrubs of Oklahoma. Oklahoma Geological Survey Circ. No. 4: 41 pp.

SHERMAN, Althea (Edited by Fred J. Pierce: Althea Sherman died in 1943)
1952   Birds of an Iowa dooryard. Boston Christopher Publishing House 270 pp.

SHOEMAKER, Hurst H.
1939   Social hierarchy in flocks of the canary. Auk, 56: 381-406.
1942   Colour discrimination in canaries. Trans. Ill. Acad. Sci., 35: 217-219.

SOPER, J. Dewey
1930   Discovery of the breeding grounds of the blue goose. Can. Field-Nat., 44: 1-11.

SPEIRS, Doris Huestis
1968   Eastern evening grosbeak, western evening grosbeak and Mexican evening grosbeak. In: Life histories of North American cardinals, grosbeaks, buntings, towhees, finches, sparrows and allies. Smithsonian Inst. U. S. National Mus. Bull. 237: 206-256. (Reprinted by Dover.)

STEVENSON, Robert Louis
1907   Walking tours. In: Virginibus Puerisque and other papers. New York Charles Scribner's Sons 233 pp.

STONE, Witmer
1915   Editorial. Auk, 32: (1): 136-139.
1919   William Brewster (obituary). Auk, 36: (4): 628.
1924   Review of Nice's "The birds of Oklahoma". Auk, 41: (4): 621.

STRESEMANN, Erwin
1927-34 Aves. In: Kukenthal-Krumbach, Handb. Zool., 7: (2): 1-889.

STRONG, R. M.
1939   A history of the Wilson Ornithological Club. Wilson Bull., 51: (1): 54.

STRONG, Reuben Myron
1939-48 Bibliography of birds. 4 vols. Field Mus. Nat. Bist., Zool. Ser. 26.

Pts. 1-2: 937 pp. 3: 528 pp.

STUDINKA, L.
1938   The life history and plumages of Montagu's harrier, *Circus pygargus.* Proc. VIII Intern. Ornith. Congr. (Oxford, July, 1934): 757 (Abstr.)

SUTTON, George Miksch
1938   Some findings of the Semple Oklahoma expedition. Auk, 55: (3): 501-508. See p. 506 on worm-eating warbler.

SUTTON, George Miksch
1967   Birds of Oklahoma. Norman Univ. Okla. Press 674 pp.

TATE, R. C.
1924   Some birds of the Oklahoma Panhandle. Proc. Okla. Acad. Sci. (Feb., 1923). Vol. 3.

TAVERNER, Percy Algernon
1926   Birds of western Canada. Ackland Canada, Geol. Surv., Biol. Ser. No. 10. Victoria Mem. Mus. Bull. No. 41: xxi + 380 pp.

THOMAS, Ruth
1950   Crip come home. New York Harper & Bros. 175 pp.

THOMSON, A. Landsborough
1926   Problems of bird migration. London Witherby 350 pp.

THOREAU, Henry D.
1843   A walk to Wachusett. Boston Miscellany. Vol. 3. January. p. 31.
1862   Walking. Atlantic Monthly, 9: 657.
1892   The Maine Woods. Boston Houghton Mifflin & Co. iii + 328 pp.
1906   The journals of Henry David Thoreau. Boston Houghton, Mifflin Co. See journal of 1850-51. Sept. 3, 1850: "As I went under the new telegraph wire, I heard it vibrating like a harp high overhead. It was as the sound of a far-off glorious life, a supernal life, which came down to us, and vibrated the lattice-work of this life of ours." See also p. 365.
1912   The Thoreau calendar. Quotations from the works of Henry David Thoreau for every day in the year. Selected by E. M. Evors. London Frank Palmer See p. 40 (selection for May 13).

TIEDEMANN, F.
1808-14 Zoologie, Anatomie und Naturgeschichte der Vögel. Landeshut & Heidelberg. 3 vols.

TINBERGEN, N.
1936   Zur Sociologie der Silbermöwe, *Larus a. argentatus* Pont. Forpflanzungsbiologie d. Vögel, 12: 89-96.

TINBERGEN, Niko
1939   The behavior of the snow bunting in spring. Trans. Linn. Soc.
          New York, 5: 1-94.

TINBERGEN, N.
1939   In the life of a herring gull. Natural history. 43: 222-229.

TOWNSEND, Charles W.
1913   Sand dunes and salt marshes. Boston D. Estes & Co. viii + 311 pp.

TRAUTMAN, Milton Bernard
1940   The birds of Buckeye Lake, Ohio. Univ. Mich. Mus. Zool., Misc.
          Publ. No. 44: 466 pp. 15 pls.

TRAUTMAN, Milton B.
1976   A partial bibliography of Margaret Morse Nice. Ohio State Univ.,
          Mus. Zool. Mimeo: 12 pp.

VOGT, William
1936   (Editorial on reviews by Margaret Morse Nice.) Bird-Banding.

WALKINSHAW, Lawrence Harvey
1939   Nesting of the field sparrow and survival of the young. Bird-
          Banding, 10: 109-114; 149-157.
1945   Field sparrow, 39-54015. Bird-Banding, 16: 1-14.
1949   The sandhill cranes. Bloomfield Hills, Mich. Cranbrook Inst. Sci.
          Bull. 29: x + 202 pp.

WHEELOCK, Irene Grosvenor
1904   Birds of California. Chicago A. C. McClurg & Co. xxciii + 578 pp.

WIDMANN, Otto
1907   A preliminary catalogue of the birds of Missouri. Trans. Acad.
          Sci. St. Louis, 17: (1): 1-288.

WODZICKI, Count Kazimerz
1939   Répartition et écologie de la cicogne palogne (*Ciconia c. ciconia*
          L.) dans le sud et sudest. Proc. 9th Intern. Ornith. Cong. (Rouen,
          1938): 445-451.

WORDSWORTH, William
1807   Poems. 2 vols. (See "Ode to duty")

WRIGHT, Mabel Osgood
1895   Bird craft, a field book of 200 song, game and water birds. New
          York Macmillan and Co. xvi + 317 pp. 15 pls.
1896a   Four-handed folk. New York. Macmillan and Co.
1896b   Tommy-Anne and the three hearts. New York Macmillan and
          Co. xvi + 322 pp.

Acknowledgements

The editor has been blessed by having a most distinguished, though unofficial, editorial committee. It was comprised of: Dr. Marjorie Nice Boyer, of Brooklyn, New York, the author's second daughter: Mr. Edward S. Morse, of Boston and South Londonderry, Vermont, the author's youngest brother; Dr. Viola Pratt and Miss Claire Pratt of Toronto; and Dr. J. Murray Speirs, of Pickering, Ontario, the editor's husband.

Dr. Boyer sent a critique of the manuscript and was also able to locate the source of a rare children's book cited by her mother in the text. Her older sister, Constance, sent helpful suggestions.

To Edward S. Morse, we really owe the fact that the book has been published. It was he who encouraged his sister to write and complete her autobiography. It was he who wrote to the president of the Margaret Nice Ornithological Club suggesting the club's sponsorship of the book's publication. It was he who supplied all the genealogical data, assembled the family photographs and helped the editor to make a good selection. It was he who had the manuscript beautifully typed and supplied the editor with several copies. He answered many questions, as a mounting file of letters could testify.

Deep gratitude to Claire Pratt for her editorial expertise, and her preparation of the extensive Index and Family Trees. Our thanks to Viola Pratt, the gifted secretary of MNOC, who prepared a summary of each chapter and who with her daughter, took over the larger part of the proof-reading.

My husband, Murray, has given daily support, from that August afternoon when the huge parcel arrived. He read each page as I laid it down and shared my joy in the manuscript. A few months later, he typed out, from the card file, the "Literature Cited" section of the work.

Gratitude to the staff of the library of the Royal Ontario Museum: to Eugene Wilburn and especially to Maureen Whitney and Patricia Trunks who literally spent hours of their time researching for the book. To Dorothy Richardson of the Bird Room for her help with Javanese species.

Our thanks to the Main Library of Metropolitan Toronto and to the Science Library of the University of Toronto: to the staff of the Port Union branch of the Scarborough Public Library, and especially to Gaile Woodcock who devoted her day off to finding for us a needed book in a Toronto library. To Dr. Ronald Orenstein who visited the Josselyn Van Tyne Memorial Library of the Wilson Ornithological Society (housed in the Museum of Zoology, University of Michigan, Ann Arbor) to enquire, on our behalf, for the loan of the rare First Edition of "The Birds of Oklahoma". Our gratitude to Janet Hinshaw, Librarian, for sending the little book so quickly and another needed item. Material has also been mailed from the American Physiological Society and from the Oklahoma Academy of Science. To their secretaries, our thanks.

Dr. William J. Beecher, of the Chicago Academy of Science, kindly allowed us to use, as a chapter in the book: "Jan Joost Ter Pelkwyk, Naturalist" which first appeared in *The Chicago Naturalist* in 1946. Mount Holyoke College, South Hadley, Massachusetts, allowed us to use: "When Wednesday was a Holiday," which appeared in the *Mount Holyoke Alumnae Quarterly* in the fall of 1976. Our thanks to the librarian of the Williston Memorial Library for the loan of the photograph of Dr. Margaret Morse Nice taken on the campus after she had received an honorary Doctor of Science degree in 1955.

We are deeply indebted to Professor Dr. Konrad Lorenz for his Foreword, but also for the living photograph of him (taken after his return from Russia) with the starling on his shoulder!

Dr. H. Albert Hochbaum kindly sent us the photograph of the three Nices, taken at the Delta Wildfowl Research Laboratory in the 1950s.

We are grateful to the Linnaean Society of New York for the use of some of the original drawings by Dr. Nice of baby birds which appeared in her book: *Development of Behavior in Precocial Birds* in 1962: to the Illinois Audubon Society for the use of illustrations from an article called: "California Spring" published in June, 1949 in *The Audubon Bulletin*; and for the drawing of a flamingo from an article: "A Plea for the Pencil" published in the *Passenger Pigeon* also in 1949.

The letterhead for the Margaret Nice Ornitholigical Club was designed by the Canadian artist, Erik Thorn. His singing song sparrow in silhouette has been adapted by Sylvia Hahn for the cover of the book. The handsome lettering is the work of Julian Mulock. The Erik Thorn design has been used as a heading for the chapters especially concerned with song sparrows. The heading and tailpiece for Chapter XXVIII are drawings by Joost ter Pelkwyk, from the original article in *The Chicago Naturalist*. All the other headings and two tailpieces are taken from publications credited above — the author's own loving creations.

We are grateful to Edwin R. Haynes and the staff of the Haynes Printing Company Ltd. of Cobourg, Ontario, for their care and courtesy.

Finally, how to thank our publisher, Barry L. Penhale? He came one Saturday afternoon in the winter to discuss the possible publication of the book. He left about 5:00 o'clock, and, as the story goes, drove straight home, took off his overcoat and sat down to read. He finished the manuscript at 2:00 a.m. Sunday morning. Not only had he read the autobiography with a deep, sympathetic understanding, being a lover of nature, but he was really stirred and enthusiastic. He has done everything in his power to make the publication of this book as a joyous experience.

The Editor.

Index

MARGARET MORSE NICE
Receiving an Honorary Doctor of Science degree, Mount Holyoke College,
South Hadley, Massachusetts, U.S.A. 1955.

THE HOUSE OF ELY

Richard Ely = Joan Phipps
(d. Plymouth, 1660)

(emigrated from Plymouth, Devonshire, Eng.
between 1660 & 1663. D. 1684)

Richard (2nd son)
(b. 1656 in Plymouth. Emigrated with his father. Settled in Lyme, Conn.)

Richard = Phoebe Hubbard
(1697 - 1777)   (d. 1772)

Josiah = Phoebe Dennison
(1739 - 1826)   (1747 - 1802)

Richard = Mary Ely Peck
(1777 - 1856)   (1778 - 1853)

Zebulon Stiles = Sarah Duncan
(1819 - 1902)   (1824 - 1880)

Margaret Duncan = Anson Daniel MORSE
(1855 - 1940)   (1846 - 1916)

Edward Stiles   Grace   Mary   William Northrop

Anson Ely   Sarah Duncan

Margaret = Leonard Blaine NICE
(1883 - 1974)   (1882 - 1974)

Harold Ely   Katharine Duncan   Edward Stiles

Janet Duncan = Henry FREDERICKS
(1923 -)

Constance Ely
(1910 -)

Marjorie Duncan = Carl BOYER
(1912 -)   (1906 - 1976)

Barbara Stewart = A. Stanley THOMPSON
(1915 -)   (1914 -)

Eleanor Margaret
(1918 - 1927/8)

Hugh Eisenhart = Gretchen Glazier
(1939 -)

Timothy Howard = Marilyn Abel
(1941 -)

Russell Stuart = Mary Thackster
(1944 -)

Sarah Lewis   Katherine Ely
(1974 -)

Daniel Christopher
(1971 -)

Allison Eleanor
(1974 -)

Michael Christopher
(1978 -)

Bruce Roger   Michael Stuart

Steven Kirk = Mary Graham
(1945 -)   (1947 -)

Jonathan
(1973 -)

Credit: The Ely Ancestry. Calumet Press. New York, 1902, page 32.

THE HOUSE OF MORSE

John Moss (early settler, New Haven Colony, Conn.)
(- 1664) signed Planters Associates 4, 4, 1639

Mercy Moss = Elizabeth
(1649 -)

John Moss = Jane Thompson
(1677 -) (m. Dec. 22, 1707)

John Moss
(c. 1710)

Daniel = Rebeccah

Rev. Daniel Munson Moss = Delia Northrop
(1875 - 1860) (m. 1813) (1792 - 1867)

Harmon MORSE = Elizabeth Murray Buck
(1815 - 1901)

Harmon Northrop   Elizabeth D.

Anson Daniel = Margaret Duncan Ely
(1846 - 1916)   (1855 - 1940)

Anson Ely
(1879 - 1966)

Sarah Duncan
(1881 - 1960)

William Northrop
(1882 - 1977)

Margaret = Leonard Blaine NICE
(1883 - 1974)   (1882 - 1974)
(m. Grey Rocks, Mass., Aug. 12, 1909)

Harold Ely
(1885 - 1896)

Katharine Duncan
(1888 - 1975)

Edward Stiles
(1892 -)

Constance Ely
(1910 -)

Marjorie Duncan = Carl BOYER
(1912 -)   (1906 - 1976)

Barbara Stewart = A. Stanley THOMPSON
(1915 -)   (1914 -)

Eleanor Margaret
(1918 - 1928)

Janet Duncan = Henry FREDERICKS
(1923 -)   m. June, 1949

Hugh Eisenhart = Gretchen Glazier
(1910 -)

Timothy Howard = Marilyn Abel
(1941 -)

Russell Stuart = Mary Thackster
(1944 -)

Kenneth Duncan
(1948 -)

Daniel Christopher   Allison Eleanor
(1971 -)   (1974 -)

Michael Christopher
(1978 -)

Sarah Lewis
(1974 -)

Bruce Roger

Katharine Ely
(1977 -)

Michael Stuart

Steven Kirk = Mary Graham
(1945 -)   (1947 -)

Jonathan
(1973 -)